THE ENSIGNS OF THE TWELVE TRIBES OF ISRAEL
THE ROYAL ARCH BANNERS

The Royal Arch Banners

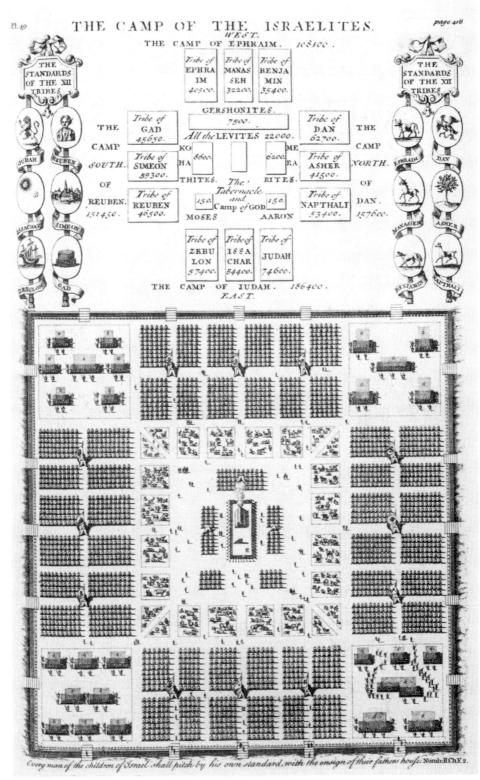

PLATE 1: *The camp of the Israelites plan showing the twelve Tribes and their ensigns*

The *ENSIGNS* of the
Twelve Tribes of Israel

Harry Mendoza

© 1989
Harry Mendoza

ISBN 0 907655 48 3
British Library Cataloguing in Publication Data

Mendoza, Harry
    The Royal Arch banners : the ensigns of
    the twelve tribes of Israel.
    1. Freemasonry. Symbolism
    I. Title
    366′.1′0148

Royalties to Vascular Surgery Research (Frenchay) C/o R A Gilbert,
4, Julius Road, Bishopston, Bristol BS7 8EU

Printed and bound in Great Britain by
Butler & Tanner Ltd, Frome and London

SECTIONS

ILLUSTRATIONS

FOREWORD

Harry Mendoza is a leading authority on the ensigns and banners displayed in the Royal Arch and he has written and lectured widely on the subject. A Past Master of Quatuor Coronati Lodge, he has made a study of aspects of the Royal Arch to which he is devoted. It has been my good fortune to have had the benefit of his scholarship on the Committee of General Purposes and in the Royal Arch Ritual Working Party.

I wholeheartedly commend this book to all Royal Arch Freemasons as a source of knowledge and pleasure, and as a valuable point of reference for sustaining the interest of newly joined Companions.

Maj-Gen. D. A. Beckett CB DSO OBE
Past President Committee of General Purposes

Harry Mendoza

ACKNOWLEDGEMENTS

The author is grateful to the Committee of General Purposes of Supreme Grand Chapter of Royal Arch Masons of England for permission to arrange for photographs to be taken of those items displayed in the coloured plates. He also appreciates and readily acknowledges the assistance of the Librarian to Grand Lodge, John Hamill, and his staff, and to the many others who passed information, and in some cases photographs to him. Special mention should be made of the staff at Jews' College, London.

He also wishes to place on record his appreciation to the Grand Scribe E of the Supreme Grand Chapter of Royal Arch Chapter of Freemasons of Scotland for permission to reproduce plates from their Constitution and Laws.

ABOUT THE AUTHOR

Harry Mendoza has written many articles on masonic matters and is well-known as a speaker in the Craft – and even more so in the Royal Arch.

He had the honour of being appointed Prestonian Lecturer in 1984, his paper being entitled *Getting and giving masonic knowledge*.

In 1976 he was elected a Full Member of Quatuor Coronati Lodge, the premier Lodge of Masonic Research, and after having served in each of the 'progressive' offices, he became Master in 1980. His Inaugural Address was entitled *Anno Lucis et al*, in which he showed that the abbreviation A.L. did not always stand for Anno Lucis.

He was a founder member of Euclid Chapter of First Principals No. 7464 and had the honour of being its first elected MEZ. He is also a member of London First Principals Chapter, No. 2712, where he has held office as Scribe N. and Third Principal.

In 1982 he was elected a member of the Committee of General Purposes and is still serving. He was invited to become a member of the Working Party when it was first set up to examine possible changes in Royal Arch ritual.

Introduction

The ensigns of the twelve tribes of Israel

Many papers have been written under a variety of headings on the banners or ensigns depicted on the staves that are seen in a Royal Arch Chapter. This book brings much of this information together. It also deals with other important aspects that have not been dealt with in detail in the past, such as:

the relationship between the sons of Jacob and the tribes of Israel;

the colours of the ensigns;

why the tribes of Israel are referred to in the Royal Arch;

the association of the ensigns with the signs of the zodiac;

and there are many other matters.

Sources of reference use variously the terms ensigns, banners. standards and flags. Generally speaking, in this book, the term 'ensigns' has been used when referring to the distinctive bearings borne by the twelve tribes, and the term 'standards' when making special reference to the distinctive bearings borne by the four leading divisions of the army of Israel, though the word 'banners' is used in Section 12, as that is how they are described in the *Constitutions and Laws* of the Supreme Grand Chapter of Royal Arch Freemasons of Scotland.

It must be stressed that this book deals with the twelve tribes of Israel only in relation to the ensigns that are attributable to them; it does not deal with the history, the geographical locations or the ultimate dispersal of the tribes.

The quotations from the Volume of the Sacred Law, unless otherwise stated, have been taken from the *Authorized Version* of the Holy Bible (AV) first published in 1611 and still widely used. It is recognized, though, that there are many other versions of the Bible which give a different wording to that used in the AV. In some cases quotations are also given from these sources; the modern wording used often helps to clarify the point under discussion. This is particularly so in regard to the choice of the descriptive bearings found on some ensigns.

The main Biblical sources used are as follows:

JOSEPHUS (AD 37–?95); a Jewish historian. The *Jewish Antiquities* covers in twenty books the history of the Jews from the creation of the world to the outbreak of war with Rome. Written in Greek; Whiston's translation used.

THE MIDRASH The Oral Law or the Tradition of Judaism which has been handed down in the form of a running commentary on the Pentateuch by generations of teachers who have devoted their lives to a study of the Hebrew Scriptures. Every word of the Scriptures was considered to have a definite meaning, and every single letter used was taken into account. New lessons were constantly being extracted by Rabbis, generation after generation. The various works making up the *Midrash* date from about the second century AD.

THE PENTATEUCH AND HAFTORAHS Edited by the Chief Rabbi, Dr. J. H. Hertz, 1938. (Hertz).

THE KNOX VERSION OF THE HOLY BIBLE A translation from the Latin *Vulgate* in the light of the Hebrew and Greek originals. First published 1985. (Knox).

GOOD NEWS BIBLE The Bible in Today's English Version. Published by the United Bible Societies, 1976. (GNB).

It is hoped that the information contained in this book will enable a suitable response to be given to practically any question that may be asked on the banners of the twelve tribes of Israel. Further, the book has been so arranged that any of the Sections may be read at a Royal Arch Convocation when there is no work to be done.

HARRY MENDOZA   *1989*

The names of the twelve tribes of Israel

From whom did the twelve tribes of Israel get their names? The answer most frequently given to this question is 'From the sons of Jacob.' Is this correct?

The birth of Jacob's sons is recorded in *Genesis* 29, 30 and 35. The sons were as follows.

By Leah	Reuben	Simeon	Levi
	Judah	Issachar	Zebulun
By Bilhah	Dan	Naphthali	
By Zilpah	Gad	Asher	
By Rachel	Joseph	Benjamin	

The names of the twelve tribes of Israel are:

Reuben	Simeon	Judah
Issachar	Zebulun	Gad
Asher	Dan	Naphthali
Benjamin	Ephraim	Manasseh

It will be seen that the names of the tribes do not entirely correspond with the names of the sons of Jacob; Ephraim and Manasseh have replaced Levi and Joseph. The answer to the question posed above, therefore, would appear to be not entirely correct.

Just before he died, Jacob adopted Manasseh and Ephraim, the two sons of Joseph, and tribes were named after them instead of after their father. It would seem, therefore, that the twelve tribes of Israel were named after ten of the sons of Jacob and his two adopted sons, the children of Joseph.

Genesis 49. 28., however, would seem to contradict this. It says

'And these are the twelve tribes of Israel.' To whom does the word 'these' refer? A brief reference is made to each verse below.

Verses 1 and 2	refer to Jacob calling his children together
Verses 3 and 4	refer to Reuben.
Verses 5 to 7	refer to Simeon and Levi.
Verses 8 to 12	refer to Judah.
Verse 13	refers to Zebulun.
Verses 14 and 15	refer to Issachar.
Verses 16 and 17	refer to Dan.
Verse 18	is considered by Jewish scholars as probably being part of the blessing bestowed upon Dan, and by some Christian scholars to be a prophetic foresight of the Messiah.
Verse 19	refers to Gad.
Verse 20	refers to Asher.
Verse 21	refers to Naphthali.
Verses 22 to 26	refer to Joseph.
Verse 27	refers to Benjamin.
Verse 28	says 'And these are the twelve tribes of Israel'.

This last verse would seem to state that the twelve tribes of Israel *were* named after the sons of Jacob. However, a comment on *Genesis* 49. 28 found in *A Catholic Commentary on Holy Scriptures* (Thomas Nelson and Sons Ltd, 1953) says '. . . the predictions concern not so much the sons in person, as the tribes named after them.'

The reason why Levi was not to become head of a tribe is because God decreed that the House of Levi, the Levites, should be separated and distinguished from the main body of the Israelites as they were the priests and had special duties to perform. (*Numbers* 3. 9).

One explanation for excluding Joseph but including his sons Ephraim and Manasseh is that Joseph was the son of Rachel, Jacob's favourite wife, and in her honour he adopted Joseph's sons as his own. The modern wording of the *GNB* helps to illustrate this, as is shown by *Genesis* 48. 5–7.

'Jacob continued, "Joseph, your two sons, who were born to you in Egypt before I came here, belong to me; Ephraim and Manasseh are just as much my sons as Reuben and Simeon. If you have any more sons, they will not be considered mine; the inheritance they get will come through Ephraim and Manasseh. I am doing this because of your mother Rachel. To my great sorrow she died in the land of Canaan, not far from Ephrath, as I was returning from Mesopotamia. I buried her there beside the road to Ephrath."' (Ephrath is now Bethlehem).

Another explanation is that Jacob considered that Reuben, his firstborn, had acted in a wicked manner by sleeping with his father's concubine and therefore forfeited his right, as the firstborn, to a double portion of the inheritance (*Deuteronomy* 21. 17), Joseph, on the other hand, by his success in Egypt, had become the saviour of the family and therefore merited the double portion.

SECTION 2

The origins of the distinctive bearings associated with each tribe

The Symbolical Lecture tells us that 'the ensigns on the staves borne by the Companions are the distinctive bearings of the twelve tribes of Israel'.

The Volume of the Sacred Law does not tell us what was depicted on the ensigns. This information comes from commentators on the Bible text who, in general, base their interpretations on the words used by Jacob just before he died. (*Genesis* 49). These words have come to be known as 'The Blessing of Jacob'. 'Blessing', however, is a misnomer in some cases, since three of his sons, Reuben, Simeon and Levi were in fact cursed because of deeds they had committed which their father thought wicked (though some say that Simeon and Levi as individuals, were not cursed, but rather their actions); other sons are treated with either a jest or satire.

The words used by Jacob are said to be prophetic anticipations of the future destinies of the tribes.

It is important to remember that the whole subject of associating particular emblems with specific tribes is a matter of tradition. As stated above, the Volume of the Sacred Law does not tell us what was depicted on each of the ensigns. The matter is discussed in the *Midrash* which, by its very nature, reflects different views (See Introduction); it is not surprising, therefore, to find a reference to different emblems for the same tribe.

What are the distinctive bearings normally associated with each of the tribes, and on what words are they based? The relevant detail is given below; the names are given in the same order as recorded in *Genesis* 49. References in this Section to the *Midrash* have been taken from the *Encyclopaedia Judaica* (6. 1334).

Reuben (*Genesis* 49. 3–4)

'Reuben, thou art my firstborn, my might, and the beginning of my strength, the excellency of dignity, and the excellency of power. Unstable as water, thou shalt not excel; because thou wentest up to thy father's bed; then defilest thou it; he went up to my couch.'

Reuben was the first of Jacob's children. One Biblical commentator considers the phrase 'unstable as water' as denoting a haughty, arrogant disposition which, like swelling water, overflows or breaks through all restraints. Another considers that Jacob is saying that Reuben's cardinal sin was weakness of will, lack of self-control and firmness of purpose and that he would 'bubble over like water' in uncontrolled vehemence of passion. This is a reference to Reuben's incest with his father's concubine (*Genesis* 35. 22.), though it is not the Jewish traditional view that Reuben had carnal relations with Bilhah). Nothing good or praiseworthy is latterly recorded in respect of Reuben or his posterity.

The distinctive bearing associated with Reuben shows waves of the sea ('unstable as water'); sometimes it shows a man ('my firstborn'). The *Midrash* tells us that the device for Reuben was a mandrake. This is considered to be a reference to the mandrake Reuben found for his mother (*Genesis* 30. 14). The mandrake is said to induce fertility. Commenting on the verse just quoted, Rabbi Mosheh ben Nachman (Nachmanides), said the mandrake resembled the human form as it had the shape of the human head and hands.

Another device, unusual for Reuben, can be seen in an illustration of the Duke of Sussex's *Pentateuch* dating from the fourteenth century. It shows four knights holding banners with emblems of the four major tribes of the army of Israel. The unusual feature is that the banner for Reuben depicts an eagle.

There are many references to eagles in the Volume of the Sacred Law; for example, *Exodus* 19. 4., in a reference to the exodus of the Children of Israel from their Egyptian bondage, and *Deuteronomy* 32. 11., in a reference to God protecting the Children of Israel. It is difficult, however, to see how these, or indeed any of the many other references to an eagle, could be associated with Reuben.

Simeon and Levi (*Genesis* 49. 5–7)

'Simeon and Levi are brethren; instruments of cruelty are in their habitations. O my

soul, come not thou into their secret; unto their assembly, mine honour be not thou united; for in their anger they slew a man, and in their self-will they digged down a wall. Cursed be their anger, for it was fierce; and their wrath, for it was cruel; I will divide them in Jacob and scatter them in Israel'.

These verses recall the murderous attack on the Shechemites (*Genesis* 34. 25ff). The Simeonites and the Levites became intermingled and dispersed amongst the other tribes.

The weapons in the verse refer to the swords with which Simeon and Levi slew the Shechemites, so it is not surprising that the distinctive bearing associated with Simeon is a sword. Sometimes Levi appears on the same ensign; when this is so, Levi is associated with a dagger. This may have been a knife, in reference to the circumcisions of the Shechemites (*Genesis* 34. 24.).

PLATE 2: *An unusual Simeon and Levi ensign in the William Waples Museum, Sunderland, showing a sword and an axe on which is superimposed a shield emblazoned with a cross patée*

The *Midrash* says Simeon's device was a city. This is a reference to the city of Shechem, where Simeon and Levi committed what their father considered their heinous offence.

An unusual ensign can be found in a set in the William Waples Museum, Sunderland. It shows a sword and an axe in saltire on which is superimposed a shield emblazoned with a cross patée. The axe and sword are undoubtedly meant to refer to the 'instruments of war'. But this is the only ensign I have seen portraying a shield emblazoned with a cross patée.

Just why the cross patée was used is unknown; I am unaware of any especial significance being attached to it. It has a long history; according to *A Complete Guide to Heraldry* (page 11; A. C. Fox-Davies, revised by J. P. Brooke-Little), the cross patée was prefigured on a shield in the Bayeux Tapestry.

The following notes from *The Pentateuch and Haftorahs* (Ed. Dr. J. H. Hertz, Chief Rabbi; page 911) will be of interest.

> We note the omission of Simeon (from the 'Blessing of Moses,') who is joined with Levi in Jacob's Blessing, Gen. 49. 5. The probable explanation is that Jacob had foretold that both Simeon and Levi should have their territories divided up among the other tribes. As Simeon's possessions consisted of only 19 unconnected cities within the territory of Judah (*Joshua* 19. 2–9), the tribe of Simeon was regarded as included in Judah.
>
> In blessing Levi, Moses prays that the privilege of guarding the Urim and Thummim may remain with Levi, who had proved his fidelity to the Divine cause in the Wilderness. (The Urim and Thummim were objects connected with the breastplate of the High Priest.)

Judah (*Genesis* 49. 8–12)

> '*Judah, thou art he whom thy brethren shall praise; thy hand shall be in the neck of thine enemies; thy father's children shall bow down before thee. Judah is a lion's whelp; from the prey, my son, thou art gone up; he stooped down, he couched as a lion; who shall rouse him up? The sceptre shall not depart from Judah, nor a lawgiver from between his feet, until Shiloh come; and unto him shall the gathering of the people be. Binding his foal unto the vine, and his ass's colt unto the choice vine; he washes his garments in wine, and his clothes in the blood of grapes. His eyes shall be red with wine, and his teeth white with milk.*

The lion is said to refer to the vigour and nobility of Judah. One commentator notes that the verse quoted likens Judah first to a lion's whelp, then a lion couched and finally as an old lion, This, it is said, is meant to express the beginning, increase and full growth of the power of the tribe of Judah.

The sceptre is an emblem of kingship; so, too, is a crown. The Royal House of David is descended from Judah.

The descriptive bearing associated with Judah is a lion couchant. On some ensigns a sceptre is also shown, and on others, both a sceptre and a crown.

There are some who argue that in this case the crown refers to something other than royalty, since the sceptre itself is sufficient to indicate this. They give as a possible reason for the crown a Christian significance, basing their arguments on the words *nor a lawgiver from between his feet until Shiloh come*. Some Biblical scholars give a Messianic meaning to this phrase, particularly those of the Christian faith.

Verse 10 seems to have presented the translators of the Bible with much difficulty. For comparison purposes, three other versions are shown.

> HERTZ   *'The sceptre shall not depart from Judah. Nor the ruler's staff from between his feet, as long as men come to Shiloh; And unto him shall the obedience of the people be.'*

> KNOX   *'Juda shall not want a branch from his stem, a prince drawn from his stock, until the day when he comes who is to be sent to us, he the hope of the nations.'*

> GNB   *'Judah shall hold the royal sceptre, and his descendants will always rule. Nations will bring him tribute And bow in obedience before him.'*

The crown is often used as a symbol in Christianity, possibly being based on *James* 1.12. 'Blessed is the man that endureth temptation; for when he is tried, he shall receive the crown of life.'; or possibly *Rev.* 2.10, 'Be thou faithful unto death and I will give thee a crown of life.'

It might be of interest to mention that the *Talmud* (a collection of early Jewish Biblical discussions with the comments of generations of teachers who devoted their lives to the study of the Scriptures), referring to the death of the patriarch Jacob, says 'And the sons of Jacob carried the bier in which rested their father's remains, as he commanded them; and there rested on the bier a sceptre and a crown of gold.'

The explanation for the sceptre and crown might possibly be found in an earlier paragraph which reads

'And Pharaoh issued a proclamation requesting the citizens of Egypt to honour Joseph by participating in Jacob's funeral and showing the last marks of respect to him. And the citizens in large numbers acquiesced in the wishes of the king.'

Zebulun *(Genesis* 49. 13)

'Zebulun shall dwell at the haven of the sea; and he shall be for an haven for ships; and his border shall be unto Zidon.'

This verse refers to the favourable geographical position of the territory that was alloted to Zebulun, where ships could come and berth in safety.

The distinctive bearing on the ensign borne by Zebulun is a ship.

Issachar *(Genesis* 49. 14–15)

'Issachar is a strong ass couching down between two burdens; And he saw that the rest was good, and the land that it was pleasant; and bowed his shoulder to bear, and became a servant unto tribute.'

A strong ass indicates great physical power. The tribe of Issachar was to possess rich territory, but its people became indolent and preferred to submit to tribute rather than to take up the sword against their enemies.

There may be a pun on the name here. The meaning of Issachar is given in Peake's *Commentary on the Bible* as 'man of hire'. As seen in the verse above, the tribe became 'a servant unto tribute'.

There is another meaning given to the name Issachar; it is 'man of reward'. The *GNB* brings this out quite clearly; *Genesis* 30. 18. *'Leah said "God has given me my reward, because I gave my slave to my husband"; so she named her son Issachar.'*

The *GNB* rendering of *Genesis* 49. 14–15 is *Issachar is no better than a donkey That lies stretched out between its saddlebags. But he sees that the resting place is good And that the land is delightful. So he bends his back to carry the load And is forced to work as a slave.'*

The usual device seen on Issachar's ensign is an ass couching between two burdens.

The *Midrash* tells us that Issachar's ensign bore a sun and a moon. This is probably a reference to *1 Chronicles* 12. 32., the first part of which reads *'And of the children of Issachar which were men that had an understanding of the times, to know what Israel ought to do.*' This was thought to be a reference to the tribe of Issachar being associated with astrology. An ensign showing this distinctive device is part of a set belonging to Hutchinson Chapter No. 318, Darwen, E. Lancs.

Dan (*Genesis* 49. 16–17)

> '*Dan shall judge his people, as one of the tribes of Israel. Dan shall be a serpent by the way, an adder in the path, that biteth the horse heels, so that his rider shall fall backward.*'

The first sentence of this verse contains a pun on the name Dan, which means 'to judge.'

The distinctive bearing on the ensign for Dan is a snake biting the heels of a horse whose rider is about to fall off backwards. This is an obvious reference to the wording in the verse above. The *adder in the path* is probably a reference to the cerastes, a horned viper that conceals itself in the sand and which will bite the heels of a passing horse, causing it to rear and throw its rider backwards.

Occasionally one sees the ensign for Dan bearing a serpent. This is an obvious reference to the verse quoted above; 'Dan shall be a serpent by the way'. The *Midrash* indicates either a serpent or a lion's whelp as the distinctive bearing for Dan, the latter being based on *Deuteronomy* 32. 22. And of Dan he said, Dan is a lion's whelp; he shall leap from Bashan.'

The serpent is shown as a device for Dan in Bibles dating from as early as 1593. Just when the bearing was changed to a snake biting the heels of a horse with its rider falling off, is not known.

According to some Bible commentators Rabbi ibn Ezra (1092–1167) is stated as having quoted a tradition that the standard for Dan bore an eagle. Such a device is included in the set belonging to Hutchinson Chapter, mentioned earlier. Sometimes the eagle has a snake in its talons; an example can be seen in the set of ensigns belonging to Chapter of Economy, No. 76, Winchester. These devices are discussed in detail in Section 10 of this book.

There is nothing in the verses relevant to Dan in either *Genesis 49* or *Deuteronomy 33*, suggesting an eagle, though *Genesis 49. 18.* might possibly have a bearing on the matter; it says 'I have waited for thy salvation, O Lord.' Hertz comments that this '... is probably intended as part of the blessing bestowed upon Dan, who was in the most exposed position among all the tribes of Israel. Thy salvation i.e. deliverance wrought by Thee.' This could be an oblique reference to both *Exodus*, 19, 4. ('Ye have seen what I did unto the Egyptians, and how I bear you on eagles' wings, and brought you unto myself') and *Deuteronomy* 32. 11. ('As an eagle stirreth up her nest, fluttereth over her young, spreadeth abroad her wings, taketh them, bearing them on her wings'). The connection with Dan, however, is not at all obvious.

Gad (*Genesis* 49. 19)

'Gad, a troop shall overcome him, but he shall overcome at the last.'

According to Hertz, there is a play on the name in this verse. The Hebrew word for Gad can mean 'a troop' or 'a marauding band'. The Chief Rabbi thought that perhaps the translation of the verse should be 'A raiding band raids him, but he will band himself against their heel.' This is well expressed in the modern language of *GNB*: 'Gad will be attacked by a band of robbers, but he will turn and pursue them.' Gad had succeeded in repelling the Ammonites, Moabites, and Aramaeans who were constantly raiding his borders. Jephtha was of this tribe.

The distinctive bearing on the ensign borne by Gad is a troop of horsemen. Occasionally one sees instead, a flag or pennant bearing a lion rampant, possibly an allusion to *Deuteronomy* 33, 20; 'And of Gad he said, Blessed be he that enlargeth Gad; he dwelleth as a lion, and teareth the arm with the crown of the head.' The *GNB* reads 'About the tribe of Gad he said; 'Praise God, who made their territory large, Gad waits like a lion to tear off an arm or a scalp.'

Gad was famed for courage and success in war. An example of a pennant bearing a lion rampant for Gad can be seen in the frontispiece of the 1599 edition of the *Barker Bible*. Sometimes the pennant is shown with a semée (or background) of stars. It is rare for a Chapter ensign to show this device, but the set belonging to Hutchinson Chapter No. 381, mentioned earlier, shows a shield bearing stars.

There are a few cases where the distinctive bearing for Gad is a camp or tent; this accords with the *Midrash*.

Asher (*Genesis* 49. 20)

'Out of Asher his bread shall be fat, and he shall yield royal dainties.'

This is another pun; the name Asher means 'happy' or 'fortunate.' The meaning is reflected in the blessing bestowed upon him.

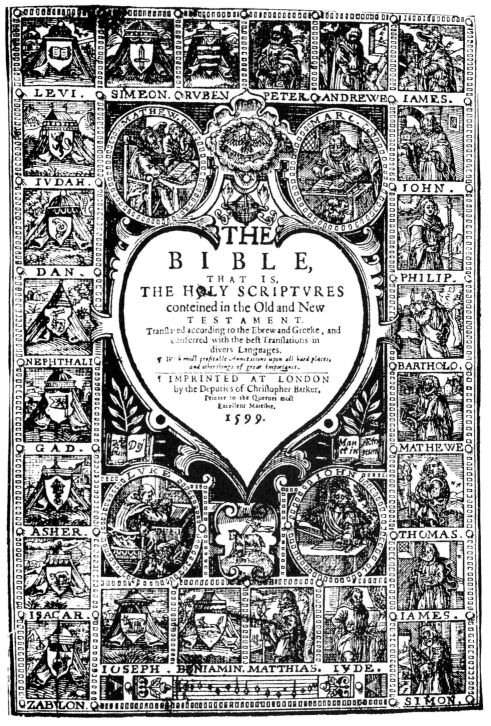

PLATE 3: *Title page of the* Barker *Bible (1599), showing on the left, the ensigns of the twelve Tribes and on the right, the twelve Apostles, with the four Evangelists within the central panel*

'Royal dainties' means delicacies fit for the tables of kings. This is brought out in the versions of the verse in other Bibles:

Knox 'Rich in wheat shall Aser's [*sic*] lands be; he shall send out delicacies for the tables of kings.'

GNB 'Asher's land will produce rich food, He will provide food fit for a king.'

The territory of this tribe was fruitful and prolific and produced an abundance of the necessities of life and the choicest fruits.

The distinctive bearing on his ensign is a flourishing tree or golden cup or urn. The tree is probably meant to be an olive tree; the urn or cup the vessel for storing the oil from the olives, oil being a symbol for fatness or plenty. The following verses from the *GNB*: *Judges* 9. 8–9 are worth noting:

> '*Once upon a time the trees got themselves together to choose a king for themselves. They said to the olive tree, "Be our king". The olive tree answered, "In order to govern you, I would have to stop producing my oil, which is used to honour gods and men."*'

Naphthali (*Genesis* 49. 21)

'*Naphthali is a hind let loose; he giveth worldly goods.*'

The words 'he giveth worldly goods' are considered to refer to the eloquence of this tribe, especially to the *Song of Deborah* which followed the victory of Barak over Jabin. (*Judges* 5)

The *Septuagint* version of this verse is: 'Naphthali is a slender terebinth, which putteth forth goodly branches.'

The *Vulgate* uses the masculine '*cervus emissus*', '*a stag let loose,*' *A Catholic Commentary on Holy Scriptures* (160f) says: Perhaps with MT (Massoretic Text); 'Nephthali [*sic*] is a free-roaming hind' with reference to branched antlers. The allusion would then be to Nephthali's spirit of freedom and eagerness to defend it.'

This can be compared with the alternate verses given in *GNB*. 'Naphthali is a spreading tree that puts out lovely branches', or 'Naphthali is a deer that runs free, who bears lovely fawns.'

All versions refer to the fecundity of the tribe and to the fertility of their land.

The distinctive bearing on Naphthali's ensign is a hind, a reference to the first version of the verse quoted. Occasionally one sees the ensign bearing a terebinth tree, a reference to the *Septuagint* version quoted earlier.

Joseph

As stated in Section I of this book, Joseph is not included in the twelve tribes of Israel, his place being taken by his two sons, Ephraim and Manasseh.

Ephraim

The distinctive bearing on the ensign borne by Ephraim is probably derived from *Deuteronomy* 33, often referred to as The Blessing of Moses. Verse 17 reads; 'His glory is like the firstling of a bullock, and his horns are like the horns of unicorns; with them he shall push the people together to the ends of the earth; and they are the tens of thousands of Ephraim, and there are the thousands of Manasseh.'

The Biblical commentators say that 'the firstling bullock' is a reference to Ephraim to whom Jacob gave preference over Manasseh, Ephraim's older brother (*Genesis* 48. 20)

The *GNB* version of *Deuteronomy* 33 is 'Joseph has the strength of a bull, the horns of a wild ox. His horns are Manasseh's thousands and Ephraim's ten thousands. With them he gores the nations And pushes them to the ends of the earth.'

The distinctive bearing on Ephraim's ensign is an ox or bullock.

Manasseh

The *Midrash* tells us that the device borne on the ensign for Manasseh was a wild ox; this is a reference to the horns of a unicorn, the Hebrew word for wild ox often being translated as 'a unicorn.' A unicorn is sometimes seen on Manasseh's ensign.

The more usual device for Manasseh, however, is a luxuriant vine, planted by the side of a wall, the tendrils of the vine overhanging the wall. This is a direct reference to the words Jacob used in his blessing of Joseph, Manasseh's father (*Genesis* 49. 22). 'Joseph is a fruitful bough, even a fruitful bough by a well; whose branches run over the wall.' The *GNB* alternate version is 'Joseph is like a tree by a spring; a fruitful tree that spreads over a wall.'

Another device occasionally seen for Manasseh is a palm tree. The reason for this probably comes from *Deuteronomy* 33. 14. (*GNB* version). Referring to Joseph, Moses said 'May their land be blessed with sun-ripened fruit, Rich with the best fruits of each season.'

Incidentally, there are many occasions in the Volume of the Sacred Law when the term 'half-tribe' is used. This does not refer to the fact that the inheritance of Joseph was split into two half-tribes of Manasseh and Ephraim. According to the Chief Rabbi, Dr. J. H. Hertz (*Pentateuch and Haftorahs*, p. 710) 'The word "half" in the phrase "half-tribe of Manasseh" is not to be taken in a precise mathematical sense. It denotes a section. According to *Numbers* 26. 29–32, there were eight sub-tribes of Manasseh, six of whom were alloted territory on the west of the Jordan.'

Benjamin (*Gen.* 49. 27)

'Benjamin shall raven as a wolf; in the morning he shall devour the prey; and at night he shall divide the spoil.'

The phrase *'shall raven'* has also been translated as *'shall tear'*; it refers to the war-like character of the tribe.

The distinctive bearing on Benjamin's ensign is a wolf, a direct reference to the verse quoted.

The Benjamin ensign in the set at the William Waples Museum at Sunderland (see above under *Simeon and Levi*) is unique. It does not show a wolf, but rather warlike horsemen brandishing weapons. The inspiration for this comes from the wording printed in the Lectures on the Banners which are found in some rituals. The wording for Benjamin is '. . . a green banner, emblazoned with a wolf because it was ever a warlike and cruel tribe.' Biblical evidence for the warlike and cruel nature of the tribe of Benjamin can be found in the Book of Judges.

Unlike Scotland (see Section 12), the Supreme Grand Chapter of England does not lay down an 'official' device for each ensign, though by and large, the distinctive bearings used by Chapters follow the pattern of those outlined above. Inevitably, however, there are occasional differences, some of which are due to bad copying whilst others are not so easily explained. There is at least one Chapter using ensigns for the *sons* of Jacob, i.e. including a separate ensign for Levi and another for Joseph, Ephraim and Manasseh being left out. The differences occur not only in the device used, but also in the colour of the ensign.

One artist who drew plates and vignettes for Bibles was Philip

PLATE 4: *A Benjamin ensign to be found in the William Waples Museum at Sunderland depicting warlike horsemen brandishing weapons*

James de Loutherbourg. He was born in Germany in 1740. Later he came to England and was elected a Royal Academician, specializing in Biblical subjects. He died in Chiswick in 1812. A copy of one of his plates called 'The Standards of Israel' can be seen in a Bible known as *The Illustrated Family Bible* (John Kitto, first published in 1828). de Loutherbourg follows the usual devices for six of the tribes; the other six have devices as follows:

Gad;	a vertical lance or banner
Judah;	an old lion
Ephraim;	a bunch of grapes on a vine
Manasseh;	a palm tree
Dan;	a serpent
Asher;	an urn filled with foliage

PLATE 5: *The de Loutherbourg woodcut in the Illustrated Family Bible (1828) and subsequent editions by John Kitto. The ensigns have the names of the Tribes inscribed in Hebrew*

de Loutherbourg's designs are featured as a masthead on the first issue of *The Weekly Gleaner*, published in San Francisco, bearing the date Friday, 16 January, 1857.

There is another feature of the de Loutherbourg ensigns; each has embroidered on it the name of the tribe in Hebrew. This idea has been copied on occasions, though one set has the Hebrew name for Asher on the ensign for Ephraim.

The following Table gives the names of the tribes in both Hebrew and English. The meaning of the name is also given. The order in which they are shown is the order in which the ensigns are placed in a Royal Arch Chapter (See Section 6).

Judah	יְהוּדָה	Praise
Issachar	יִשָּׂשכָר	Man of reward
Zebulun	זְבוּלֻן	Dwelling
Reuben	רְאוּבֵן	Behold, a son
Simeon	שִׁמְעוֹן	Hearing
Gad	גָּד	A troop
Ephraim	אֶפְרַיִם	Doubly fruitful
Manasseh	מְנַשֶּׁה	Causing forgetfulness
Benjamin	בִּנְיָמִן	Son of the right hand
Dan	דָּן	Judge
Asher	אָשֵׁר	Happy
Naphthali	נַפְתָּלִי	Wrestling

Before leaving this Section, mention should be made of a set of ensigns belonging to Bonavallum Chapter, No. 1304, Horncastle, Lincolnshire. One of their members, E Comp I. McFeeters, has prepared some notes on them. He says: 'In most Chapters the ensigns are silken banners but here they are discs of art board with brass fittings to attach them to the top of the staves. The discs are painted with the name of the tribe on a scroll on one side and the emblem on the other. Such ensigns are rare in England and unique in Lincolnshire.'

By and large the emblems are similar to those found in most other Chapters. The main differences are as follows. The comments below are taken from the notes prepared by E Comp McFeeters.

ISSACHAR: '. . . an ass bent beneath its burdens. But our ass has collapsed beneath its burden, its mouth is open and it looks to be braying its last heehaw.'

REUBEN: '. . . a man. Looking at it in detail, he is surrounded by water and in the background are the hills from which it has flowed. The man is almost naked, with just a coarse and scanty cloak. This could suggest that he is just coming from the bed of his father's concubine, or that it is showing his poverty—that, indeed, he is not excelling. So every aspect of Jacob's statement is covered in this banner.'

GAD: '. . . a vertical lance. This could indicate "He shall overcome at the end"—for after mediaeval tournaments the victorious knight would hold his lance aloft.'

EPHRAIM: '. . . a fox—an emblem that might have been appropriate to Jacob himself in his method of obtaining the birthright of Esau—but this has no connection with Ephraim. . . . So what happened? I think our artist was probably a schoolmaster who had spent many years combatting the Lincolnshire dialect. The chief characteristics of the dialect are lengthening and splitting the vowels and the transposition of aspirates. In Lincolnshire, an 'en lays a hegg'. So I am convinced that the artist was firmly told "We must 'ave a banner for Hephraim; it wants a hox on it." So our artist painted a fox with a fall of water beneath to show that it was due to a defect in aspiration peculiar to their dialect.'

PLATE 6: *An Ephraim ensign belonging to Bonavallum Chapter No. 1304, Horncastle, which bears a device that clearly represents a fox*

There is no doubt that the ensign for Ephraim bears a device that clearly represents a fox; but why? The ingenious explanation given above, which the writer says is speculation, may possibly be right; he puts it forward in all seriousness. It may sound somewhat far-fetched, but I cannot think of a better reason. And who would want to!

Latin inscriptions on the ensigns

Some sets of Chapter ensigns bear Latin inscriptions usually taken from the *Vulgate* version of the Bible.

In the year AD 382, Pope Damasus commissioned Jerome to produce a Latin Bible. Jerome translated the whole of the Old Testament from the Hebrew text, and the work was finished in the year AD 405. The *Books of Apocrypha* were then completed, this work taking only a few months.

The new Latin version was immediately accepted by the Church, but over the next few centuries there were textual changes. The Council of Trent in 1546 made the *Vulgate* the authorized text of the Roman Church. Further revisions were made under the direction of Pope Clement VIII who declared, in 1592, that it was 'never again to be altered.' However, according to *A Catholic Commentary on Holy Scriptures*; (page 9) 'The official Clementine edition of 1592 being inadequate, the work of preparing a critical edition of the *Vulgate* has been in the hands of a special Benedictine Commission since 1907, and since 1933 has become the special work of the Monastery of St. Jerome in Rome. The task of the monks is to restore the text of St. Jerome, as far as that is possible.'

The notes which follow show:

(a) the relevant extract from the *Vulgate*;
(b) the Latin quotation usually found on each ensign, with a generally accepted, but not necessarily accurate, English translation, and
(c) other Latin quotations that are known to be used on some ensigns, again with a similar English translation,

Mistakes in spelling are frequently found, some of which may be included here.

Judah

Vulgate	*Catulus leonis Juda . . . requiescens accubuisti ut leo . . . quis suscitabit eum?* A lion's whelp is Judah . . . thou hast lain reclining like a lion . . . who will rouse him?
Usual quotation	*Accubuit ut leo quis suscitabit.* As a lion he reclined; who will rouse him.
Known variations	*Accubuit ut leo.* He lay down (He has lain down) like a lion.
	Accumbit ut leo. He lies down like a lion.
	Catulus suscitabitur. The (lion's) whelp will be roused.
	Vivit leo de tribu Juda. The lion of the tribe of Judah lives.

The wording in the last quotation comes from *Revelations* 5. 5.

'Et unus de senioribus dixit nihi; Ne fleveris; ecce vicit leo tribu Juda, radix David, aperire librum, et solvere septem signacula ejus.' The *AV* reads 'And one of the elders said to me; Weep not, behold the Lion of the tribe of Judah, the Root of David, hath prevailed to open the book and loose the seven seals thereof.'

The ensign in Supreme Grand Chapter uses this last version, the only difference being that the first word is given as '*Vivat*'; this gives the meaning as 'Long live the lion of the tribe of Judah . . .'

Issachar

Vulgate	*Asinus fortis accubans inter terminos.* A strong (-built) ass lying between the boundaries
Usual quotation	*Accubans inter terminos.* Lying (reclining) between the borders.
Known variation	*Intra onera accumbens.* Lying reclining within loads (burdens)

Zebulun

Vulgate	*In littore maris habitabit.* He shall dwell on the shore of the sea.

PLATE 7: *The ensign of the Tribe of Judah with a Latin inscription*

PLATE 8: *The ensign of the Tribe of Issachar with a Latin inscription*

PLATE 9: *The ensign of the Tribe of Zebulun with a Latin inscription*

PLATE 10: *The ensign of the Tribe of Reuben with a Latin inscription*

PLATE 11: *The ensign of the Tribe of Simeon with a Latin inscription*

PLATE 12: *The ensign of the Tribe of Gad with a Latin inscription*

PLATE 13: *The ensign of the Tribe of Ephraim with a Latin inscription*

PLATE 14: *The ensign of the Tribe of Manasseh with a Latin inscription*

PLATE 15: *The ensign of the Tribe of Benjamin with a Latin inscription*

PLATE 16: *The ensign of the Tribe of Dan with a Latin inscription*

PLATE 17: *The ensign of the Tribe of Asher with a Latin inscription*

PLATE 18: *The ensign of the Tribe of Naphthali with a Latin inscription*

PLATES 19–22: *The four Principal Banners depicting a Man (Reuben), a Lion (Judah), an Ox (Ephraim) and an Eagle (Dan)*

PLATE 23: *The Harris Tracing Board for the Royal Arch showing how the ensigns are arranged in Chapter*

PLATE 24: *An example of an Aaron's Breastplate, belonging to Leicester and Rutland Chapter of First Principals, No. 1896. It shows the colours thought to be attributed to the precious stones and from which the colours of the ensigns are taken*

Plate 25: *A Royal Arch Apron showing the T over H 'badge'*

Usual quotation   As in *Vulgate*.

Known variation   *Ad portum navium, ipse ad portum navium.*
                  To the haven of (for) ships, himself to the
                  haven of (for) ships.

Reuben
Vulgate   *Primogenitus meus . . . effusus es sicut aqua non
                  cresces.*
                  My firstborn . . . thou are unrestrained like
                  (as) water, thou shalt not thrive (grow).

Usual quotation   *Aquarum instar ruens.*
                  Hastening (rushing) like waters.

Known variations *Primogenitus meus.*
                  My firstborn.
                  Ecce filius aquarum instar ruens.
                  Behold my son rushing like the waters.
                  (flood).

Simeon and Levi
Vulgate   *Vasa iniquitatis bellantia . . . dividam eos in Jacob,
                  et dispurgam eos in Israel.*
                  Fighting vessels (utensils) of injustice . . . I
                  will divide them in Jacob, and scatter them in
                  Israel.

Usual quotation   *Vasa iniquitatis bellantia.*
                  Fighting implements of injustice.

Known variations *Dividam et dispergam.*
                  I will divide (separate) and scatter (them).
                  Instrumenta violentia in habit.
                  Impetuous instruments in (their) habiti(a-
                  tion(s)).

Gad
Vulgate   *Ipse accingetur retrorsum.*
                  He himself shall be armed.

Usual quotation   *Ipse tandem devincet.*
                  He at last will subdue.

Known variation   *Turma populabitur cum sed ipse.*
                         The troop (squadron) will be destroyed but
                         yet not him.

Ephraim
Vulgate.   —

Usual quotation   *Amans trituram.*
                         Fond of threshing.
                         Loving to thresh.

Known variation   *Actionibus ipsius.*
                         By his own efforts.

Manasseh
Vulgate   —

Usual quotation   *Ramus foecundus juxta fontem.*
                         A fruitful bough near a well (spring).

Benjamin
Vulgate   *Benjamin lupus rapax, mane comeddit praedam, et*
                         vesperi dividet spolia.
                         Benjamin is a ravening wolf, devouring the
                         prey in the morning, and dividing the spoils
                         in the evening.

Usual quotation   *Manus comedit praedam et vesperi dividet spolia*
                         In the morning he eats the prey and in the
                         evening divides the spoil.

Known variations   *Ut lupus erit qui mane vorat et vesperi partitur.*
                         He will be like a wolf which eats greedily in
                         the morning and in the evening it (i.e. the
                         spoil) is shared.
                         Lupus qui discerpit mane comedit.
                         The wolf which tears (its prey) in pieces eats
                         in the morning.

Dan
Vulgate   *Coluber in via, cerastes in semita.*
                         A snake on the road, a horned snake on the
                         footpath.

Usual quotation   *Coluber in via.*
A snake on the road (in the way).

Known variation   *Surgens juxta viam qui pasco equitem.*
Rising up close to the road (art thou) who feeds upon (consumes) a horseman (rider).

Asher
Vulgate   *Et praebebit delicias regibus.*
He will provide delicacies for kings.

Usual quotation   *Praebebit delicias regibus.*
He will provide delicacies for kings.

Known variation   *Pinguis panis ejus et proebebit delicias.*
His bread is fat and shall furnish (provide) delicacies.

Naphthali
Vulgate   *Cervus emissus.*
A stag let loose.

Usual quotation   *Cerva emissa.*
Hind (deer) let loose.

Known variation   *Ecce, cerva emissa quae proefert.*
Behold, a hind let loose that brings forth (gives birth).

Connaught Chapter No. 1971, Aldershot has a set of ensigns that bear unusual and original Latin quotations. The Petition for the Chapter was signed on 25 April, 1898; there were ten Petitioners, one solicitor and nine Army men. Three of these belonged to the Army Medical Service; two to the Somerset Light Infantry; 1 from the Army Chaplain Department; 1 from the Northumberland Fusiliers; 1 from the Hants Volunteers. The tenth was a Colonel, but his Regiment is not known; he was the MEZ. I suggest the mottoes may well have some connection with the Regiments of the Petitioners. The Latin, with English translation, is given below, together with one of the Regiments using the motto.

Judah   *Nec aspera terrent.*   Nor do difficulties deter. Motto of The Royal Fusiliers (City of London Regiment).

Issachar	*In arduis fidelis.* Steadfast in difficulties Motto of Royal Army Medical Corps,
Zebulun	*Per mare per terram.* By land, by sea, Motto of Royal Marines.
Reuben	*. . . retrorsum.* . . . backwards.
Simeon	*Cede nullis.* Yield to none. Motto of The Light Infantry.
Gad	*Quo fas et gloria ducunt.* Whither right and glory lead, Motto of The Royal Regiment of Artillery.
Ephraim	*Nil sine labore.* Nothing without labour. Motto of The Royal Corps of Transport.
Manasseh	*Viret in aeternum.* It flourishes for ever. Motto of the 13th Royal Hussars.
Benjamin	*Ecce, ferus hostis.* Behold, a savage foe.
Dan	*Quis separabit?* Who will separate? Motto of The Irish Guards.
Asher	*Ne obliviscaris.* Forget not. Motto of Argyll and Sutherland Highlanders.
Naphthali	*Nisi Dominus frustra.* In vain without the Lord. Motto of The King's Own Scottish Borderers.

Latin inscriptions on the four Principal Banners are unusual, but they appear on a set owned by the Chapter of Union, No. 310.

Man	*Sapientia et intelligentia.* Wisdom and understanding.
Lion	*Robur et imperatum.* Strength and command.
Ox	*Patientia et sedulitas.* Patience and assiduity
Eagle	*Promptitudo et alacritas.* Speed and alertness (readiness).

The colours of the Royal Arch ensigns

In the printed Lectures on the ensigns which are found in some Royal Arch rituals, we are given the colour of each ensign (with the exception of Reuben); they substantially correspond to the colours of the ensigns used in Supreme Grand Chapter.

The *Midrash* tells us that the colour of the flag [*sic*] for each of the tribes corresponded to the colour of the precious stones on the breastplate of Aaron, the High Priest.

To associate a colour with each ensign it is necessary to associate each tribe with a particular stone. This necessitates the consideration of

(a) the names of the stones used in the breastplate;
(b) the colour(s) associated with each stone;
(c) the names engraven on the stones, and
(d) the order of the stones in the breastplate.

It is as well to start with the relevant verses from the Bible; they are as follows:

Exodus 28. 17–21

17. And thou shalt set in it settings of stones, even four rows of stones; the first row shall be a sardius, a topaz, and a carbuncle; this shall be the first row.
18. And the second row shall be an emerald, a sapphire and a diamond.
19. And the third row a ligure, an agate, and an amethyst.
20. And the fourth row a beryl, and an onyx, and a jasper; they shall be set in gold in their inclosings.
21. And the stones shall be with the names of the children of Israel, twelve, according to their names, like the engravings of a signet; every one with his name shall they be according to the twelve tribes.

The following quotation should also be noted.

Josephus (*Antiquities. Book 3., 7.5*) says the stones shall be 'in the order according to which they were born.' This is a reference to *Exodus. 28.* 9–10 which says 'And thou shalt take two onyx stones, and grave on them the names of the Children of Israel; six of their names shall be on one stone, and the names of the six that remain on the other stone, according to their birth.' This had nothing to do with the breastplate; it referred to the stones on the shoulder pieces of the ephod, a priestly garment that draped from the shoulders. The reason for the names on the stones is found in *Exodus* 28. 12: 'And Aaron shall bear their names before the Lord upon his two shoulders for a memorial.' According to Rashi (Rabbi Solomon ben Isaac, 1040–1105) 'So that the Holy One, blessed be He, will see the names of the tribes written before Him, and He will remember their righteousness.'

The names of the stones

Some years ago an eminent masonic scholar, the Rev. Canon W. W. Covey Crump (a Past Master of Quatuor Coronati Lodge), pointed out that the description of gems has for some time now been based on a chemical and crystallographic classification which was unknown in Biblical days. Different gems, if similar in appearance, were at one time regarded as identical in nature. It is probably for this reason that the names of the stones differ in various sources. The following Table illustrates the difficulty in identifying the names of the stones used in each row. The information has been taken from the following; no two sources giving the same detail.

> *Josephus; The Book of Antiquities.*
> *The Authorized Version of the Bible.*
> *A Bible bearing the date 1769.*
> *The Pentateuch and Haftorahs. (*Ed. Hertz*).*
> *The Knox Version of the Holy Bible.*
> *The Bible in Today's English Version. (GNB).*
> *The New International Version of the Holy Bible.*
> *The Midrash*

The figures in the Table represent the number of times the particular stone is mentioned in the eight sources.

The first row

Sardius.*	5.	Topaz.	7.	Emerald.	2.
Ruby	2.	Chrysolite.	1.	Carbuncle	2.
Cornelian	1.			Smaragd.	1.
				Garnet.	1.
				Green felspar.	1.
*or Sardonyx				Beryl.	1.
Total	8.		8.		8.

The second row

Carbuncle.	3.	Sapphire.	6.	Diamond.	3.
Emerald.	3	Jasper.	1.	Emerald.	2.
Turquoise.	1.	Lapis Lazuli	1.	Sapphire.	1.
Purple Garnet.	1.			Jade.	1.
				Jasper	1.
Total	8.		8.		8

The third row

Ligure.	3.	Agate.	7.	Amethyst.	6.
Jacinth.	3.	Amethyst.	1.	Agate.	1.
Turquoise.	2.			Jasper	1.
Total	8.		8.		8.

The fourth row

Beryl.	4.	Onyx.	6.	Jasper.	5.
Chrysolite.	3.	Cornelian.	2.	Green felspar.	1.
Topaz.	1.			Cornelian.	1.
Total	8.		8.		8.

The colours of the stones

Even if we could positively identify the stones used, we would still have problems regarding their colour. Some of them can be in a variety of colours, as the following list shows. The information has been taken from a large Bible printed in Birmingham in 1769, supplemented where appropriate by information from *The Shorter Oxford English Dictionary*, the latter being shown in brackets. The names of the stones are in alphabetical order.

Colour of the stones

Agate	Partly transparent, partly opaque; generally variegated with veins disposed in the most elegant manner.
Amethyst	Violet colour, bordering on purple or nearly the colour of red wine.
Beryl	Pale green, now generally known by the name of Aqua Marine from its resemblance to sea-water.
Carbuncle	Species of ruby, glowing red colour. (Varying from deep crimson to pale rose).
Chrysolite	(Pale, yellowish green).
Cornelian	(Deep, dull red, flesh coloured or reddish-white).
Diamond	(Colourless, or variously tinted).
Emerald	Lively green, transparent and free from the least mixture of any colours.
Felspar	(Usually white or flesh coloured).
Garnet	(Usually transparent, deep red).
Jacinth	(Reddish-orange).
Jade	(Translucent, bright green, bluish or whitish).
Jasper	Generally green, spotted with yellow, brown or white.
Lapis-Lazuli	(Bright blue).
Ligure	Thought to be a kind of jacinth, agate or amethyst; nearly the colour of amber.
Onyx	Various species of this gem; the ground is often the colour of the human nail, variegated with zones in the most regular manner, and often of a brown colour.
Ruby	(Varying from deep crimson to pale rose).
Sapphire	Fine blue colour.
Sardius	Red, flaming colour; half transparent, sometimes with a yellow cast in it. Also known as cornelian.

Smaragd	(Bright green).
Topaz	Transparent and of a beautiful yellow or gold colour.
Turquoise	(Opaque or translucent sky-blue or pale green).

Another source of information is *Miscellanea Latomorum*, a collection of masonic notes and queries published by Quatuor Coronati Lodge, No 2076 (EC). One correspondent to that publication (Vol. 25, page 107) supports the information he gives with the statement 'This is the most authentic arrangement I can find. It is by a great Hebrew scholar in a Lecture at the Metropolitan College S.R.I.A.' Unfortunately, the Hebrew scholar is not identified.

The following Table shows the colours of the stones
as given in three different sources.

Tribe	The Midrash	The Lectures	Misc. Lat.
Reuben	Red	*not stated*	Red
Simeon	Green	Yellow	Yellow
Levi	White, black and red	—	Green
Judah	Azure	Crimson	Blood red
Issachar	Black	Sky blue	Blue
Zebulun	White	Purple	Green
Dan	Like sapphire	Light green	Bright blue
Gad	Grey	White	Purple
Naphthali	Wine	Blue	Red and green
Asher	Aquamarine	Purple	White
Joseph	Black	—	Blue and black
Benjamin	Mixture of all twelve colours	Dark green	Blue and green
Ephraim	Black embroidered with a picture of Egypt	Dark green	—
Manasseh		Flesh colour	—

The colours of the ensigns used by Supreme Grand Chapter of England are those listed under the heading *The Lectures* in the Table on page 47, red being used for Reuben. These colours are not specified in *Royal Arch Regulations*; they are so specified in *The Constitution and Laws of the Supreme Grand Chapter of Royal Arch Freemasons of Scotland*. (See Section 12).

The names engraven on the stones

To associate a colour with each ensign it is necessary to consider whether the names to be engraven on the stones were those of the twelve sons of Jacob, which would include Levi and Joseph but exclude Ephraim and Manasseh, or the names of the twelve tribes of Israel, which would include Ephraim and Manasseh, but exclude Levi and Joseph.

Exodus 28. 21 says 'And the stones shall be according to the names of the Children of Israel ... they shall be for the twelve tribes.' Does the name 'Israel' refer to Jacob? *Genesis* 32. 28 says 'Thy name shall no more be called Jacob, but Israel.' This interpretation would mean that Levi and Joseph should be included and Ephraim and Manasseh excluded. This then raises the difficulty of the colour of the ensigns for Ephraim and Manasseh.

The order of the stones on the breastplate

We have seen that *Josephus* said the stones shall be 'in the order according to which they (i.e. the sons of Jacob) were born.' As previously stated, this referred to the stones on the shoulder pieces of the ephod, not to the stones on the breastplate. So far as the latter is concerned, the Volume of the Sacred Law gives the names of three stones for each of the four rows, but no indication of the way they were to be read. Should it be from left to right as English is read, or from right to left as Hebrew is read? If the latter (this seems more likely), then the order would have been as shown in the Table on page 49.

The name of the stone is given in each case, the details being taken from *The Pentateuch and Haftoras* (Ed. Dr. J. H. Hertz, Chief Rabbi). The name of the comparable stone in the A.V. is given in parenthesis where it differs from Hertz. The Biblical verse mentioning the birth of each son is also shown.

The order of the stones on Aaron's breastplate
(assuming they were read from left to right)

Levi (*Genesis* 29. 34) Smaragd (Carbuncle)	Simeon (*Genesis* 29. 33) Topaz	Reuben (*Genesis* 29. 32) Carnelian (Sardius)
Naphthali (*Genesis* 30. 8) Emerald	Dan (*Genesis* 30. 6) Sapphire	Judah (*Genesis* 29. 35) Carbuncle (Emerald)
Issachar (*Genesis* 30. 18) Amethyst	Asher (*Genesis* 30. 13) Agate	Gad (*Genesis* 30. 11) Jacinth (Ligure)
Benjamin (*Genesis* 35. 18) Jasper	Joseph (*Genesis* 30. 24) Onyx	Zebulun (*Genesis* 30. 20) Beryl

(Zebulun was given preference over Issachar in Jacob's blessing).

Despite the clear statement that there were four rows of three stones, many Bible illustrators have indicated three rows of four stones. An illustration in a Bible printed in 1595 shows the High Priest wearing a breastplate with four rows, each row having three stones, as in diagram (i) below. However, illustrations in later Bibles show the High Priest wearing a breastplate with three rows of four stones, as in diagram (ii) below. Could this have resulted in the names being read from top to bottom, i.e. the four rows of three stones?

(Diagram i)

(Diagram ii)

Bernard Jones, in his book *Freemasons' Book of the Royal Arch* (revised edition, pages 208–209) shows two photographs of breast-plates, both four rows of three stones, one with the names of the sons of Jacob engraven in the following order.

LEVI	SIMEON	ASHER
ZEBULUN	ISSACHAR	JUDAH
GAD	NAPHTHALI	DAN
JOSEPH	BENJAMIN	REUBEN

It will be noted that the order does not correspond to the order in which the sons were born, whichever way the names are read (See Section 12 regarding the official Jewel worn by the Third Grand Principal in Scotland).

The peculiar qualities of the stones

The following information is taken from *The Legends of the Jews* (Ginsberg; Vol. III pp 169–172). It will be noted that the stones given for each of the sons does not always match the stone(s) referred to in the Table on page 49.

'The twelve stones differed not only in colour, but also in certain qualities peculiar to each, and both quality and colour had a special reference to the tribe whose name it bore.

Reuben's stone was the ruby that has the property, when grated by a woman and tasted by her, of promoting pregnancy, for it was Reuben who found the mandrakes which induce pregnancy.

Simeon's stone was the smaragd, that has the property of breaking as soon as an unchaste woman looks at it, a fitting stone for the tribe whose sire, Simeon, was kindled to wrath by the unchaste action of Shechem.

Levi's stone was the carbuncle that beams like lightning, as, likewise, the faces of that tribe beam with piety and erudition. This stone has the virtue of making him who wears it, wise.

Judah's stone was the green emerald that has the power of making its owner victorious in battle, a fitting stone for this tribe from which springs the Jewish dynasty of kings that routed its enemies. The colour green alludes to the shame that turned Judah's countenance green when he publicly confessed his crime with Tamar.

Issachar's stone was the sapphire for this tribe devoted themselves completely to the study of the Torah, and it is this very stone, the sapphire, out of which the two tables of the law were hewn. This stone increases the strength of vision and heals many diseases, as the Torah likewise, to which this tribe was devoted, enlightens the eye and makes the body well.

The white pearl is the stone for Zebulun, for with his merchant ships he sailed the sea and drew his sustenance from the ocean, from which the pearl, too, is drawn. The pearl also has the quality of bringing its owner sleep, and it is all the more credit to this tribe that they nevertheless spent their nights on commercial ventures to maintain their brother tribe, Issachar, that lived only for the study of the Torah.

Dan's stone was a species of topaz, in which was visible the inverted face of a man, for the Danites were sinful, turning good to evil, hence the inverted face in their stone

The turquoise was Naphthali's stone, for it gives the owner speed in riding, and Naphthali was 'a hind let loose.'

Gad's stone was the crystal, that endows its owner with courage in battle, and hence served this warlike tribe that battled for the Lord as an admonition to fear none and build on God.

The chrysolite was Asher's stone, and as this stone aids digestion and makes its owner sturdy and fat, so were the agricultural products of Asher's tribe of such excellent quality, that they made fat those who ate of them.

Joseph's stone was the onyx, that has the virtue of endowing him who wears it with grace, and truly by his grace, did Joseph find favour in the eyes of all.

Jasper was Benjamin's stone, and as this stone turns colour being now red, now green, now even black, so did Benjamin's feelings vary to his brothers.'

Chagall's Jerusalem windows

This Section would not be complete without a reference to a modern artist's ideas of colours associated with the individual tribes of Israel. Marc Chagall, a distinguished French-Jewish artist, has designed for the synagogue of the Hadassah Hebrew Medical Centre in Jerusalem, what has been described as 'twelve magnificent stained glass windows . . . symbolizing the twelve sons of the patriarch Jacob from whom came the twelve tribes of Israel.'

Chagall is said to have worked for two years in the research, study and final execution of the windows. In designing them he was influenced by the Blessing of Jacob (*Genesis* 49) and the Blessing of Moses (*Deuteronomy* 33). In selecting the colours to be used, he was influenced by *Exodus* 28. 15–21. The windows are arranged in threes, just as were the jewels in Aaron's breastplate. Each window represents a tribe of Israel and is placed in the same order as that which Jacob used when he blessed his sons.

The dominant colours used in the windows are blue, red, yellow and green. The choice of colours is emotional, rather than any attempt to follow the Biblical narrative. In an introductory text to

The Jerusalem Windows (published by Michael Joseph), the author Jean Leymarie says 'The basic harmony between the blues and the reds, interrupted by intermediate violet tones—sapphires and rubies punctuated by amethysts—balances the wonderful audacity of the three green windows against the three yellow ones—emeralds and chrysolites with topaz reflections.'

The basic colour of each of the windows is as follows.

Reuben	Light blue on a white base, evoking clean air and transparent foaming sea. (*Genesis* 49. 4. '*Unstable as water.*')
Simeon	Sombre blue, establishing a grave and nocturnal atmosphere. (*Genesis* 49. 6. '*For in their anger they slew a man*'.)
Levi	Yellow. The window has been designed to emphasize the religious functions that were to be assumed by this tribe.
Judah	Crimson, punctuated with white, which is meant to symbolize power, the blood of battles and the 'blood of grapes' (*Genesis* 49. 11. '*He washed his garments in wine and clothes in the blood of grapes.*')
Issachar	Light green, described by Jean Leymarie as 'tender and calm,' which is the very expression of spring and paradisial joy. (*Genesis* 49. 15. '*And he saw that the rest was good, and the land that it was pleasant.*')
Dan	Dark blue. The design includes a three-branch candelabrum, rising as a tree of judgement, entwined by a horned viper. (*Genesis* 49. 16–17. '*Dan shall judge his people ... Dan shall be a serpent by the way.*')
Gad	Sombre green, punctuated by blood red depicting the tumult of battle, a reference to the tribe's constant defence of nomadic invasions. (*Genesis* 49. 19. '*Gad, a troop shall overcome him, but he shall overcome at the last.*')

Asher	Soft green, indicative of peace and happiness. (*Genesis* 49. 20. '*His bread shall be fat and he shall yield royal dainties.*')
Zebulun	A ship sailing on a vermilion sea. (*Genesis* 49. 13. '*Zebulun shall be a haven for ships.*')
Naphthali	Lemon-yellow. (*Deuteronomy* 33. 23. '*O Naphthali, satisfied with favour, and full with the blessing of the Lord.*')
Joseph	Gold. The messianic meaning of Jacob's blessing is emphasized by two hands holding a ram's horn (shofar).
Benjamin	Blue, with a wolf coloured violet and carmine and with bloodshot eyes, standing over its headless prey. (*Genesis* 49. 27. '*Benjamin shall raven like a wolf.*')

No attempt has been made to describe the windows in detail. This information can be found in *The Jerusalem Windows*, mentioned earlier, to which reference is strongly recommended.

Early references to ensigns and the twelve tribes of Israel in the Royal Arch

References to Royal Arch Chapters appear in England in the 1760s, but we are not given any idea how the Chapter was furnished, nor do we have any evidence of the ritual used in those early days.

We know that the Grand Lodge of the Antients came into being about 1751. Their *Constitutions* went by the name *Ahiman Rezon*, the first edition of which was published in 1756. Therein we find that the author, their Grand Secretary, Laurence Dermott, included what he called '*Ahabat Olam, a prayer repeated in the Royal Arch at Jerusalem.*' There was, of course, no Royal Arch at Jerusalem, but the prayer has for many years been said daily by orthodox Jews. Immediately following this prayer, Dermott tells us that he firmly believes the 'Royal Arch to be the Root, Heart and Marrow of Free-Masonry.' It is quite evident that this Grand Lodge actively encouraged the Royal Arch.

The other Grand Lodge at that time, the premier Grand Lodge, did not recognize the Royal Arch, but that did not stop some of its members becoming exalted. A few of them, acting in their private capacity, decided in 1766 to set up the Grand and Royal Arch Chapter of Jerusalem, from which our present-day Supreme Grand Chapter is descended. It is worthy of note that amongst those members was none other than the Grand Master himself.

The instrument setting up this historic body is known as *The Charter of Compact*; it can be seen today in the Exhibition at Freemasons' Hall, Great Queen Street, London. (See illustration plate 22.)

A careful examination of this important document reveals that although it refers to the Jewel, the apron to be worn (which had to

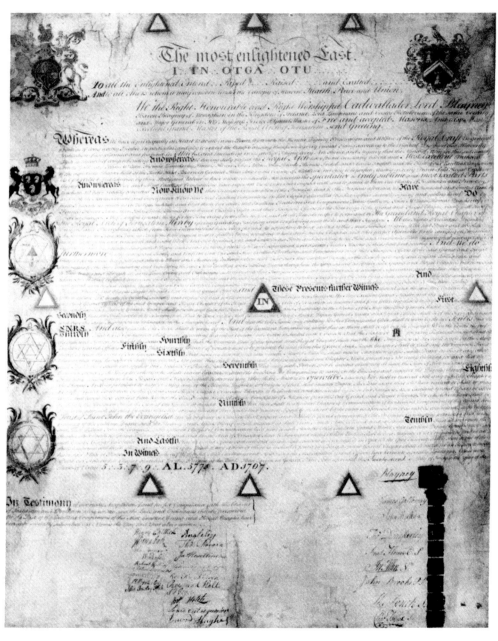

PLATE 26: *The Charter of Compact which established the first Grand Chapter. It refers to the T over H 'badge' that had to be properly displayed on the Royal Arch Apron (see plate 25 for an early example)*

show a letter T over a letter H) (see PLATE 25), and the indented Ribbon or Sash of the Order, it made no reference to staves or banners. The only reference to ensigns is in the eighth clause: 'EIGHTHLY That none calling themselves Royal Arch Masons shall be deemed any other than Masters in Operative Masonry; nor shall be received into any regular Chapter of the Royal Arch or permitted to reap or enjoy any of the Benefits, Dignities, or Ensigns of that Most Excellent Degree ...'

It was not until 1778 that this Grand Chapter issued what it called its *Abstract of Laws for the Society of Royal Arch Masons*. One of these Laws says: '... that in the Grand Chapter all officers and twelve senior Companions bear upon their Staffs as Ensigns ...' This was repeated in subsequent editions of the Laws, the only change being the word 'staves' for the word 'staffs.'

The reference to 'all officers' is probably meant to refer to those named in the Laws as making a complete Chapter, namely the three Principals, the three Sojourners, and the two Scribes. There were other Grand Officers, e.g. Presidents of the Council, Grand Treasurer, Grand Recorder (from 1787), Grand Sword Bearer (from 1779), Grand Standard Bearer (from 1779), plus other Offices which were filled occasionally, together with a small number of Grand Superintendents. It is thought unlikely that any of these would be included in the phrase 'all officers' referred to above.

The three Sojourners may well have carried staves bearing the distinctive bearing of the tribe of Judah, as they were of that tribe. (There are some Chapters today who remind us of this by displaying three Judah ensigns in the west, behind the Sojourners).

Each of the three Principals and one of the Scribes may have carried a stave bearing the emblem shown on each of the four Principal Banners. The other Scribe might possibly have carried a stave with an ensign showing the T over H emblem, but this is thought to be unlikely; it is sheer supposition without a shred of evidence to support it.

We cannot be certain what 'the proper ensigns' referred to in the Laws were meant to be, but those carried by 'twelve of the senior Companions' may well have been the distinctive bearings of the twelve tribes of Israel.

In 1807 the Grand Lodge of the Antients published their *Laws and Regulations for the Instruction and Government of the Holy Royal Arch Chapter*. Like the Charter of Compact mentioned earlier, these Laws made no reference to staves, banners or, indeed, to ensigns.

Four years after the Union of the two Grand Lodges in 1813, a so-called United Grand Chapter came into being. It was renamed Supreme Grand Chapter in 1822. Neither in the first, nor in any subsequent edition of their Regulations, has there ever been a mention of staves, banners or ensigns.

There is a paucity of evidence regarding the use of ensigns in a Royal Arch Chapter. Apart from what has already been quoted, the earliest reference is found in an inventory, taken in 1791, of the property belonging to the Royal Arch Chapter of St James, formerly No. 60, now No. 2. The Chapter was founded in 1788. The relevant entry is '14 Banners painted; 4 Grand Standards, Gilt Staves, with fringes . . .'

The earliest-known ensigns so far discovered belong to Chapter of Economy, No. 76, Winchester. These are small metal discs attached to staves, the name of the tribe being painted on one side and the emblem on the other. They have been in use since the Chapter was consecrated in 1803. There are a few similar sets extant in other parts of the country.

Now let us turn our attention to what little we have in the way of early Royal Arch manuscripts. The earliest of these is probably a French document thought to date from about 1760. Here, too, we draw a blank regarding staves, banners or ensigns.

The first such document to give a tiny hint that the twelve tribes of Israel were possibly connected with the Royal Arch comes from what is known as *The Kirkwall Scroll*. Bernard Jones, in his book *Freemasons' Book of the Royal Arch* (p. 241), tells us that this scroll, which is in the possession of the Scots Lodge Kirkwall, Kilwinning, No. 382 (known to have been working from 1736), is of strong linen, eighteen-and-a-half feet long, five-and-a-half feet wide, and, so far as height is concerned, more than occupied the west wall of the lodge room. It is roughly painted on both sides in oil. It portrays amongst many other things, emblems of a number of masonic degrees, including the Royal Arch. There are eight panels, two of which have obvious Royal Arch connections. One of these shows the Tabernacle in the Wilderness with the tents of the twelve tribes of Israel around it, and, in each corner, one of the four emblems found on the principal Banners, i.e, a man, a lion, an ox and an eagle. Bernard Jones says that the scroll may have been designed for use as a floor-cloth somewhere in the 1736–1750 period.

There is another hint in a Royal Arch manuscript written in catechetical form in Sheffield, about 1785. It contains the essence of much of our present-day ritual, including the Sojourner's reference to his being of the same tribe as the Principals and being entrusted with a staff as an ensign of office. There is also a Section headed 'The Mystical Knowledge of the Temple'. This is highly Christian in content and bears a very strong resemblance, indeed almost word-for word, to a section in an early masonic catechism of about 1710, known as *The Dumfries manuscript*.

Another feature of this Royal Arch manuscript is that it refers to the three Grand Lodges we commemorate. Regarding the first or Holy Lodge we are told that it was founded in the Tabernacle of the Wilderness; that it was called the Holy Lodge '. . . because the command of God was there and with His holy fingers wrote the two Tablets of Stone, which He delivered to Moses for our sake'; that the furniture was the same as the furniture of King Solomon's Temple and that 'Moses built an Altar under a Hill and fix't 12 Pillars according to the 12 Tribes of Israel.'

In another Royal Arch manuscript known as *The Commins manuscript*, two pages of which have a watermark dated 1795, there are a couple of questions and answers that have a bearing on the matter with which we are concerned. Firstly, 'Pray, what reasons have we for the use of these staves?' The answer refers to Moses and his rod. The next question is 'Why do we use the arms at the top?' The answer is 'To commemorate the wonders the Lord wrought for the Children of Israel during their travels in the wilderness when they first set up Standards round their encampment and about which each tribe was to pitch their Tents. The device being emblematic of the prophecy of what should happen to their posterity in after ages.'

By the early part of the nineteenth century we have manuscript documents which indicate quite clearly that by this time chapters included in their furnishings twelve ensigns showing the distinctive bearings of the tribes of Israel. A few of these refer to the staves being emblematic of Aaron's rod, making reference to its miraculous qualities. Aaron's rod figures in the ceremony known as 'Passing the Veils' which used to be a pre-requisite for the Royal Arch, as it still is in Scotland, Ireland, and in the Province of Bristol.

In one manuscript ritual (Deptford '*Banks*' c1808) in the Library at Freemasons Hall, London, we find the following list of names against each being a brief description of the ensign appropriate to the tribe:

Reuben	Agitated water
Simeon and Levi	A sword
Judah	A lion couchant
Zebulun	A ship
Issachar	An ass between two burdens
Dan	A serpent
Gad	A flag
Asher	A bull
Naphthali	A hind let loose
Joseph	A cup
Benjamin	A wolf

Note that these are the *sons* of Jacob; Joseph and Levi being included, Ephraim and Manasseh being excluded. Note also that although all twelve sons are mentioned, only eleven ensigns are described; Simeon and Levi being shown together.

Only two call for special comment; Joseph and Asher. It seems to me that the scribe has made a mistake; the cup should, I believe, have been shown on the ensign for Asher. (*Genesis* 49. 20) and the bull on the ensign for Joseph (*Deuteronomy*. 33. 17, and in particular the *GNB* version of same verse).

But the feature of particular interest in this manuscript is that it says 'The officers have banners as follows:

Z	A lion couchant
H and J	Mitre and Crown
E and N	Mitres
PS	A lion passant
Other 2 Sojs	A lion passant and crown

(Note. A lion couchant is represented as lying down, but head erect and alert; not to be confused with a lion dormant, depicted as lying down, eyes closed and head resting on extended forepaws. A lion passant is represented as walking).

Were these the Ensigns referred to in the *Abstract of Laws for the Society of Royal Arch Masons?*—'and that in the GRAND CHAPTER all Officers and twelve of the senior Companions, bear upon their Staffs as Standards the proper Ensigns.' Unfortunately, we do not know.

As to the reasons for the particular ensign, one can only hazard a guess. I suggest the lion couchant was given to Z because of his connection with the Royal House of David. The lion in heraldry has a long association with Royalty. Lions have been on the Arms of England since about the time heraldry began; they were originally known heraldically as leopards.

I assume the entry for H and J is meant to be a mitre for one and a crown for the other; not a mitre and a crown for each. As written, one would assume the mitre was for Haggai, but logically it should be for Joshua, the High Priest; it is the mitre that appears on his sceptre. (Incidentally, it was Joshua, or Jeshua, who was the High Priest, not his father Josedek, who was himself the son of a High Priest, but who never held that high office).

But why a crown for Haggai; or, indeed, Joshua? Neither was of Royal descent.

There is no difficulty in assigning a mitre for Ezra; he was a priest as well as a scribe. But Nehemia? Perhaps the reason is that he greatly assisted Ezra with religious reforms.

One would expect the ensigns to be borne by the Sojourners to show an affinity with Judah; after all they were of his tribe. In some Chapters today there are three Judah ensigns hanging in the west above the three Sojourners to remind us of this. But why 'passant', especially when Judah's ensign shows a lion couchant (though occasionally one sees the lion dormant). And why is the principal Sojourner's the only one of the three without a crown? Perhaps the more relevant question should be why is a crown shown on the other two! Any answer to these questions must be speculative.

One other point of interest about this manuscript; it makes no mention of the four Principal Standards.

One masonic author, Rev. F. de P. Castells, says that amongst the earlier editions of William Preston's Lectures '. . . there is a curious passage which reads; "There are in Freemasonry Twelve Original Points, which form the basis of the system and comprehend the whole Ceremony of Initiation. Without the existence of these Points no man ever was, or can be, legally and essentially received into the Order. Every person who is made a Mason must go through these twelve forms and ceremonies, not only in the first Degree, but in every subsequent one".' The twelve Points are then listed. Castells goes on to say that this teaching was omitted at the Union of the two Grand Lodges in 1813. Preston, he says, does his best to make the essentials of the ritual correspond with the personal characteristics of the twelve sons of Jacob as described in *Genesis* 49. He gives the following summary. The first sentence in each case represents what he calls Preston's 'Twelve Original Points'.

THE ENSIGNS OF THE TWELVE TRIBES OF ISRAEL

1. The Opening of the Lodge.
   Reuben; the beginning of his (Jacob's) strength.

2. The preparation of the candidate.
   Simeon; Simeon prepares instruments of slaughter.

3. The report of the senior deacon.
   Levi; whose people gave a signal to Simeon.

4. The entrance of the candidate.
   Judah; that tribe was the first to cross the Jordan.

5. The prayer.
   Zebulun; when being blessed he was preferred to Issachar.

6. The circumambulation.
   Issachar; thriftless and indolent, needing a leader.

7. The advancing to the pedestal.
   Dan; lapsed into idolatry; in want of God's truth.

8. The Obligation.
   Gad; denotes Jephtha's vow, who was of that tribe.

9. The intrusting.
   Asher; inheritor of fatness and royal dainties.

10. The investiture of the candidate.
    Naphthali; satisfied with favour and full of blessing.

11. The closing of the lodge.
    Benjamin; the youngest, who closed his father's strength.

During the latter years of his life, E. Comp, Colin Dyer, *OSM*, a Past Master of Quatuor Coronati Lodge, was the leading authority on William Preston. He could find no evidence to support the claims and comments of Castells.

The early Royal Arch manuscripts to which reference has been made mention the distinctive bearings of the twelve tribes of Israel, some of them quoting the appropriate Biblical reference. Not one of them, however, gives a hint as to the reason for the inclusion of the twelve tribes in the Royal Arch ceremony. This aspect will be dealt with in Section 7.

The arrangement of the ensigns in a Royal Arch Chapter

Let us now consider how the staves bearing the ensigns are arranged in a Royal Arch Chapter. There are six on the south side and six on the north side, as follows.

North side	*South side*
Judah	Issachar
Naphthali	Zebulun
Asher	Reuben
Dan	Simeon
Benjamin	Gad
Manasseh	Ephraim

Is there any significance in the order in which the ensigns are placed? Yes, there is. We turn again to the Volume of the Sacred Law, *Numbers* 2.2.

> '*Every man of the children of Israel shall pitch (his tent) by his own standard, with the ensign of their father's house; far off about the tabernacle of the congregation shall they pitch.*'

On the east side were;	Judah, Issachar and Zebulun.,
On the south side were;	Reuben, Simeon and Gad.
On the west sided were;	Ephraim, Manasseh and Benjamin,
On the north sided were;	Dan, Asher and Naphthali

There are some interesting comments to be found in Rabbinical writings regarding these positions, some of which are summarized below; they are taken from *Commentary on the Torah* (*Numbers* 2. p 20ff) by Nachmanides (Rabbi Mosheh ben Nachman 1194–c.1270). The relevant Biblical verses are given in parenthesis.

In the east were;

Judah	the sovereign. He was the first to start journeying. (*Judges* 1. 2)
Issachar	who studies the Torah (the Mosaic Law) The Torah is called 'light' (*Proverbs* 6. 23) and
Zebulun	who is wealthy. (*Genesis* 49. 13) and *Deuteronomy* 33 19)

Thus the tribes placed in the east,

> Judah (sovereignty),
> Issachar (knowledge) and
> Zebulun (wealth)

all represented aspects of 'light' which originates in the east.

In the south, from whence come the dews and the rains which bring blessings to the world, shall pitch

Reuben;	for he is master of repentance, which is a good quality. He was the first of the brothers who tried to save Joseph and return him to his father. (*Genesis* 37. 22).
Simeon;	to atone for his having caused anguish to his father. (*Genesis* 49. 5–7)
Gad;	who has the qualities of heroism (1 Chronicles 12. 8*ff*) and between them

'And they shall set forth in the second rank' (*Numbers* 2. 16) because repentance is second to the study of the Torah.

In the west, the storehouses of snow, hail, cold and heat, were;

Ephraim; Manasseh and Benjamin	These three tribes, to whom God grants strength (*Psalm* 80. 3) are the most able to resist the destructive aspects of the natural elements.

In the north whence comes darkness to the world, were;

Dan;	who darkened the world through the idols which Jeroboam made (1 *Kings*, 12. 29)
Asher;	to illuminate the darkness, as it is said of him, 'he shall dip his foot in oil' (*Deuteronomy* 33. 24), and
Naphthali;	who is full of blessings, as it is said of his tribe 'O Naphthali, satisfied with favour and full with the blessing of the Lord.' (*Deuteronomy* 33. 23)

'They shall set forth hindmost' (*Numbers* 2. 31) 'for whoever worships idols goes backward, not forward.' (*Jeremiah* 7. 24).

The *Talmud* tells us that just before Jacob died, he turned to his children and said

> 'Thus shall ye carry me after my death to my resting place in the cave of Machpela. Ye, my sons, and not your children shall bear me. Judah, Issachar and Zebulun shall carry the eastward corner of my bier; Reuben, Simeon and Gad shall carry the south; Ephraim, Manasseh and Benjamin at the western end; and Dan, Asher and Naphthali to the north. Levi shall not carry or help to carry my bier, for his descendants will bear the Ark of God's Covenant through Israel's host; neither shall Joseph assist in carrying, for he is a king; his sons shall take his place, and walk beside his brother Benjamin. As I have spoken, do; diminish not from my words.'

In a Royal Arch Chapter the ensigns are placed in the same order, but for practical reasons we do not put any ensigns in the east or west. We place Judah in the north-east, Issachar in the south-east, and next to him we place Zebulun. That looks after the tribes that should be in the east. For those that should be in the west we place Ephraim in the south-west and Manasseh and Benjamin in the north-west. This arrangement allows the Principals a clear view down to the west.

The 'standard' referred to in the Biblical verses quoted was the large field-sign of each of the four leading divisions making up the tribes who were encamped around the Tabernacle in the Wilderness. In the Royal Arch we refer to these standards as the Principal Banners which hang in the east (see Section 10).

The 'ensign of their father's house' was a smaller banner carried at the head of each of the twelve tribes. In the Royal Arch these traditional ensigns are on the staves which are placed in the north and south of the Chapter.

In some Royal Arch Chapters there are three additional Judah ensigns; these are placed in the west and are meant to represent the Principal Sojourner and his two assistants, who were of that tribe.

Why were the twelve tribes of Israel included in the Royal Arch?

This is a question that is occasionally asked but, so far, no satisfactory answer has been given. In this attempt to do so, let us start by looking at an old masonic document dated 1726, known as *The Graham manuscript*. This is an important masonic document and it is distinctly Christian in content. It gives part of our third degree legend, but with Noah rather than Hiram as the principal character. The part of the document to which reference will now be made is in catechetical form.

In answer to the question 'How many Lights belong to a lodge?', the respondent answers 'Twelve.' He is then asked what they are and his answer includes 'The ffather [*sic*], son and Holy Ghost.' Later he is asked to draw reference to these Lights. His reply, using the archaic spelling of the day, is 'We draw refferance from the 12 patriarches and also from the 12 oxen we reid of at the 7 chapter of first king that caryed up the molten sea of brass which was tipes of the twelve disciples was to be tought by christ . . .'

Who were these twelve patriarchs? The word patriarch is derived from the Greek language. According to Young's *Concordance* the word patriarch does not appear in the Old Testament. It does, however, appear in the New Testament, and in particular at *Acts* 7. 8 where we find '. . . and Jacob begat the twelve patriarchs.' So, the twelve patriarchs are the twelve sons of Jacob.'

We now turn to another important reference, a book called *The Testaments of the Twelve Patriarchs*. This is an early Jewish pseudepigraphic work dealing with the sons of Jacob. (Pseudepigrapha are books ascribed to various Biblical personalities far more ancient than the writings themselves). It is said that *The Testaments of the Twelve Patriarchs* was written between 137 and 107 BC. There are passages in the book which give clear hints at salvation through Jesus

Christ. The following quotation from the *Encyclopaedia Judaica* (Vol. 13, 185–7) will be of interest. '*The Testaments of the Twelve Patriarchs*, though originally written in Greek, are one of the most important sources for the understanding of Jesus' message. In the context of Jewish thought, they are one of the most sublime documents of Jewish ethics in Antiquity,'

Our next reference is to the title page of what is generally called *The Barker Bible* of 1599. Here is a quotation from the description of that book, taken from the *Historical Catalogue of Printed Bibles* (printed by The British and Foreign Society). 'The woodcut border to the first general title is a frame having twenty-four small compartments, showing on the left—the tents of the twelve tribes; on the right—figures of the twelve Apostles; the inner part exhibits the four Evangelists . . . The same border is used for the N.T. title.'

The ten sons and two grandsons of Jacob, whose distinctive bearings we show on the twelve Royal Arch staves, were considered by learned Christians to be the fore-runners (or, to use the more usual term, antetypes) of the twelve Apostles of Christ.

What was the task of those twelve Apostles? Was it not to spread the knowledge of the WORD? Let one of the Apostles answer that; I quote the first verse of the Gospel according to St. John. 'In the beginning was the WORD, and the WORD WAS WITH God; and the WORD was God.' This verse played a prominent part in the Royal Arch ritual before it was revised in 1834–5. And is it not entirely compatible with the words in the closing stages of the Mystical Lecture? 'This Supreme Degree inspires its members with the most exalted ideas of God, and leads to the exercise of the purest and most devout piety; a reverence for the incomprehensible J. . ., the eternal ruler of the Universe, the elemental life and primordial source of all its principles, the very spring and fount of all its virtues.'

There are many instances in Biblical books of reference, and indeed, in the New Testament, that testify to an association of the twelve tribes of Israel with the twelve Apostles. For example, *Blakes Bible Dictionary*, under the heading *Apostles* says, 'The number twelve corresponds to the twelve tribes of Israel'. The *Encyclopaedia Judaica*, under a similar heading, says 'In Christian tradition the immediate followers of Jesus number twelve, most probably a symbolic number signifying the twelve tribes of Israel.' Later on, under the same heading it says 'The original association of 'The Twelve' with the tribes of Israel is held by some scholars to have had an eschatological significance', and then it refers to *Matthew* 19. 28 and *Revelation* 21. 12. The word 'eschatological' means 'The science of the last four things, death, judgement, heaven and hell.'

The view has been expressed by some masonic historians that

a) Freemasonry in the early days was essentially Christian;

b) that the author of the earliest masonic *Constitutions*, Anderson, in his First Charge opened the door to those of other faiths;

> (... 'tis now thought more expedient only to oblige them (*i.e. Masons*) to that Religion in which all Men agree, leaving their particular Opinions to themselves; that is to be good Men and true, or Men of Honour and Honesty, by whatever Denominations they may be distinguish'd ...')

c) that the third degree was incomplete in that a 'word' was lost, thus giving rise to

d) a 'completion degree' which would at the same time restore Freemasonry to its essentially Christian character.

Whatever may be the truth of any or all these assumptions, it is a fact that early Royal Arch Masonry was essentially Christian in character. In looking at the history of our masonic ceremonies, with their apparent emphasis on events recorded in the Old Testament, we must remember the aphorism of St. Augustine; 'The New Testament lies hidden in the Old and the Old Testament is manifested in the New.'

I suggest that it is with this aphorism in mind we find the reason for the inclusion of the twelve tribes of Israel in the Royal Arch; namely their Christian allusion as antetypes of the Apostles of Christ.

Of course, it could be pointed out that there is evidence that Jews were being exalted into the Royal Arch in the 1750s, and that one is therefore entitled to ask why *they* should seek to participate in a ceremony with such a strong Christian influence. The answer is simple. They would interpret the ritual and consider the ensigns and descriptive bearings from a Jewish standpoint, and would be able to draw therefrom the same high moral lessons drawn by those who looked through the eyes of a Christian.

The banner bearers mentioned in the Bible

The Lectures on the ensigns tell us the name of the prince who carried each of the 'banners', together with the name of his father. This information corresponds to that given in *Numbers 2* in which we are also told where each prince was to pitch his tent in relation to the Tabernacle, and the order in which they were to march.

With regard to the twenty-four names given, the Editor of *The Pentateuch and Haftorahs* pp. 568–9 (Dr. J. H. Hertz, Chief Rabbi) points out that:

nine contain the Divine Name EL, which means God;

three contain the name TZUR, which means Rock, a frequent appellation of God, and in

three others SHADDAI occurs, which is usually translated 'Almighty'.

Their names, and the meaning of the names, are shown in the Table at the end of this Section.

It is not known precisely when the Lectures on the ensigns first appeared. The earliest known printed version is in *The Perfect Ceremonies of the Supreme Order of the Holy Royal Arch* printed in London by A. Lewis in 1877. This is believed to be the first reference in the Royal Arch to the princes who, according to the Volume of the Sacred Law, bore the banners of the tribes of Israel.

As pointed out in Section 5, in the first edition of *Abstract of Laws for the Society of Royal Arch Masons*, 1778, there is a reference to 'all officers and twelve senior Companions bear upon their Staffs as Standards the proper ensigns' but we do not know what these proper ensigns were.

It is also interesting to note that a Grand Standard Bearer was appointed in the Royal Arch in 1779; his name was Comp. Cornelius

Vanderstoop. It would be interesting to know what Standard he carried.

Remember that the Grand Chapter, the body that appointed the Grand Standard Bearer, was set up by members of the premier Grand Lodge acting in their private capacity and without the authority of that Grand Lodge which is on record as saying it did not recognize the Royal Arch. Because of this the Standard carried by the Royal Arch Grand Standard Bearer was hardly likely to be anything connected with the premier Grand Lodge.

It might have been a Standard that bore the Armorial Bearings of the First Grand Principal at that time, Comp. Captain George Smith. It should be noted that there are no known Armorial Bearings for the first Grand Chapter.

Incidentally, this same Capt. George Smith was expelled from the Society in 1775 for 'uttering an instrument purporting to be a certificate of the Grand Lodge recommending two distressed brethren'.

The Standard could not have borne the triple tau because that was as yet unknown in the Royal Arch (see Section 11), though it might possibly have been the emblem T over the letter H that had to be worn on the Royal Arch apron, though this is considered unlikely.

Perhaps, like present-day Royal Arch Grand Standard Bearers, the early Royal Arch Grand Standard Bearers did not carry a Standard at all! (As a matter of interest, the *Masonic Year Book Historical Supplement* indicates that the first Grand Standard Bearer in the Craft was not appointed until 1882, but the Order of Procession for the Grand Assembly of Freemasons for the Union of the two Grand Lodges of England in 1813 shows that the Royal Standard was carried!).

Illustrations of Jewels to be worn in the Royal Arch were first published in the 1843 edition of *Royal Arch Regulations*. That for the Grand Standard Bearer showed a Standard bearing two equilateral triangles, in the centre of which was a circle enclosing a triple tau. The equilateral triangles soon became a six-pointed star.

Name of tribe	Name of prince	Name of prince's father	Meaning of name
Reuben	Elizur	Shadeur	God is my rock. Shaddai is a light.
Simeon	Shelumiel	Zurishaddai	(Either) at peace with God (or) my friend is God. My rock is Shaddai.
Judah	Nahshon	Amminadab	Serpent. The (divine) Kinsman is generous
Issachar	Nathaniel	Zuar*	God hath given. Little.
Zebulun	Eliab	Helon*	God is father. Strong.
Ephraim	Elishama	Ammihud	God hath heard. The (divine) Kinsman is glorious.
Manasseh	Gamaliel	Pedahzur	God is my reward. The rock hath redeemed.
Benjamin	Abidan	Gideoni*	The father hath judged. My great warrior.
Dan	Ahiezer	Ammishad-dai	The (divine) brother is a help. The people of Shaddai.
Asher	Pagiel	Ochran*	The lot or fate of (i.e. given by) God. Troubler.

The banner bearers

Name of tribe	Name of prince	Name of prince's father	Meaning of name
Gad	Eliasaph	Deuel (or Reuel)	God hath added. God is a friend.
Naphthali	Ahira	Enan*	The (divine) brother is a friend. Fountain.

Note Those marked* have been taken from Young's *Analytical Concordance to the Holy Bible*; the meaning is not given in Dr. Hertz's *Pentateuch and Haftorahs*.

SECTION 9

The association of the ensigns with the signs of the zodiac

The earliest reference to the zodiac in Freemasonry is found in a Grand Lodge Minute dated 26 November, 1728. It says 'The Health of the twelve stewards was proposed and drank with twelve alluding to the twelve Signes of the Zodiak as well as to their Number which they returned jointly in like manner.'

So far as the Royal Arch is concerned, we have an interesting comment from Richard Carlile, who was not a Freemason. He published a number of exposures in the nineteenth century. In a section on the Royal Arch he wrote:

'The Keystone of the Royal Arch is the ancient science of the Zodiac.' The signs of the zodiac are prominent in many Chapters. They are often seen woven on the carpet on which the pedestal stands. In the frontispiece of *The Perfect Ceremonies of the Royal Arch* there is a picture of a Royal Arch tracing board on which can be seen the signs of the zodiac shown clockwise between two concentric circles.

There is no known evidence to suggest that the signs of the zodiac were specifically included in either Craft or Royal Arch ceremonies. They are briefly mentioned in some Craft Lectures of the early part of the nineteenth century, together with excursions into Platonic theory and Cabbalism, which drew from one eminent masonic scholar, Bro. P. James (*AQC* 83 p 193) the comment 'In places it is difficult to understand . . . (and) at times it becomes pure nonsense.'

It is interesting to note that the signs of the zodiac have been included in each of the three Freemasons' Halls in Great Queen Sreet, London, the first of which was inaugurated in 1779, the second in 1869 and the third, the present Hall, in 1933.

Another point of interest is that the editor of *The Freemasons' Quarterly Review* (Dr. Crucefix) which was first published in 1834, used the signs of the zodiac as its frontispiece.

Why were the signs of the zodiac used as a decoration in Freemasonry? I suggest that the reason may be because they might be considered to encapsulate the importance attached to the seventh of the liberal arts and sciences, namely astronomy, which, according to our Lectures enables us to 'discover the laws which govern the heavenly bodies, and by which their motions are directed ...' The Lecture defines Astronomy as 'that exalted science which enables the contemplative mind to soar aloft, and read the wisdom, power and goodness of the Great Creator in the Heavens.'

Efforts have been made to equate the signs of the zodiac with specified tribes of Israel. Some of the papers dealing with this subject can be found in the *Transactions* of the Dormer Masonic Study Circle, which devotes itself to what might be described as 'mystical' masonry. The explanations given have not convinced those of the 'authentic' school of masonic research.

Some years ago, a distinguished member of Quatuor Coronati Lodge, Bro. the Rev. Canon Covey-Crump PGCh wrote '... the proposed connection between the distinctive emblems on the ensigns and the ensigns of the zodiac is entirely fallacious and wasted ingenuity.' However, it must be pointed out that a connection between the signs of the zodiac and the twelve tribes of Israel had been made by Jewish scholars at least as early as 1491. They translated the Latin names of the zodiac into Hebrew and associated each of them with one of the tribes of Israel.

According to the *Encyclopaedia Judaica* (16. 1191);

The tribes encamped in the east
Judah, Issachar and Zebulun

correspond to
Aries, Taurus and Gemini.

the tribes encamped in the south
Reuben, Simeon and Gad

correspond to
Cancer, Leo and Virgo

the tribes encamped in the west
Ephraim, Manasseh and Benjamin

correspond to
Libra, Scorpio and Sagittarius

the tribes encamped in the north
Dan, Asher and Naphthali

correspond to
Capricorn, Aquarius and Pisces.

It is interesting to note that the signs of the zodiac corresponding to the leading divisions of the army of Israel in the information given above, namely Judah, Reuben, Ephraim and Dan, correspond to the signs of Aries, Cancer, Libra and Capricorn. The commentator in the *Kitto* Bible (first published in 1828) agrees. He says 'The Cabbalists have an opinion that the bearings of the twelve standards corresponds with the months of the year and the signs of the zodiac—the supposed characters of the latter being represened thereon; and that the distinction of the great standards was, that they bore the cardinal signs of Aries, Cancer, Libra and Capricorn, and were also charged with one letter of the tetragrammaton, or quadrilateral name of God.'

The *Encyclopaedia Judaica* also tells us that the signs of the zodiac figured prominently in early Jewish art; for example in prayer books and the mosaic floors of ancient Palestinian synagogues. The following quotation from that publication illustrates the point.

'Directly above the synagogue (from the third century C.E.) and using its columns, was another synagogue built in the form of a basilica with an outstanding mosaic pavement which contained (from north to south) a dedicating inscription flanked by two lions, a zodiac of a high artistic standard with the sun god Helios on his chariot in the centre and representations of the four seasons in the corners, the Ark of the Law with menoroth and other ritual articles.'

The difficulty of finding an authoritative matching of the zodiac signs with specific tribes is just as great as finding an authoritative matching of stones in Aaron's breastplate with specific tribes. There are various lists, but their authority is open to question. Some of them associate the signs with the *sons* of Jacob, i.e. including Levi and Joseph but excluding Ephraim and Manasseh; one includes Levi (Pisces), Ephraim and Manasseh (Gemini) and Jacob's daughter Dinah(!) (Virgo). This latter list is said to have been compiled by 'Asaph, the writer and historian of the Hebrews'; it is contained in a *Fragment from the Philosopher Andronicus and Asaph, the Historian of the Jews* which formed part of the John Rylands Library, Manchester.

The list given below is taken from the *Midrash (Yalkut Shimoni Leviticus 418)* which was reprinted in the *Encyclopaedia Judaica* 16. 191–2.

Sign	Tribe
Aries	Judah
Taurus	Issachar
Gemini	Zebulun
Cancer	Reuben
Leo	Simeon

Virgo	Gad
Libra	Ephraim
Scorpio	Manasseh
Sagittarius	Benjamin
Capricorn	Dan
Aquarius	Asher
Pisces	Naphthali

It should be noted that in the *Midrash* the signs of the zodiac have been likened to other Biblical personalities; for example in *Midrash Rabbah 7. 7.*

Gemini is likened to	Peretz and Zerah, sons of Judah and Tamar; *(Genesis 38. 27. 'behold, twins were in her womb').*
Libra is likened to	Job. *(Job 6. 2. 'Oh that my grief were thoroughly weighed, and my calamity laid in the balances together')*
Scorpio is likened to	Ezekiel; *(Ezekiel 2. 6. 'thou dost dwell among scorpions'),* and
Aquarius is likened to	Moses; *(Exodus 2. 17. 'Moses stood up and helped them, and watered their flock').*

Further comment on this subject is made in Section 12.

In a booklet entitled *The Hebrew Mazzaroth* (R. W. Frater, published by S.R.I.A.) the author says 'According to Ptolemy the zodiacal constellations . . . represent the twelve tribes of Israel.' This claim is probably due to a quick but inaccurate reading of a footnote in one of the sources used by the author.

Neither the Symbolical Lecture nor the Lectures on the ensigns normally make reference to the zodiac. An exception, however, has been found. The Symbolical Lecture used in a Chapter under the auspices of the Supreme Grand Chapter of the Netherlands includes the following:

'The ensigns borne by the staves arranged round the TB are the distinctive bearings of the twelve tribes of Israel, and are emblematic of the twelve signs of the zodiac. The remaining four principal banners in the East represent the Omnipresent Power as it is manifested in the world, here represented by the emblems of the four cardinal points of the compass.'

The latter part of the quotation refers to the standards of the leading divisions of the army of Israel; Judah in the east, Reuben in the south. Ephraim in the west and Dan in the north.

SECTION 10

The four Principal Standards

The four Principal Standards bear devices of a man, a lion, an ox and an eagle. When were these emblems first used in the Royal Arch? Whence did they come? What or whom do they represent? Is there any significance in the order in which they are placed?

When were they first used in the Royal Arch?

It is not possible to be sure whether the four Principal Standards with the emblems they bear were in use at the start of Royal Arch masonry, which is believed to have been during the 1740s. We have no information on the subject for that period.

What we *do* know is that in 1764 Laurence Dermott, the Grand Secretary of the Grand Lodge of the Antients, referred in their *Constitutions* to armorial bearings said to belong to Rabbi Jehuda Leon, who had been displaying in Holland, Paris, Vienna and London a model he had made of King Solomon's Temple.

Dermott quotes the emblazonment of these Arms, which can be simplified as follows;

in the first quarter	blue with a gold lion, rampant;
in the second quarter	gold, with a black ox, walking;
in the third quarter	gold, a man in a crimson robe edged with ermine and his hands erect;
in the fourth quarter	blue, with an eagle perched, its wings raised, gold.

The Grand Lodge of the Antients actively encouraged the Royal Arch. Indeed, as was said earlier, Dermott called it the 'Root, Heart and Marrow of Freemasonry.' Further, Dermott associated the Arms just described with Freemasonry, including the Royal Arch and, in 1775 that Grand Lodge adopted these Arms as their own.

They were not authorized to do so by the College of Heralds.

At the Union of the two Grand Lodges in 1813, these Arms were placed alongside those borne (without the appropriate authority) by the premier Grand Lodge. It was some years later before a Grant of Arms from the College of Heralds regularized the use of the Arms. Later the College authorized a border of lions to be added to the Arms.

We know, therefore, that the emblems of a man, a lion, an ox and an eagle have been associated with the Royal Arch from at least 1764.

Whence did the emblems come

There is some evidence that the man, the lion, the ox and the eagle were emblems used by some ancient peoples in connection with their deities. The source of the emblems so far as Freemasonry is concerned is undoubtedly the Volume of the Sacred Law. There are three references to consider.

Firstly, *Numbers* 2. vv 3, 10, 18 and 25, which give details of the encampment of the tribes of Israel whilst they were in the wilderness. As explained in Section 6, the four leading divisions of the army of Israel were Judah, Reuben, Ephraim and Dan. The Biblical commentators give the devices borne on the standards of these four as respectively, a lion, a man, an ox and a serpent or a horse rearing, his heels being bitten by a snake and the rider falling off.

Next we have the vision of *Ezekiel*, Chapter 1 of which refers to (v. 5) 'four living creatures . . . they had the likeness of a man (v. 6) . . . and every one had four faces . . . (v. 10) . . . as for their faces . . . the face of a man and the face of a lion . . . the face of an ox . . . the face of an eagle.'

The third reference is from Chapter 4 of the *Revelation of Saint John* which records 'four beasts' (v. 7) 'and the first was like a lion, and the second was like a calf, and the third head had a face as a man and the fourth beast was like a flying eagle.'

According to the *Midrash*, Rabbi Albin said four kinds of exalted beings have been created in the world. The most exalted of living creatures is man; of birds, the eagle; of cattle, the ox, and of wild beasts the lion . . . All of these received royalty and had greatness bestowed upon them, and they are set under the chariot of God, as it says, 'As for the likeness of their faces,' and then goes on to quote *Ezekiel*, 1. 10, to which reference has just been made.

The same source tells us that Rabbi Abbahu said 'There are four lordly creatures. The lord among birds is the eagle; the lord among cattle is the ox; the lord among beasts is the lion and the lord over them all is man. The Holy One, Blessed be He, took them and engraved them on the Throne of Glory, as it says, 'The Lord has established His throne in the heavens and His kingdom ruleth over it' (Ps. 103. 19).

What or whom do the emblems represent?

Our ritual tells us that the four Principal Standards represent the leading standards of the four divisions of the army of Israel, the lion representing the division headed by the tribe of Judah, the man the division headed by the tribe of Reuben, the ox the division headed by the tribe of Ephraim and the eagle the division headed by the tribe of Dan.

There is nothing in the verses relevant to Dan in *Genesis* 49, or indeed, *Deuteronomy* 33, that has any bearing or any connection with an eagle (but see comments on page 10–11, Section 2). Why, then, is an eagle used on the Principal Banner for Dan? And why do we occasionally find the eagle with a serpent in its talons on both the Principal Standard for Dan and also on his ensign? An example of the latter can be seen in a Bible published in 1756 by the Rev. Thomas Stackhouse which has a page showing *The Camp of the Israelites*, in which the descriptive bearings for the tribes are seen quite clearly; that for Dan bears an eagle with a serpent in its talons (*see* PLATE 1).

In *Commentary on the Torah* Nachmanides quotes Rabbi ibn Ezra (1092–1167), saying 'The ancient sages say that ... on Dan's standard was the figure of an eagle.' A footnote reads 'This was because of the expression "as an eagle stirreth up his nest"' (*Deuteronomy* 32. 11), and of Dan it is written that 'he was the rearward of all the camps' (*Numbers*, 10. 25) who stirred the attention of all the camps to any lurking dangers. Rashi (Rabbi Shelomoh Yitschaki Solomon ben Isaac, 1040–1105) explains the words in *Deuteronomy* 32. 11 (*The Soncino Chumash* footnote page 1161) as follows; 'The eagle, whose instinct of love and piety for her young is very great, does not enter her nest suddenly, but gradually awakens them by flapping her wings before entering.'

Neither of these comments give a satisfactory explanation of why Dan's standard bore an eagle. A request was made to the Rev.

Geoffrey Shisler, Cantor of Kenton Synagogue, to go back to the original Hebrew for a possible explanation. He has stated that he finds it exceedingly difficult to trace the reason for the suggestion that Dan's standard bore an eagle, and that the source everyone comes back to is Rabbi ben Ezra.

He also thought one source of influence might have been *Proverbs* 30. 19 'The way of an eagle in the air; the way of a serpent upon a rock'; the mode of movement of both the eagle and the serpent is unfathomable.

Another possible source, he says, is a serious suggestion made by Rabbi Solomon Zalman Netter (mid-nineteenth century), a famous commentator on the works of Rabbi ibn Ezra. Netter refers to the Hebrew in *Genesis* 49. 17, which reads;

> 'Yehi Dan nahash ngale-derech shefifon ngale orah hanoshech ngike-beh-soos vayipol rochebo ahhor.'

The letters underlined form the word 'nesher', which means 'eagle'.

Yet another suggestion is offered by the Spanish exegete and statesman Don Isaac Abarbanel, namely that the device was meant to be a combination of eagle and serpent, a kind of winged dragon.

All that can be said with a degree of certainty is that the old Biblical commentators used a great deal of imagination in relating one thing to another to establish the connection they wanted!

There is another explanation in the *Midrash* as to why Dan's standard bore an eagle. The Rabbis say that the four leading divisions of the army of Israel, namely Judah, Reuben, Ephraim and Dan, correspond to the four groups of angels surrounding the celestial Throne in the vision of Ezekiel. They then draw the conclusion that the four faces referred to in *Ezekiel* 1. 10, namely a man, a lion, an ox and an eagle, correspond to the emblems used on the standards of these four tribes.

It must be remembered that early Royal Arch masonry had a very strong Christian bias. This is reflected here in the emblems of the eagle and the eagle with a serpent in his talons.

The eagle is the emblem of St. John the Evangelist, the author of the last of the four Gospels. The opening words of that Gospel are 'In the beginning was the word, and the word was with God, and the Word was God.' These words, as mentioned earlier, played a prominent part in early Royal Arch masonry.

The serpent is an emblem of the sinful nature of mankind. The earliest Biblical indication of this is found in *Genesis* 3. 14. 'And the Lord God said unto the serpent, because thou hast done this, thou art cursed above all cattle, and above every beast of the field; upon thy belly shalt thou go, and dust shalt you eat all the days of thy life'.

The significance of the eagle with a serpent in its talons, therefore, is the triumph of the Word of God over the sinful nature of mankind.

The eagle and the serpent are prominent in many churches. The lectern, from which the Word of God is proclaimed, is quite often in the shape of an eagle with outstretched wings, one of which represents the Old Testament, the other the New Testament. The eagle is the natural enemy of the serpent and many lecterns in the form of an eagle have a serpent at the foot of the pillar, symbolizing the evil powers conquered by the Word of God.

The sinful nature of the tribe of Dan is referred to in the Lecture describing the ensigns, where we are told that 'The tribe of Dan, however, were ringleaders of idolatry and were the first to apostasize from God.' This is a reference to *I Kings* 12. 28–30, which tells of Jeroboam establishing the worship of a golden calf in the town of Dan, previously known as Laish or Shechem, which the Danites captured and destroyed by fire; they then rebuilt it and called it Dan (*Joshua* 19. 47).

It is interesting to note that Iranaeus, a second century Bishop of Lyons, suggsted the reason why the tribe of Dan is not mentioned with other tribes in *Revelation* 7 is because the Anti-Christ would be descended from this tribe.

From the time of Iranaeus each of the creatures, a man, a lion, an ox and an eagle, have been held to symbolize one of the four Evangelists, Matthew, Mark, Luke and John 'without much point', according to the Rev. N. Turner, BD, MTh, PhD. (Peake's *Commentary on the Bible*). Just why Iranaeus chose to symbolize the Evangelists by these creatures is not known; the reason often heard, however, is that the man became the symbol of Matthew because his Gospel traces the human genealogy of Christ; the lion was chosen to symbolize Mark because his Gospel begins with the words 'the voice of one crying in the wilderness', and it has been said that this suggests the roar of a lion; the symbol for Luke is an ox, the animal of sacrifice, and Luke's Gospel stresses the atoning sacrifice of Jesus; the high-soaring eagle is the symbol of John because in his narrative he rises to the loftiest heights in dealing with the mind of Christ.

Another viewpoint is that the man represents the incarnation of

Christ, the ox His passion, the lion His resurrection and the eagle His ascension.

Yet another view is found in a description of Graham Sutherland's tapestry in Coventry Cathedral which interprets the vision of St. John the Divine (*Revelation* 4, 6–8). Referring to the four creatures, i.e. the man, the lion, the ox and the eagle, the writer, R. Furneaux Jordan (*Cathedral Reborn* a souvenir publication) says

'St. John the Divine uses these four figures as symbols. He sees in these mysterious figures a representation of supremacy—they stand for everything that is noblest, strongest, wisest and swiftest in Nature. The Rabbis were supposed to believe that there four supreme orders in the world; among created beings, mankind; among birds, the eagle; among domestic animals, the ox and among wild animals, the lion. Each of them outstanding in its own particular sphere.'

Our ritual refers to 'A man to personify intelligence and understanding; a lion to represent strength and power; an ox to denote the ministrations of patience and assiduity; and an eagle to indicate the promptness and celerity with which the will and pleasure of the great I AM is ever executed.'

Incidentally, in one printed ritual (*Hornsey*) there is a footnote indicating that the Principal Standards refer to Saints Matthew, Mark, Luke and John.

There is a piece of Christian art in Chichester Cathedral which is of interest to Royal Arch Companions. It is the Piper Tapestry. An extract from the explanatory note on the Tapestry reads 'The subject is The Trinity (three central panels) 'represented by an equilateral triangle among flames, and related to this, symbols for The Father (a white light), The Son (a Tau Cross) and The Holy Spirit (a flame-like wing); and in the flanking panels, two on each side, The Elements at the top (Earth, Air, Fire, Water), and the Evangelists below them—St. Matthew (winged man), St. Mark (winged lion), St. Luke (winged ox), and St. John (winged eagle).

Is there any significance in the order of the Standards?

The order in which the Principal Standards appear in most Chapters is (starting from that above the Chair of H), ox, man, lion and eagle. This is not the order in which they are usually referred to. Is there any significance in the order in which they appear in Chapter?

Before attempting to answer that question, let us see how they appear in written or heraldic sources, the latter following the recognized description of an emblazonment where the shield is divided quarterly, i.e.

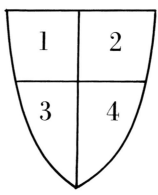

	1	2	3	4
Numbers 2, 2	Lion	Man	Ox	Eagle
Ezekiel 1, 10	Man	Lion	Ox	Eagle
Revelation 4, 7	Lion	Ox	Man	Eagle
Graham Sutherland's tapestry	Man	Eagle	Ox	Lion
The Arms of Rabbi Leon	Lion	Ox	Man	Eagle
The Arms of Grand Lodge	Lion	Ox	Man	Eagle
In most Chapters	Ox	Man	Lion	Eagle

It will be seen from this Table that the arrangement in most Chapters is different from all the other sources quoted. There is no known reason for this. Nor do we know when that order was first used. However, we *do* have some evidence in the form of a painting of a tracing board for the Royal Arch by Harris, dated 1834. It shows quite clearly that the order and layout of the ensigns and Principal Standards is the same as that used in most Chapters today. This painting was reproduced as a frontispiece for the first edition of *The Perfect Ceremonies of the Royal Arch Lecture* (1876). Incidentally, the first known printed copy of the Lecture on the Royal Arch ensigns appears in the second edition, 1877.

The triple tau

The triple tau has nothing to do with the twelve tribes of Israel, the staves borne by the Companions or the four Principal Standards. It is being included here simply because it is shown on a banner and placed in the east end of the Chapter between the four Principal Standards.

What is the triple tau? When and how did it find its way into the Royal Arch, and what is its significance?

A look at the *Charter of Compact* (i.e. the instrument setting up the first Grand Chapter and from which our Supreme Grand Chapter is descended), and some early Royal Arch jewels and aprons, will show that the original device was a letter T over a letter H. Contrary to what has been said in some quarters, this was not meant to refer to Thomas Harper, a Deputy Grand Master of the Grand Lodge of the Antients in the first part of the nineteenth century, a silversmith who designed and supplied masonic jewels.

The letters were meant to refer to the Temple of Jerusalem, as is evidenced by the post-script of a letter written by Thomas Dunckerley on 27 January, 1792. 'I wish you would amend the . . . Patent under my name . . . for the Royal Arch it is $\overline{\text{T}}$emplum $\overline{\text{H}}$eirosolyma.' (Thomas Dunckerley was a Grand Superintendent of eighteen different Provinces from 1776 to his death in 1795).

At some time during the early part of the nineteenth century, a change took place; the letters lost their serifs and the 'tail' of the letter T dropped on to the 'crossbar' of the letter H. This now gave the appearance of three capital Ts joined together at the base of the 'tail'. The symbolic nature which could be attached to this was soon seen, and shortly afterwards we begin to find references to the triple tau in Royal Arch masonry.

This brings us to the question, 'What is a tau'? It is the name given to the nineteenth letter of the Greek alphabet and is shaped like a capital T. According to the *Encyclopaedia Britannica* under the heading ALPHABET, the tau was originally a cross, either a 'plus' sign or a 'multiplication' sign. Later on it was changed to a letter T as we know it today, though in the Hebrew alphabet it was made to resemble three sides of a square, the lower side being open, and the left 'leg' being given a small 'foot' slightly protruding to the right. It is the last letter of the Hebrew alphabet and is known as tav or tov.

What is the significance of the tau? It shows yet more evidence of a Christian influence in early Royal Arch masonry. It is said that the shape of the cross on which Christ was crucified was in the form of a letter 'T' with a longish 'tail'.

There are many artists who depict such a cross in their Crucifixion paintings, especially in the Crucifixion of Christ. The following quotation from *Hall's Dictionary of Subjects & Symbols in Art* (page 82) will be of interest. 'At the site of the execution the upright post (stipes) was already set in the ground, a fixture that could be used more than once. The condemned man was led to the place bearing only the horizontal piece (patibulum) to which his hands (or wrists) were nailed to the ends of the cross-bar which was then lifted on the upright. It rested across the top, to form a "T", called the tau-cross (from the Greel letter "t") or crux commissa (joined); or was set somewhat lower down, forming the familiar crux immissa (intersecting).'

Because of the association with the Crucifixion of Christ, the cross in the form of a 'T', the tau-cross, came to have an especial significance for those of the Christian faith. The combination of *three* such crosses, with both their Golgothan and Trinitarian implications, would therefore be given a very special significance.

An eminent member of Quatuor Coronati Lodge, Bro. Ivor Grantham, one-time Librarian to Grand Lodge, suggested a possible connection between the triple tau and one of the Apocryphal Books of the New Testament, *The General Epistle of Barnabas*. Quoting from *AQC* 57 (page 283);

'... chapter eight contains three verses;

11. For the Scripture says that Abraham circumcised three hundred and eighteen men of his house. But what therefore was the mystery that was made known unto him?
12. Mark first the eighteen, and next the three hundred. For the numeral letters of ten and eight are I. H. And these denote Jesus.
13. And because the cross was that by which we were to find grace; therefore, he adds, three hundred; the note of which is T (the figure of

His cross). Wherefore by two letters he signifies Jesus, and by the third, His cross.'

Ivor Grantham goes on

'If, as some students feel, the symbol of the Triple Tau is Christian in origin, the verses quoted above may well explain the composition of the symbol;

verse 12 ... I H   I
                        H

verse 13 ... T   T
                        H

If this explanation of the origin of the triple tau is accepted, it may well be that the existence of this symbol may be traced back to the fourth century AD, when the canonical nature of the New Testament writings were determined—or possibly even to the lifetime of the twelve Apostles, if the attribution of this Epistle to St. Barnabas can be maintained.'

It is not known how much support this theory has; probably very little. Incidentally, in Hebrew numbers, the letter tav represents 400, not 300 as implied by verse 13 quoted above.

Our present day ritual refers to the tau as mentioned in *Ezekiel* 9. 4. 'And the Lord said unto him, Go through the midst of the city, through the midst of Jerusalem, and set a mark upon the foreheads of the men that sigh and that cry for all the abominations that be done in the midst thereof.' The text does not refer to the nature of the mark to be made. In the Hebrew version, the word 'tav' is used. The root from which this word comes means 'a mark, or scribble.' It may be of interest to point out, though, that in the old *Jewish Encyclopaedia* (Vol. 1 499) are reproduced old Hebrew and Samarian alphabets, where the letter tav is shown as a cross. Similarly, the *Encyclopaedia Britannica* (Alphabet) has a Table showing the Hebrew letter tav being equivalent to a cross in both the Sabaean and Aramaic alphabets.

One Rabbinical interpretation of *Ezekiel* 9. 4. suggests that the instruction was 'thou shalt tau a tau (i.e. mark a cross) upon the foreheads.'

A first reading of the text implies that the mark was to be placed on the foreheads of the righteous; 'the men that sigh and that cry for all the abominations that be done in the midst thereof.' But it would appear that there could be another interpretation, namely that the mark was to be placed on the foreheads of the *wicked*, rather than the righteous, the words 'the men that sigh and that cry' being held to mean those that clamoured or raised an outcry *for the continuation* of all the abominations. But this hardly ties up with the modern wording in the *GNB* or in *Knox*. Their versions of this verse are as follows:

GNB   'Go through the whole city of Jerusalem and put a mark on the forehead of everyone who is distressed and troubled because of all the disgusting things being done in this city.'

Knox   'Make thy way, the Lord said to him, all through the city, from end to end of Jerusalem; and where thou findest men that weep and wail over the foul deeds done in it, mark their brows with a cross.'

According to a tractate from the *Talmud* (*Shabbat* 55a), it would appear that one Rabbi interpreted this verse as meaning that *all* the inhabitants had a tau marked on their foreheads, for it reads 'God ordered the angel Gabriel to mark on the foreheads of the righteous a tau, in ink, the initial of the Hebrew word *tichyeh*, meaning 'Thou shalt live', and on the foreheads of the wicked a tau, in blood, the initial of the Hebrew word *tamuth* meaning 'Thou shalt die.' This is yet another Biblical interpretation.

An English translation of the *Vulgate* gives the meaning as 'write the letter TAW.' A later translation gives 'mark their foreheads with a cross', adding a footnote which says 'Literally with a TAW. This was the last letter of the Hebrew alphabet ... and a cross was the symbol for it.'

It must be remembered that the sign of the Cross on the forehead is a fundamental tenet of the Christian faith, used in both Baptism and Extreme Unction.

In Jewish literature there is an interesting comment by Rashi (Rabbi Solomon ben Isaac, 1040–1105. Referring to the anointing of Aaron the High Priest, he says, 'This anointing was in the form of a X; he (Moses) put a drop of oil on his (Aaron's) head and another drop between his eyebrows and joined them with his finger into this shape, X.'

It is also interesting to note that according to *Hall's Dictionary of Subjects & Symbols in Art* (page 78) we are told 'By tradition the mark made on the door-posts on the eve of the Passover was a tau-cross.'

As has been seen, there is some Biblical evidence to suggest that the tau had a special meaning. How much greater significance, then, can be given, especially by those of the Christian faith, to three taus joined together, the triple tau!

Let us recall the words of the Mystical Lecture; 'The union of the taus alludes to the Deity, by whom the gloomy, horrific and unshapen chaos was wrought into perfect form and peaceful existence.' I suggest that to Companions of the Jewish faith, it could also serve to remind them of three important Hebrew words, all beginning with the letter 'tav', namely

Torah	the study of the Mosaic Law;
Tefilah	prayer, and
Teshuba	return to the ways of the righteous.

One might ask 'Why is the triple tau shown on a Standard at the east end of the Chapter, and is there any significance in the colours used?'

The answer to the first part of the question is probably quite simply that at the revision of the Royal Arch ritual in 1834–5, the triple tau was given a degree of significance. This is evidenced to some degree by the phrase used in the Mystical Lecture, namely that the triple tau was 'affixed to the summonses of Royal Arch masons on occasions of more than usual importance.' A very similar phrase appears in the first known printed copy of the Royal Arch ritual, published by Claret in 1845. There is little doubt that, just as it appeared on Royal Arch summonses, so it also appeared in Convocations of Royal Arch Chapters. The importance attached to it would warrant a special position, and where better than in the east, above the Chair of the Principal Officer of the Chapter.

As to the colours, it will be recalled that we are told in the Mystical Lecture that the pedestal discovered was white, with a gold plate; 'white being an emblem of innocence, and gold of purity.' This is reflected in the pedestal in the Chapter which on its front has engraven (again as the Lecture tells us), a triple tau. The manufacturers of the Royal Arch furniture would have undoubtedly been influenced by the wording of the Lecture; hence, I suggest, the colours used, both on the pedestal and on the Standard.

A comparison with the Grand Chapters of Scotland and Ireland

This Section does not deal with the differences between the Royal Arch in the Grand Chapters of England, Scotland and Ireland, but rather with the differences regarding the various matters referred to in this book. However, it should be made clear that the Supreme Grand Chapter of Royal Arch Freemasons in Scotland is an autonomous body, being in no way directly connected with the Grand Lodge of Scotland. Further, both Scotland and Ireland have different masonic qualifications for the Royal Arch from those required in England.

Scotland

The Supreme Grand Chapter of Scotland is quite specific in the colour and devices of the Banners of the Order, as they are officially known. Law 37 of their *Constitutions and Laws* is quoted by kind permission of their Grand Chapter.

37. *Banners of the Order*

1. The Banners of the Order consist of two great and twelve small, the latter being those of the Twelve Tribes. The border of each of the small Banners shall be uniform—indented blue and crimson, as on the Aprons and Sashes of the Order. The shape shall be as shown on Plate XIII.

2. The great Banners shall be of the colours and devices as follows;

(i) Crimson, with the four-headed Animals and the motto *In Domino fiducia omnis.* (In the Lord is all our trust).

(ii) Dark Green, with the Signs of the Zodiac.

3. The Banners of the Twelve Tribes shall be of the colours and devices as follows;

Judah	Crimson; device, a Lion couchant surmounted by a Crown and Sceptre, and the Hebrew word יהודה
Issachar	Sky Blue; device, an Ass crouching beneath its burden and the Hebrew word יששכר
Zebulun	Purple; device, a Ship, and the Hebrew word זבולן
Reuben	Red; device, a Man erect, and the Hebrew word ראובן
Simeon	Yellow; device, a Tower and the Hebrew word שמעון
Gad	White; device, a Troop of Horsemen and the Hebrew word גד
Ephraim	Dark Green; device, an Ox and the Hebrew word אפרים
Manasseh	Flesh-colour; device, a Vine by the side of a well and the Hebrew word מנשה
Benjamin	Dark Green; device, a Wolf and the Hebrew word בנימן
Dan	Light Green; device, an Eagle with a Serpent in its talons and the Hebrew word דן
Asher	Purple; device, a Cup and the Hebrew word אשר
Naphthali	Blue; device, a Hind let loose and the Hebrew word נפתלי

The small Banners

It will be noted that by and large the colours and devices are very similar to those in general use in England, apart from the fact that they all have the name of the Tribe in Hebrew. The main differences are;

Reuben	'a Man erect' instead of waves of water.
Simeon	'a Tower' instead of a sword.
Dan	'an Eagle with a Serpent in its talons' instead of a horse rearing, its heels being bitten by a snake, and the rider falling off backwards.

The position of the small Banners is the same as that of the twelve ensigns used in England, though sometimes the Banner of the leading Tribe at each point of the Compass is placed between the other two, i.e.

Judah between Zebulun and Issachar in the east;
Reuben between Simeon and Gad in the south;
Ephraim between Manasseh and Benjamin in the west, and
Dan between Asher and Naphthali in the north.

The great Banners

Scotland does not have the four Principal Standards used in
England; they use the two great Banners referred to in Law 37
above.

The Crimson Banner

This Banner shows a shield depicting a pair of open compasses upon
a chevron between three arches; above the shield is a castle, and
above that an All-Seeing Eye. The shield is supported by cherubim
each of which shows the four faces of the living creatures that are
mentioned in *Ezekiel* 1. 10; that on the dexter side having the faces of
a man, a lion and and an eagle; that on the sinister side the faces of a
man, an ox and an eagle. Below the shield is a motto; '*In Domino
fiducia omnis.*' (In the Lord is all our trust). The whole is surrounded
by twelve small shields, each of which bears a sign of the zodiac, the
order being as follows.

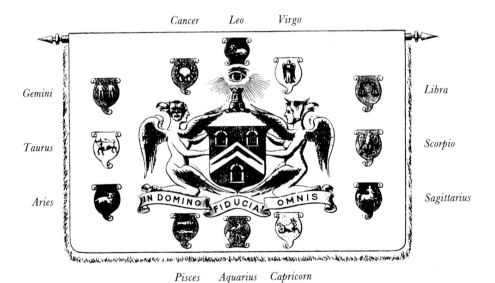

PLATE 27: *The Crimson Great Banner of the Supreme Grand Chapter of Royal Arch
Masons of Scotland; it depicts signs of the zodiac*

Scorpio is depicted as an eagle displayed, instead of the usual scorpion.

If one starts from Aries (in the 8 o'clock position) and goes round clockwise, the order is the same as that mentioned in the *Midrash* where each of the tribes is associated with a sign of the zodiac. This shows

Judah (Aries), Issachar (Taurus) and Zebulun (Gemini) on the dexter side, implying the east

Reuben (Cancer), Simeon (Leo) and Gad (Virgo) at the top, implying the south;

Ephraim (Libra), Manasseh (Scorpio) and Benjamin (Sagittarius) on the sinister sided, implying the west; and

Dan (Capricorn), Asher (Aquarius) and Naphthali (Pisces) at the bottom, implying the north.

This is the same order as the Banners are placed in Chapter.

The Green Banner

This shows the Ark of the Covenant with two Cherubim on top, each showing three faces as in the Crimson Banner. Above the Cherubim is the All-Seeing Eye; the whole is surrounded by the signs of the zodiac within a circle, the order being as given below. On the dexter side, in the upper corner, are the Volume of the Sacred Law with the square and compasses; in the lower corner, the theorum of Pythagoras; on the sinister side, in the upper corner, an equilateral triangle within a circle, and in the lower corner, the tools used by the Sojourners.

The order of the zodiac signs, together with the associated tribes as mentioned in the *Midrash* (shown in parenthesis) is

In the

1	o'clock position the sign of	Gemini	(Zebulun)
2		Taurus	(Issachar)
3		Aries	(Judah)
4		Pisces	(Naphthali)
5		Aquarius	(Asher)
6		Capricorn	(Dan)
7		Sagittarius	(Benjamin)
8		Scorpio	(Manasseh)
9		Libra	(Ephraim)
10		Virgo	(Gad)
11		Leo	(Simeon)
12		Cancer	(Reuben).

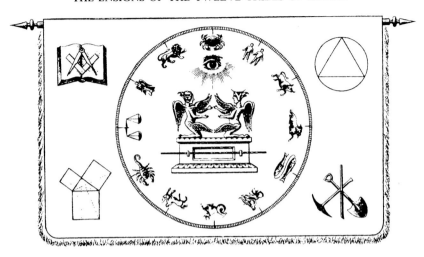

PLATE 28: *The Green Great Banner of the Supreme Grand Chapter, Scotland; it depicts signs of the zodiac (though in a different order to those on the Crimson Banner), together with masonic emblems*

Scorpio is represented on this Banner by the usual scorpion, not an eagle displayed, as shown on the Crimson Banner.

It will be seen that the order of the zodiacal signs on the Green Banner go in an anti-clockwise direction; thus starting from Aries (in the 3 o'clock position) the relevant compass points would appear to be;

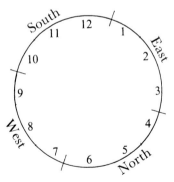

Jewels

Some of the Jewels worn by the Officer-bearers in Scotland show six of the signs of the zodiac; namely

Virgo	Leo	Cancer
Gemini	Taurus	Aries

the order being as shown on the Crimson Banner (plate 27).

The Royal Arch Jewel worn by all the Companions shows, on both the obverse and the reverse, ten of the signs of the zodiac, the triple tau taking up the space where the other two should be. The order is as used on the Green Banner (plate 28).

Aaron's Breastplate

The Jewel worn by the Third Principal is a breastplate of twelve stones, four rows of three, each stone bearing the name of one of the sons of Jacob. The names are inscribed in Hebrew and are shown in the following order.

Levi	Simeon	Reuben
Zebulun	Issachar	Judah
Gad	Naphthali	Dan
Benjamin	Joseph	Asher

If read from right to left (as in Hebrew) they do not accord with the instructions given in *Exodus* 28. 9–10 (plate 30).

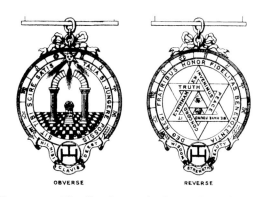

OBVERSE   REVERSE

PLATE 31: *The Jewel worn by Companions of the Supreme Grand Chapter, Scotland. Note signs of the zodiac*

PLATE 30: *Aaron's Breastplate worn as a Jewel by the Third Grand Principal, Supreme Grand Chapter, Scotland. Notice the names of the Tribes in Hebrew*

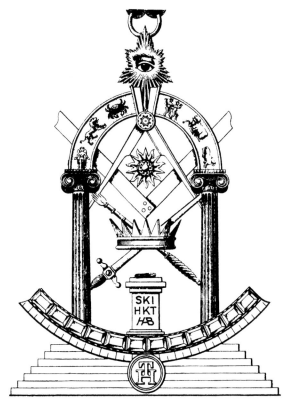

PLATE 29: *The Jewel of the First Grand Principal of the Supreme Grand Chapter, Scotland. Note signs of the zodiac on Arch*

Ireland

The Supreme Grand Royal Arch Chapter of Ireland uses a different legend in its ritual to that used in England and Scotland; they deal with the repair, rather than the rebuilding, of the Temple. The names of their Principal Officers also differ from those used in the other two Constitutions.

The twelve tribes of Israel are not mentioned in their proceedings, and they do not display the ensigns or Standards used in England, or the Banners used in Scotland. Further, there is no reference to either the signs of the zodiac or Aaron's breastplate.

Summary of Main Points

- The ensigns on the banners used in Royal Arch Chapters take their names from the ten sons and two grandsons of Jacob. Joseph and Levi (sons) are replaced by Ephraim and Manasseh (grandsons).

- The distinctive bearings on the ensigns are traditionally associated with the interpretations given by Biblical commentators on the words used by Jacob when he blessed his children.

- Some sets of ensigns show a Latin quotation. This is usually the appropriate wording from *Genesis* 49 of the (Latin) *Vulgate*.

- The colour of the ensigns represents the colour of the precious stones worn on the breastplate of Aaron, the high Priest.

- The earliest reference in the Royal Arch to ensigns depicting the distinctive bearings of the twelve tribes of Israel is towards the end of the the eighteenth century. There is manuscript evidence dating from the early nineteenth century that clearly indicates such ensigns were part of Royal Arch Chapter furnishings.

- The arrangement in Chapter of the staves bearing the ensigns follows that described in *Numbers* 2, which gives details of how the tribes pitched their tents during the journey in the Wilderness of Sinai. For practical reasons, however, no staves are placed in the east or west of the Chapter.

- The possible reason why the twelve tribes of Israel were included in the Royal Arch is because the early Royal Arch was essentially Christian in character; a connection was seen between the twelve tribes and the twelve Apostles. The aphorism of Saint Augustine is relevant. 'The New Testament lies hidden in the Old and the Old is manifest in the New.'

- The Royal Arch Lectures tell us who bore the banners in the Wilderness. This information is based on *Numbers* 1. 5–15.

- The signs of the zodiac have been associated with Freemasonry for about 250 years. They also formed part of the decoration of the first and second Freemasons' Halls and can be seen in the present Freemasons' Hall in Great Queen Street, London. They have been shown in the furnishings of Royal Arch Chapters for many years. In Scotland they are shown on the two great Banners, on the Jewels worn by some of the Officers and on the Jewel of the Order.

- The Principal Standards are said to bear the devices of the leading divisions of the army of Israel. This seems unlikely so far as the device shown on Dan's Standard is concerned. *Ezekiel* 1. 5–6 and *Revelation* 4. 7 are more likely sources. The man, the lion, the ox and the eagle have been used since the second century AD to symbolize the Gospel writers, Matthew, Mark, Luke and John.

- The triple tau was originally the letter T over the letter H. It was shown in this fashion on early Royal Arch documents, aprons and Jewels. In time the letters lost their serifs and the 'tail' of the T dropped on to the 'crossbar' of the H, thus giving the appearance of three capitals Ts, joined to each other at the 'tail'. The symbolic nature of this was soon seen and shortly after (about 1810 or so) we begin to find references to the triple tau.

- The Constitutions and Laws of Supreme Grand Chapter of Royal Arch Freemasons of Scotland gives precise details of the shape, colours and devices of the Banners of the Twelve Tribes of Israel. Their position in Chapter is the same as that in England. Precise details are also given for the two great Banners.

- The Supreme Grand Royal Arch Chapter of Ireland uses a different legend from that used in England and Scotland. The twelve tribes of Israel are not mentioned in their proceedings; they do not display the ensigns, banners or Standards used in England or Scotland; nor is there any reference to Aaron's breastplate or the signs of the zodiac.

GENERAL INDEX

INDEX OF SOURCES QUOTED

Stoicism

*How To Integrate This Powerful
Philosophy To Become More Balanced,
Productive, And Reach Your Full
Potential*

Table of Contents

Chapter 6: Practical Exercises of Stoicism

1. Be Mindful of Each Situation

2. Focus on What Is Truly Important

3. You Must Get to Know Yourself

4. Accept Whatever Comes Your Way

5. Negative Visualization

6. Everything Is the Same

7. Imagine Your Death

8. Use a Reserve Clause

9. Always Work on Self-Improvement

10. What You Own Is Borrowed from Nature

11. Morning Reflection

12. Evening Reflection

13. Your Health Matters

14. Voluntary Discomfort

15. Speak and Act Wisely

16. Remember Moderation

17. Manage Your Time Wisely

18. Become an Eternal Scholar

19. Learn That Pain and Challenge Are Virtues

20. Live Simply

21. Courage and Calmness over Anger

22. Your Strength Is Compassion

23. Pick a Role Model

24. Act Good, Don't Just Avoid Acting Evil

25. Don't Worry About Fame

26. Beat Your Fear

27. Life Is a Challenge

28. Judging Is Harmful

29. Remember Your Blessings

30. Look at the Bigger Picture

31. Find the Best People for Your Company

Introduction

You might have chosen this book because you want to focus on finding ways to help you release negativity and remain calm in a chaotic world. You may have selected this title because you found a quote from a famous Stoic philosopher from Ancient Rome and want to know more. You might even have chosen this book simply to further your personal education on the philosophy of Stoicism.

The world is busy - your world is busy. Some days, you may feel that there is no way to handle situations which are put in front of you. You react in a way that is irrational and later causes you guilt. You replay situations in your mind over and over as you ask yourself why you reacted in such an irrational way, and how you could have acted more rationally.

We have all been in these situations at some point in our lives. This book is intended to help guide you towards a better solution and more rational actions. Not only will you receive an understanding of the Stoic philosophy, but over 60 practical exercises that you can use in your daily life, as well. This book will help you reach your highest self, so you can act more calmly and stop agonizing over situations which you cannot control.

We will begin by discussing the different parts that make up Stoicism. People often feel that Stoicism is a complicated philosophy due to its varying definitions and aspects. However, once you gain a sense of these aspects, you will find that Stoicism is easy to understand and even easier to implement. The first chapter will discuss eudaimonia and how Stoics believe that through reaching your highest self, you will reach your greatest happiness, which is what eudaimonia is all about. Chapter 1 will also discuss the four main cardinal virtues of Stoicism, which are (1) practical wisdom, (2) justice, (3) courage, and (4) self-discipline.

Chapter 2 will give you a history lesson on Stoicism. You will learn how the philosophy came to be, who its founder was, and receive an overview of some of the most influential ancient teachers of Stoicism.

Chapter 3 will take a deeper look into the history of Stoicism by discussing the various phases of Stoicism, which are defined as Early, Middle, and Late Stoicism. Through this chapter, you will learn a bit more about some of the philosophy's famous influencers and how they helped develop Stoicism through the ages. This chapter will also discuss how Stoicism found its way back into the mainstream and where it stands today.

Chapter 4 will focus on some of the main benefits you will find when you start practicing Stoicism. This chapter is meant to help prepare you for the good that will come out of practicing the various exercises discussed in a later chapter throughout your day.

Chapter 5 will focus on how Stoicism can help you through the process of grief. No matter who you are, you will be faced with the death of a loved one or friend one day. No matter how much you prepare for the passing, you will still have to go through the same grieving process as everyone else. Chapter 5 discusses the typical stages of grief and how Stoicism can help you through these stages. Stoics do not fear death, because it is inevitable. Therefore, the philosophy of Stoicism has practical exercises and teachings which can help you handle the process of grief the best you can.

Chapter 6 will give you dozens of exercises you can try throughout your day and will also help you prepare before you begin your exercises. It's important to remember that you shouldn't just dive into and begin the exercises. You will be able to focus on and continue to practice the exercises more effectively if you have the correct mindset.

Chapter 7 will help you if you are struggling to implement any of the exercises. This chapter will give you tips which can help you overcome any struggles you face as you start to practice the exercises. This chapter will also briefly discuss the consequences of not implementing the Stoic exercises.

Before we go further into this book, I want to take the time to thank you for purchasing this book. I hope that the contents will inspire you to seek out your higher self and help you discover how beautiful life can be with the right mindset and tools to grow.

Chapter 1: What Is Stoicism?

The philosophy of Stoicism states that practitioners do not complain about the hardships and pain that they face in their lives. However, Stoicism is about so much more than just powering through pain and difficulty. The Stoic philosophy teaches you how to overcome the difficult times so that you can become constructive and resilient. People will often fall into the shadows of stress, depression, or anxiety when they are faced with situations that they feel they cannot handle. Stoicism teaches you to release your inner negativity, so you can handle whatever life throws at you with peaceful strength. Stoicism focuses on using techniques and exercises so that people can control themselves during times of crisis. The philosophy maintains that you can do this by focusing on what matters.

Stoicism is about understanding that you cannot control external factors in your environment, but you can learn to control your impulses, emotions, and actions. Stoicism is an action philosophy, which means that you must act on what the philosophy teaches. As a real world example, imagine your supervisor is a procrastinator, which is a trait that Stoics do not practice. You are unable to control your supervisor's actions, but you can manage your own. Instead of acting impulsively and emotionally, you will learn through Stoicism to calmly come up with a solution to discuss with your procrastinating supervisor.

Eudaimonia

Take a moment to imagine the highest version of yourself. Imagine that you have reached your greatest good, the best you that could possibly exist. You are no longer making mistakes or feeling anger, and you know exactly the correct way to act in all situations. For Stoics, this is the goal in life. Stoics continuously work to improve themselves so that they can reach eudaimonia.

To Stoics, eudaimonia means living in peace and happiness with your highest self. Every moment, you are living in harmony with yourself and your quality of life. Eudaimonia focuses on more than the emotion of happiness; it focuses on your overall experience. The founder of Stoicism, Zeno, stated eudaimonia the best when he said, "happiness is a smoothly flowing life."

Principles to Help You Achieve Eudaimonia

There are three main principles which will help you achieve eudaimonia. These are (1) focusing on what you can control, (2) living with arete, and (3) taking responsibility for your actions.

Focusing on what you can control is a crucial factor in Stoicism. While we can control our actions, we cannot control environmental situations or the ways other people act. Instead, we must learn to accept the circumstances we cannot control. By going with the flow of what you can't manage and making the best of each situation, you will reach eudaimonia.

To live with arete, or virtue, means you strive to be your best self in every moment. Of course, no one is perfect. While you won't always be able to be your best self in every moment of your life, you can do your best to *be* your best in every situation. Some moments will be more comfortable than other moments. Your goal is to try to close the gap between your current self and your highest self. If in every moment you try to express your best self, you will, over time, slowly close this gap.

Through taking responsibility for your actions, you will maintain eudaimonia. This principle helps you realize what you can control and what you cannot control. In the process, you learn to control your actions, which help you reach your highest self. This is because you stop giving situations you cannot control power. Instead, you take responsibility for yourself and what you can control - you.

Four Cardinal Virtues

Other than the three principles, there are also four cardinal virtues which Stoics follow in their everyday lives: (1) practical wisdom, (2) justice, (3) courage, and (4) self-discipline.

Practical wisdom, or phronesis, helps you understand the difference between good, indifferent, and bad. Practical wisdom is the knowledge which helps give you happiness. It directs you to what actions will make you happy and what actions will not. It helps you make the decision to know what you need to get done and what you don't have to get done. Wisdom helps you understand the most important things in your life. Through practical wisdom, you realize what you need to do during your precious time here on Earth.

Justice, or dikaiosune, is the way you treat other people. Justice helps you realize that there is no need for gossip, and it's not your place to judge other people. This virtue helps you deal with general morality. For a Stoic, justice is more than just what is right, what is wrong, and how people should be treated in a legal sense. It's how you treat people daily, no matter how they treat you.

Courage, or andreia, is not letting fear control you. When you have courage, you are able to think rationally when you are solving a problem, because you control your fear. You can still have courage and feel fear - the trick is to control the emotion of fear instead of allowing fear to control you. You're able to incorporate Stoic exercises during the situation so you can remain calm as you deal with what you are facing. Seneca, a Roman Stoic philosopher, believed that you can't have courage without fear.

Self-discipline, or sophrosyne, is doing what is right even in times when you feel a different way. Self-discipline, which some people refer to as moderation, will help you keep on track with your highest self. It is self-discipline that will tell you that you need to be compassionate when someone is being rude to you. When Epictetus discussed self-discipline, he talked about a person's moral conscience.

When you strive to become your best self, you focus your time on doing well in all four of these virtues and don't waste your energy on the negative. These virtues are important to follow every day, because they assist in the formation of your actions and words. The more often you follow these four cardinal virtues, the quicker you will be able to reach eudaimonia.

Stoicism teaches people to live by virtue. However, the philosophy further teaches that only humans can live by virtue. Virtue cannot be a part of nature or animals.

You can only find virtue within yourself. Stoicism started as a philosophy for the masses and continues to be this type of philosophy to this day. Stoics believe that everyone is capable of learning and practicing Stoicism in their daily lives. It's up to you whether you decide to live according to the virtues or not. To learn the philosophy of Stoicism and practice its exercises are actions that are completely within   your   power.

Chapter 2: The History of Stoicism

Around 300 B.C., Zeno of Citium found himself in Athens, Greece, after a shipwreck. At first, Zeno started to follow the school of philosophy known as Cynicism, but he soon began teaching his own beliefs, which became known as Zenonism. However, Zenonism would quickly become Stoicism after Zeno spoke at the Stoa Poikile, also known as the Painted Porch.

Unlike many other schools of philosophy at the time, Stoicism became a philosophy for everyone. Other schools were taught in private locations, but Zeno taught Stoicism in public where anyone could listen. Because of this, many people referred to Stoicism as the "philosophy of the street."

One of the biggest influences of Stoicism came from the philosophical question of how people can live the good life. In order to teach people how to have a good life, Zeno focused on using situations found in everyday experiences. Zeno taught that you could reach your best self through challenging circumstances. One of the biggest differences between Cynicism and Stoicism was that Zeno taught people to live a simple life.

Because Stoicism was available to everyone, this school of philosophy quickly became popular. People from all walks of life were listening to the words taught on the steps of the Painted Porch. Epictetus first heard about the teachings of Stoicism as a slave. His wealthy master allowed him to listen to the teachings of Musonius Rufus. Over time, Rufus became Epictetus' mentor and once freed, Epictetus started teaching the philosophy of Stoicism himself.

Today, we know more about some eras of Stoicism than others. This is because some texts have survived through time, while other were lost. For example, you can still read Marcus Aurelius's *Meditations*, which was his journal. As I will discuss more in Chapter 3, Marcus Aurelius became a famous Stoic philosopher in the third or Late Stoa Era, which is the era from which the majority of Stoic texts survived. There are very little to no texts which remain from the Early or Middle Stoa Eras.

Over the years, Stoicism grew from Athens towards the Romans. Some of the major Stoics of this time were Seneca, Epictetus, Musonius Rufus, and Marcus Aurelius. Throughout its first five centuries, the significant leaders of Stoicism helped shape the school of philosophy. Each leader would focus on one of the philosophy's three basic principles of logic, ethics, and physics. They would all help to expand the school of philosophy and bring their thoughts and beliefs into the philosophy of Stoicism.

Stoicism continued to grow for five centuries and remained a philosophy for everyone, and people from all walks of life became interested in Stoic teachings. Both the poor and the rich would stop and listen to the Stoic philosophers discuss their beliefs, teachings, and exercises. However, all this popularity could not keep the philosophy of Stoicism from fading into history. But, unlike most philosophies of its time, Stoicism would make a comeback during the 1970s and continue to hold its own well into the 21st century.

Chapter 3: Stoicism Through the Ages

A Look at Some Leading Stoics

Marcus Aurelius (121 C.E. - 180 C.E.)

One of the most notable ancient Stoics is Marcus Aurelius. Known for his famous work, *Meditations*, Marcus wrote down his Stoic advice. He discussed how Stoics should handle various situations in life, from realizing that no one is perfect to imagining your own death. Overall, *Meditations* is similar to a diary. Marcus

Aurelius is known to have written at least one entry a day. His famous book is actually the combined work of a dozen short books, all of which were written like diaries. In these books, Marcus would reflect on his thoughts and the events of his days. He would discuss how he believed certain situations should be handled and how he handled many situations he faced.

As a child, Marcus Aurelius wasn't big into philosophy. This part of his life came a bit later, when he was given *Discourses* by Epictetus. From that moment on, Epictetus became one of Marcus Aurelius's main influences in the philosophy of Stoicism. He devoted his life to teaching himself Stoicism. Aurelius spent most of his time writing about his exercises and the things he learned. He didn't spend a lot of time lecturing like many other Stoics did. Instead, he became a popular Roman Emperor as he continued to practice Stoicism.

Musonius Rufus (30 C.E. - 100 C.E.)

Musonius Rufus was a teacher of the Stoic philosophy. While he is not often talked about, he established his own school, which helped spread the philosophy further into Rome. Unfortunately, not much is known about Rufus's Stoic teachings because unlike Marcus Aurelius, Rufus didn't take much time to write things down. During his career, Rufus taught many students. One of his students would become equally famous as a Roman Stoic, Epictetus.

Epictetus (55 C.E. - 135 C.E.)

Born a slave, Epictetus was able to listen to Musonius Rufus with his master's approval. Once Epictetus gained his freedom, he continued to learn under Rufus and become one of the most influential Stoics of all time, not to mention an incredibly popular Stoic teachers during his era. Like Rufus, Epictetus established his own school, where he was free to teach Stoicism as he pleased. His school became extremely popular. Unfortunately, similar to his role model Rufus, Epictetus didn't write much of the information from his lectures down.

Three Main Eras of Stoicism

Scholars state that there are three main eras of Stoicism. The first era is called Early Stoa, which began with the school's founding in 300 B.C.E. The main leaders of this phase were Zeno of Citium, Cleanthes, and Chrysippus. The fourth leader of Stoicism, Zeno of Tarsus, marked the start of the Middle Stoa era. Other leaders of this era included Diogenes of Babylon, Antipater of Tarsus, and Panaetius. Posidonius came at the end of the Middle Stoa, around the First Century B.C.E. The Late Stoa era is often referred to as the Roman Imperial Period. Starting in the First Century C.E., Musonius Rufus, Seneca, Epictetus, and Marcus Aurelius became Stoicism's significant figures.

Here's a look at the approximate timeline of the three eras discussed above:

- Early Stoa (300 - 100 B.C.) starts with Zeno and continues to Chrysippus, who became the third head of the School of Stoicism.

- Middle Stoa (100 - 0 B.C.) starts in the late second century and into the first century B.C. A couple of the most famous Stoics during Middle Stoa were Posidonius and Panaetius.

- Late Stoa (0 - 200 A.D.) finishes the first century and goes into the second century C.E. Many famous Stoics lived in this period, such as Musonius Rufus, Marcus Aurelius, Seneca, and Epictetus.

Unfortunately, no written texts from the Early and Middle Stoa timeframe survive today. However, there are some texts from the Late Stoa Era. This doesn't mean the history of Stoicism is completely lost. We know that during the early days of Stoicism, many famous Stoics helped mold the philosophy, such as Cato, Seneca, Cleanthes, Epictetus, and Marcus Aurelius. These Stoics would take the teachings of Zeno and meld their own beliefs with his. They would sometimes add to the previous teachings or debate the teachings of Stoicism. For instance, Epictetus, as mentioned, was a slave when he first started to listen to the Stoic teachings. Then, once he gained his freedom, he started to teach Stoicism himself. While he taught the original teachings of the philosophy, he also added his own beliefs, which he wrote down in *The Enchiridion*.

When people think of the days of Early Stoicism, they think of Zeno and how he started the school of thought because he didn't care for the materialistic world. Another reason Zeno started Stoicism was because he didn't believe that the people had to experience pain in order to get to pleasure, which was a key idea at the time. Zeno started many of the beliefs that Stoics still teach today, such as ethics.

After Zeno, the next leader of Stoicism became Cleanthes, who followed Zeno's teaching very closely but did add some of his own beliefs. After Cleanthes, Chrysippus took over the school and focused mainly on logic, though he did take time to teach physics and ethics as well. Historians often credit Chrysippus with bringing Stoicism into the mainstream. After his time as a leader, Stoicism became the most popular philosophy. Zeno of Tarsus took over as leader of Stoicism after Chrysippus, and he was followed by a man named Diogenes. The last leader under the Early Stoa Era was Antipater.

The Middle Stoa Era began with Stoicism becoming popular in Rome. Panaetius was one of the first leaders under this era. While he was less interested in teaching logic, he focused a lot on physics. Next, Posidonius took over as the leader and focused on building the school of thought in Rome. It was here that Cato the Younger and Cicero would join in on the Stoic teachings and way of life. Out of the two, Cato has become the more popular Stoic, and he also changed a few of the beliefs as he focused on several previous Stoic leaders such as Zeno, Chrysippus, Panaetius, and Posidonius.

The Late Stoa Era held many famous Stoics, such as Epictetus, Seneca, and Marcus Aurelius. The leaders of this era focused on ethics more than logic or physics. Because this is the era original writings survived from, historians know the most about the Late Stoa Era compared to the first two eras. *Epistulae Morales ad Lucilium* by Seneca and *Ta eis heauton* or *Meditations* by Marcus Aurelius are two of the era's most notable surviving works. There are also *Discourses* and the *Enchiridion* by Epictetus, which is essentially a Stoicism handbook. To this day, people say that this handbook is one of the best ways to start learning about Stoicism. However, *Meditations* is probably the work that is easiest to find. This work focuses on self-discipline and how you can improve yourself in the ways of a Stoic.

A Stoic Comeback

Cognitive Behavioral Therapy is a hands-on psychotherapy treatment which focuses on goals and problem-solving. It's a short-term therapy which aims to change the way people think and solve their problems so that they can overcome difficulties and reach their goals. CBT is also used to help turn the negative thinking into positive. For example, if someone goes to a cognitive behavioral therapist to treat their anxiety, the therapist would figure out the negative thought patterns of the person. These negative thought patterns would be the reason for the person's anxiety. Therefore, the therapist would use techniques to help the person think more positively, which in return would reduce the person's anxiety.

Ever since Stoicism started to make a comeback during the 1970s, many famous people have turned to Stoicism. If you're a football fan, you may be happy to learn that Coach Pete Carroll uses Stoicism in his football tactics. A famous historical figure who followed Stoicism was President Theodore Roosevelt. Warren Buffett, an investor, and Microsoft's founder Bill Gates have also used techniques of Stoicism to help them succeed in their careers.

There are many famous singers and actors/actresses who are also followers of Stoicism. LL Cool J is one singer who has been known to follow Stoicism. Actress Brie Larson has quoted from Marcus Aurelius' *Meditations*, along with actress Anna Kendrick. JK Rowling, Ralph Waldo Emerson, and John Steinbeck are just a few famous authors who are known to follow the ways of Stoicism.

Because Stoicism is so helpful for so many people, it has become a staple in the self-help area. Many books with a self-help focus have started to take exercises and principles from the Stoic philosophy and use them to help people overcome obstacles and find ways to better their lives. One of these self-help books was written by Ryan Holiday and Stephen Hanselman. The book is called *The Daily Stoic: 366 Meditations on Wisdom, Perseverance, and the Art of Living*. This book has a list of Stoic exercises that you can read and practice daily. Another book which can help is called *The Little Book of Stoicism: Timeless Wisdom to Gain Resilience, Confidence, and Calmness*, which was written by Jonas Salzgeber.

Through the ages, Stoicism has developed into a popular philosophy, was almost forgotten by the passage of time, and finally found its way back into people's lives in a way that its early leaders would never have imagined. Stoicism has been focused on turning the bad into the good. Reframing negatives into positives has been at the heart of Stoicism - however, this doesn't mean that we should avoid our shadows, and the necessary inner work should always be done to help us become more whole and balanced human beings. To just focus on one aspect means you're potentially missing out on something. The next chapter will help you discover the many benefits of Stoicism, and later, we'll look at how you can reap those benefits by incorporating Stoic habits into your daily life.

Chapter 4: Benefits to You as a Practicing Stoic

"The chief task in life is simply this: to identify and separate matters so that I can say clearly to myself which are externals not under my control, and which have to do with the choices I actually control. Where then do I look for good and evil? Not to uncontrollable externals, but within myself to the choices that are my own…" – Epictetus.

When you practice Stoicism, you will find there are many benefits to your daily life. Some of these benefits including controlling your emotions, accepting what you can control over what you can't control, and prioritizing. You will become completely honest, you won't procrastinate, and with each step, you will get closer to reaching your highest self.

Of course, there are more benefits than those laid out in this chapter. Some of the benefits of Stoicism will pertain more to you than others, because you become focused on what you want to achieve. You become focused on your version of your highest self, and only you know what this self looks like. For example, you might be able to handle your emotions better in a stressful situation than your friend, who is also working towards achieving her best self. Therefore, you won't focus as much on practical exercises which help you control your emotions as your friend will. However, you might find that you aren't 100% honest with your flaws, which means you will focus on this aspect of Stoicism more. You will work on admitting and accepting your flaws by learning to realize that everyone has flaws and you don't have to be ashamed by yours. Instead, you will strive to work on these flaws so that you can reach your best self. Let's look at a few more benefits that may or may not pertain to you.

Stoicism Helps You Control Your Emotions

Stoics manage their emotions through various practical exercises and self-discipline. It's important to remember that Stoicism isn't about becoming emotionless; it's about taking control of your emotions. You will still have all your human emotions and you will still feel them, but you will be able to manage them internally instead of externally.

There are many reasons why controlling your emotions is vital. First, you will think more rationally about the situation you are facing. Second, you will have more control in the situation. Third, you will become a better problem-solver, and fourth, you will become closer to reaching your highest self.

When we are faced with difficult or emotional situations, our emotions often take over. When this happens, we start to act as our emotions want us to act, which isn't generally rationally because emotions tend to be more irrational. We have all acted this way at some point in our lives. Maybe you were criticized over a presentation or something you wrote, and you immediately became defensive. Instead of thinking about and analyzing the criticism, you immediately defended yourself as if you were right and the other person was wrong.

When you control your emotions, you can control the situation with more ease. For example, instead of acting defensively upon receiving criticism, what if you listened to what the individual had to say, thought of what you presented, and analyzed the situation? Through this process, you might realize that what the individual said was correct. You can then thank the person for their criticism and let the person know how you will incorporate the criticism. This creates a far more pleasant scenario than flying off the handle does.

Through controlling your emotions to a situation, you will become a better problem-solver. Because you think more rationally about the situation, you will be able to think of solutions to any problems you face. When our mind is clouded by our emotions, our thoughts are often clouded as well, which affects the entire thought process that goes into developing a solution to a problem.

Controlling emotions is a vital part of Stoicism and reaching your highest self. When you learn to control your emotions, you will be able to control everything else in your life. The more you use various practical exercises to control your emotions in any situation, the closer you become to reaching your version of your best self.

Accepting What You Can Control and What You Can't Control

Our world is full of factors that we can't control. Stoics believe that one of the main problems within people of this world is that they try to control things that are not in their control. People want to control everything in their environment, and they often feel that they can. However, as Stoicism teaches, there is very little we can actually control within our environment.

After incorporating practical Stoic exercises, you will gain an understanding that you can really only control your thoughts, emotions, and actions. You can't control how other people think or act. You will also learn that you can't control the outcome of a situation. In every situation, you can only control you, which means you can't control the other people and factors that are involved. For example, you can control how much you study for an exam, but you can't control what is on the exam. You can control the research and work you put into your job, but you can't control what other people will think of the end result.

Accepting what you can and can't control is a major benefit of Stoicism, because it helps bring a sense of peace to situations, especially if the situations don't go your way. By accepting the outcome, you will be in harmony with your work and actions, your environment, and the overall situation. This harmony will further help you feel the peace within yourself and will bring you closer to your highest self.

Stoicism Will Help You Learn How to Make Rational Decisions

There are many practical exercises you will learn in the next chapter that will help you learn how to make rational decisions. There are several factors which go into making rational decisions instead of irrational decisions. Some of these factors include controlling your emotions, learning to accept what you can and can't change, and knowing your version of your best self.

The main goal for the philosophy of Stoicism is to become your best self. All of your actions and thoughts, the practical exercises you choose to incorporate, and all the other work you do to better yourself is helping you reach your best self. It's important for you to know who your best self is so you can always keep your best self in mind when you're making any decision. Doing this will help you make rational decisions that get you closer to your goal.

Stoicism Will Help You Let Go of Greed

We live in a materialistic world. We also live in a world where people always seem to want more. No matter how much money people have, they always seem to want more money. Even if they are living comfortably or are fabulously wealthy, they always want to bring in more money. They want to be able to buy the newest and best things. They want to have a bigger house. When Stoics look at this, they see people who are full of greed.

For Stoics, greed is a negative emotion. It's similar to the emotions of anger and frustration. Negative emotions often bring out the worst in people instead of the best. When Seneca discussed greed, he stated, "For greed all nature is too little." Stoics are one with nature. They feel that everything they have is borrowed from nature, which means it is nature that we must thank for what we have in our lives. When people continuously want more, they are not in harmony with nature, and therefore cannot be in harmony with themselves. This also means that you would not be in harmony with your best self.

In order to get a step closer to your highest self, you need to let go of greed. There are many practical exercises of Stoicism that help you learn how to let go of greed. For example, in the next chapter, you will learn how to live simply or eliminate the unnecessary items from your life. Stoics lived as minimalists, which means that many of the exercises will help you achieve the same lifestyle.

When you live like a minimalist, you are happy with what you have in your environment. You are grateful for the items nature has given you. With this harmony, you are able to let go of your wants and focus on your needs. This helps you let go of any greed you feel and become happier with your life and more in harmony with your best self.

Stoicism Teaches You How to Prioritize

People often struggle with prioritizing. It doesn't matter who you are; there has been a time in your life where you have placed something with less importance in front of something more important. This could have been something as small as a couple of tasks at your job, all the way to something serious like putting your work before your health.

Struggling with prioritizing often brings people stress and anger. These negative emotions can lead us down a more dangerous path, one which divides us further from our highest self. Furthermore, negativity brings negativity. When you hold negative emotions, such as anger, you're more likely to feel negative overall. This negativity can influence the people around you.

The philosophy of Stoicism is full of various practical exercises which will not only help you prioritize, but will also aid you in feeling more confident and positive about the decisions you're making.

Stoicism Will Help You Stop Procrastination

"In your actions, don't procrastinate. In your conversations, don't confuse. In your thoughts, don't wander. In your soul, don't be passive or aggressive. In your life, don't be all about business." – Marcus Aurelius.

For many people, procrastination can be as big of a problem as prioritizing. In Stoicism, you learn that procrastination is your enemy. Seneca and Marcus Aurelius talked a lot about procrastination because, like so many of us, they too procrastinated.

Seneca understood that sometimes it was hard for people to get motivated. He talked about how he struggled with motivation himself. Seneca told people that to feel motivated, they had to realize that no one lives forever. Seneca asked why we would decide to procrastinate when we know that we will one day take our last breath. Seneca believed that procrastination meant that we forgot we were mortal.

When discussing procrastination and how he worked to overcome it, Marcus Aurelius stated to look at the things surrounding him. He noticed that everything, even the plants and the trees, had their tasks. He noticed how they performed their tasks every day, no matter what. Through these types of observations and knowing he wanted to stop procrastinating, Marcus Aurelius set about accomplishing his own task because he realized that he needed to take responsibility for his own life, and he told other people to do the same.

Both Seneca and Marcus Aurelius further discussed procrastination by stating that if you stop it, you will become more self-disciplined. You will no longer whine or complain about the tasks you need to accomplish. Instead, you will realize you have to take responsibility because you are the only one who can take responsibility for the tasks that are yours. You will just get up and do them, because they are a part of your purpose.

However, this does not mean that you should ignore feelings of procrastination. Both Stoic philosophers taught that you need to acknowledge the way you feel and note your procrastination. But after you do, must still complete the task at hand. By overcoming procrastination, you will find that you're living the life you want to live as you move closer to your highest self.

Stoicism Will Teach You to Be 100% Honest

In Stoicism, honesty is more than just being honest with other people; it's also about being honest with yourself. It's about acknowledging your emotions, flaws, goals, and achievements. Being honest is about learning about yourself and the vision you see of your best self.

Marcus Aurelius talked about being honest when he stated, "If it is not right, do not do it. If it is not true, do not say it." Honesty is a big part of Stoicism, as it's something that you have to keep in mind all the time. This is more than just telling the truth when someone asks you a question. It's also making sure you don't manipulate to get what you want. It's making sure that you don't act like someone you aren't. For example, if you talk and act like you're an expert on a certain topic, make sure you're an expert. If you act like you're an expert, but you're not, then you are lying not only to others, but also to yourself.

The big problem with honesty starts when you decide to hang on to dishonesty, which can be tricky because you might not even realize this is what you're doing. In his book *Meditations*, Marcus Aurelius discusses honesty when he talks about how villains use dishonesty to get what they want. They use dishonesty as a tool, which Marcus Aurelius believed was cowardly.

Stoicism Will Help You Form Better Relationships

Another benefit of Stoicism is that you will be able to form better relationships. It doesn't matter if you want to focus on the relationship with your parents, spouse, children, other family members, friends, or supervisors. Stoicism will help you strengthen the relationships in all aspects of your life.

One of the biggest reasons Stoicism helps you improve your relationships is because you're constantly working on self-improvement. Through the dozens of exercises provided in chapter 6, you will learn how to not only forgive yourself but also forgive others. You will learn what is important, that judging is harmful, and to look at the bigger picture in every situation.

You will become balanced between spending time with yourself and spending time with others. Being alone too much can often make people feel lonely, which can turn into a negative emotion. Therefore, Stoicism helps you realize that the company of others, especially the right company of like-minded people, will help you stay energized and focused.

Stoicism Helps You Remain Mindful

Marcus Aurelius wrote of remaining mindful in his book *Meditations* when he discussed how we shouldn't focus on the fact that life is short, but we should remain mindful of it. Aurelius stated that in order to remain mindful, we should take care of our body. You want to watch what food you eat and what you drink. He stated that we should, "...look after yourself so well that your body hardly needs medical attention, drugs, or ointment."

Mindfulness means to live in the moment. You're aware of your surroundings and pay attention to everything that is going on. For example, if you're driving to work on your regular route, you shouldn't let your thoughts drift you away from your task. This usually happens when people are repeating tasks that they do every day. They become so used to their tasks that they tend to let their thoughts wander away from them. Of course, they are still able to accomplish the task, but they often wonder how, because they don't remember completing all the actions. Think about a route your drive often. Have you ever gotten to your destination and wondered when you passed the lake or the grove of trees because you didn't remember seeing these landmarks? This is an example of being mindless in a task, which is the opposite of mindfulness. If you were mindful, you'd remember all the landmarks you passed as you remained in the moment.

It's important for Stoics to remain mindful or in the moment at all times. This is because when you're mindful, you're more likely to think rationally and make the right decisions. Stoics are also more likely to realize which factors won't allow them to reach their highest self. For example, they might find that they are spreading gossip about their neighbor. Stoic philosophers such as Marcus Aurelius and Seneca taught that Stoics should not gossip.

People who are mindful are better equipped to control their emotions and actions. When people take themselves out of the moment or they are mindless, they will run on instinct. Instead of making decisions logically, they will make decisions based on their emotions and might not be able to control their instincts, which can lead you astray if emotions are playing a bigger role than logic.

One of the best ways to be mindful is to continue to focus on the task you are working on. For example, if you are listening to a conversation between your friends, you not only know what your friends are discussing, but you are also aware of your surroundings. You are aware of where you are and if other people have walked in or out of the building. Furthermore, you are also aware of the body language your friends are exhibiting. You are aware of your own body language, thoughts, and are mindful of what you are saying when you do speak. You remain aware of all the Stoic exercises that you can practice while you are with your friends, such as only talking when you find it necessary and remaining mindful of your time.

Stoicism Will Help You Reach Your Highest Self

One of the biggest benefits of Stoicism is that it will help you reach your best self. Before you start to work on the exercises in chapter 6, you should have an idea of your highest self. Through several exercises, you will gain a clearer picture of your highest self. You will continue to work to reach your highest self throughout the course of your life, so don't expect it to be an easy process. You will have to change your ways, and some of the change might be uncomfortable in the beginning. But when you practice Stoicism, the change is worth it!

Your highest self is the best person you can be. This person can be anyone you want to become. Stoics such as Marcus Aurelius and Seneca stated that one way to learn who you want to be is by thinking of your death and how you want people to remember you. Sounds morbid? It happens to be the best way to realize what your priorities and values truly are.

Chapter 5: Stoicism and Dealing with Death and Grief

Death and grief are common themes in Stoic texts because they're common themes in our lives. No matter who you are, where you live, or what you do, you are going to know and love someone who is going to die. Stoics refer to death as Memento Mori, which basically means "remember you must die."

5 Stages of Grief

In 1969, Elisabeth Kubler-Ross published a book titled *On Death and Dying*, where she proposed five stages of grief: (1) denial, (2) anger, (3) bargaining, (4) depression, and (5) acceptance. If you have ever lost a loved one, you can probably remember going through this series of stages. While these stages were not established during the days of the ancient Stoics, they were still a part of the grieving process, and Stoics like Marcus Aurelius and Seneca understood this.

Denial is the step of grief which can make us feel lost, overwhelmed, or that life is meaningless. You will feel shocked at this stage and might tell yourself that this isn't happening. Some people start to feel numb and wonder if they will be able to continue their life without the person they have lost. While we might not feel like we can survive without someone we have loved and lost, we will also begin to heal, as denial helps us cope. Denial is thought of as a defense mechanism against reality, but it also helps us begin to find peace with death.

Stoicism can guide you through the denial stage by helping you find peace with the death of your loved one. In the next chapter, you will find several practical exercises which will allow you to find peace in difficult situations. Stoicism reminds you to focus on remaining calm and realizing what factors in your life you can control and which ones you cannot. Both of these exercises will help you work through the denial phase.

Anger will start to show itself after you've come to realize that the person has passed away. Your shock and numbness will start to wear off, and you will begin to feel angry - at yourself, at the world, and even at the one who passed. You will start asking yourself why this happened, and sometimes even blame yourself for the person's death. Even though there will be other emotions felt, such as sadness, anger will become the most prominent emotion. You might take out your anger in many ways, including through your words and actions towards your family and friends.

Anger is generally not an emotion people want to feel, but it's also an emotion that you shouldn't hide during your grieving process. Like the other stages, anger is an important part of the process and will help you heal. Even though Stoics teach us not to focus on anger, you must acknowledge your anger during grief. However, you should also continue to follow the Stoic way and not allow your anger to control you. By accepting your anger, you will be able to control your anger, and this will help you get through the second stage of grief.

Bargaining is often referred to as the "if only" stage. This is the stage where you constantly wonder what you or others could have done to help the person. You might think to yourself, "If only I had brought him to the doctor earlier," or, "If only I paid more attention to the signs." Some people also tend to bargain with God or another higher power. They might say something like, "If I start to go to church every Sunday, I can wake up and this will only be a terrible dream." The emotion of guilt is very common in the bargaining stage. This is also the stage when you might feel that the loss of the person is just too painful. You might feel overwhelmed by the process of grief and start begging for an end to the whole situation.

A Stoic would see bargaining as living in the past, which is something they feel is a waste of time. Stoicism can help you overcome the stage of bargaining by realizing you have to remain in the moment. Stoicism can further help you in this stage through its method of learning what you can and cannot control. Death is something that people typically cannot control under natural circumstances - no bargaining can stop it.

Depression is the stage which follows bargaining. In this stage, guilt is still present as the feeling of being completely overwhelmed and exhausted over the death becomes more prevalent. At this stage, people feel so much loss that they sometimes have trouble coping with their day to day activities. While depression is a major mental illness, it's important to remember that this isn't the case in the process of grief. It's a natural stage, just like anger and bargaining. For some people, depression can come when they are worrying about how to pay for the funeral or figuring out burial arrangements. For others, depression comes in very short bursts and lasts only a few minutes.

Stoicism can help with depression by offering you tools to maintain a positive mindset. Ancient Stoics realized that a person's positive attitude would help them overcome difficult situations. Furthermore, people often feel depressed because they focus on the pieces of the situation they cannot control. Therefore, realizing what you can and cannot control can help you overcome depression.

Acceptance is regarded as the final stage of grief. Some people think of this stage as the time when they decide that they are okay with what happened or start to feel better. However, acceptance has nothing to do with the feeling that you will be alright. Acceptance is about truly realizing that your loved one is gone, and you will never see the person physically again. In this stage, you start to learn how to live without the person. You will start to find yourself again. You will start to feel more at ease and begin to put the pieces of your life back together.

It's important to remember that the stages of grief can go back and forth. For instance, you might be at acceptance and then go back to depression. Some stages might last for a few hours, some a few days, and some weeks or months. You will have good days and you will have bad days. You will always miss the person who passed away, of course. We never truly get over the loss of a loved one; we simply learn how to live without them. Stoicism can help.

Stoics and Grief

Stoics believe that one of the best ways to remember that life is precious and you must spend your time wisely is by keeping in mind that one day you will die. They also believe that one of the best ways you can overcome grief when a loved one dies is by remembering Memento Mori. Another way to overcome grief is to live by Seneca's words, "It's better to conquer grief than to deceive it."

Seneca did not just realize that grief was bound to happen because death is going to happen, but also that nature requires us to grieve. However, Seneca further taught that we needed to handle this grief well and not let it drive us into madness, depression, or despair. We have to keep a balanced mind as we grieve, as this will help us overcome our grief. If we don't remain balanced, we will allow grief to cause more harm than it should.

Seneca believed that one way we can overcome grief is by realizing that the person we grieve over would not want to us suffer from such emotions. He further stated that if you believe the person would want you to suffer through the tears, then this person is not worth your time or energy.

This doesn't mean that we shouldn't grieve. Seneca knew that grief was unavoidable when dealing with death. He showed this when he wrote to his mother, who had been stricken with grief, telling her, "I realized that your grief should not be intruded upon while it was fresh and agonizing..." Seneca understood that people still needed to go through the grieving process, but he also understood that we should not allow this process to consume us.

There are many Stoic exercises which can help prepare you for death. While these will be discussed in the next chapter, a couple of these exercises include negative visualization and focusing on what is important. When you use negative visualization, you imagine your loved one dying. Stoics believed that this process will help you overcome grief once the person has passed away. When you focus on what is important, you realize that your loved one will die, and therefore, you need to spend quality time with them while you are able to. This ties back into the idea of controlling what you can. You cannot stop yourself or someone you love from dying, but you can make the most of their time here.

Sometimes it's not you that is dealing with grief, but someone you love. Epictetus believed that when you see someone grieving, you have to be careful that you do not take on that grief. Stoicism teaches us to be compassionate and understand the feelings of others, including feelings of grief. Therefore, Epictetus taught that we need to find a way to allow other people to grieve but not take on the emotions ourselves. Epictetus stated, "If a friend is grieving, our goal should be to help her overcome her grief...for us to catch her grief...won't help her but hurt us."

In *Meditations*, Marcus Aurelius discusses death and grief by stating that it's necessary and expected. Aurelius taught that once we understand that death is a part of nature, we will be able to move on from grief at a healthy pace. In order to help you overcome your fear of death, you can work on your relationship with God or whatever deity you believe in. Aurelius wrote that adults should have no fear when it comes to death. The only people who should fear death are young children, because they can't understand how death is a part of nature. As an adult, you can.

Stoics felt that death should not be terrifying. In fact, they believed that if we took the fear out of death, we would be able to overcome grief. Ancient Stoics stated that death was nothing more than a transition from your human form into a new form. They believed that it wasn't an ending, but a new beginning. People should fear death just as much as they fear sleep - not at all.

Chapter 6: Practical Exercises of Stoicism

"How long are you going to wait before you demand the best for yourself?" – Epictetus.

This chapter contains almost 60 Stoic exercises for everyday use, but before we get into the exercises, I want to explain a few points. First remember that you are human. You are going to make mistakes, you will have off days, and some situations are going to be easier for you to handle than others. But this does not mean that you should handle the days or situations differently. You must practice the exercises every day and make them a main part of your life. Second, you will like some exercises more and some will work better for you than others. You might not be able to practice all the exercises, and that is okay. These practices are not strict rules that you should follow, but suggestions to help you reach your best self. You need to find exercises that work for you. Third, you don't want to jump into the exercises headfirst. If practicing Stoic exercises is something new for you, then you want to focus on easier exercises that will help you develop the habit. If you start with something that's too difficult or doesn't resonate with your needs, you are less likely to continue. Read through these practical exercises and make note of which ones you can begin implementing right away.

1. Be Mindful of Each Situation

There are a lot of details and exercises in Stoicism that you need to practice every day. This can make Stoicism a bit hard to follow for most people. One of the best techniques to use in order to begin living your life as a Stoic is to remain mindful of every moment.

When you're mindful, you are aware of what is going on around you and in your surroundings. By remaining mindful, you're better able to control your emotions, which will help you control how you react to a given situation. Furthermore, when you're mindful, you will realize when you need to utilize a Stoic exercise. As Seneca himself said, "A consciousness of wrongdoing is the first step to salvation...you have to catch yourself doing it before you can correct it."

In order to do this, you must first make sure your attention is in the current moment. You need focus on remaining aware not only of the people around you, but also your environment. You want to be aware of your actions and your thoughts. There are many ways you can focus on remaining mindful, such as utilizing mindful meditation. To try this, find a quiet location where you can sit down and meditate by focusing on your breathing and allowing your thoughts to flow in and out. Remember to be kind to yourself if you find your mind wandering. Don't talk negatively to yourself. Instead, just bring your mind back to focusing on the moment.

2. Focus on What Is Truly Important

One of the main lessons in Stoicism is focusing on what is truly important. Many of the exercises of Stoicism tie in with each other. You will find that this particular exercise is not only important on its own, it also becomes a tool to use for successfully practicing other exercises as well. For instance, this exercise ties into living simply and looking at the bigger picture.

Knowing what is truly important to you will depend on a few factors. First, you are going to have to have a clear vision of your highest self. Second, you need to know what characteristics you will have to work on to reach your highest self. Third, you must have a clear vision of your goals. Finally, you also need to know what's important to the people who surround you.

Many Stoics, such as Marcus Aurelius, discussed how important time is. Time is really one of your most valuable resources, which makes it something that is truly important. Because of this, you want to make sure you are mindful of your time and you use your time wisely.

By focusing on what is most important to you every day, you will move closer to your goals and not get caught up in what doesn't matter. This will also help you be better able to keep many other exercises in mind, as knowing what is truly important is a basis for Stoicism. The whole philosophy of Stoicism teaches us what is really important.

3. You Must Get to Know Yourself

Stoics focus on reaching their highest self. Everything they do is supposed to take them closer to their highest self. One of the first steps you will take as someone who practices Stoicism is to imagine your best self. However, you can't imagine your best self without getting to know yourself first. On top of this, you will have to continue to get to know yourself because as time goes on, you will start to change. In order to keep your mind focused on reaching your best self, you have to continue to learn about who you truly are - what you like, dislike, what your goals and values are, and who you imagine yourself to be.

4. Accept Whatever Comes Your Way

Epictetus stated, "Don't seek for everything to happen as you wish it would, but rather wish that everything happens as it actually will—then your life will flow well."

As a Stoic, you understand that you cannot control everything in your environment. You can only control your actions and thoughts towards stimuli. Therefore, it is important to practice accepting the things you cannot change. Often, people tend to fight against the situations they don't like. This causes people to lash out or react in a way that could further impair progress.

When you don't accept what happens, you begin to suffer. Once you suffer, you start to lose sight of eudaimonia and your best self. When you can accept whatever happens, you can remain happy, calm, and keep your best self in mind. You can bring yourself into harmony with the situation and realize that no one has the power to change the situation, but you have the power to react without judgement.

When teaching his students to accept their fate, Marcus Aurelius compared fate to prescriptions from a doctor. When we are sick, we go to the doctor to get medication to help us feel better. We know that we must take this medication, no matter what is prescribed to us, just as the doctor tells us to or we will not start to feel better. The fate you are handed is there to help you grow - to help you get better at using various Stoic exercises, learn how to handle your emotions, and become your best self.

5. Negative Visualization

Negative visualization can be a hard exercise to follow for many people. This is because people want to focus on positive outcomes. After all, it's a lot easier to imagine yourself receiving an A on your exam than receiving an F. The trick is to realize that negative visualization can help you prepare for the worst case scenario. When you prepare yourself, you're able to think through your reactions to the situation. This will help you stay in control of your actions. It's easier to handle certain situations when you feel prepared instead of surprised.

Think about an event you have in the near future. Maybe you need to present at a business meeting. You could imagine that you have forgotten your speech. You then go through the rational steps you would take in that situation. Think about what else could go wrong at the presentation. Think of how you should react if you stumble over your words or state a fact incorrectly and how you could best handle these situations. It's not about focusing on the negative, it's about learning how to react ahead of time so you can behave logically instead of emotionally.

If you have trouble with negative visualization, think of how often you prepare for bad situations. We have all prepared for a bad situation, such as the death of a loved one or possibly losing our job. When you prepared for these bad situations in the past, you practiced negative visualization - but you more than likely did not come up with a solution. As a Stoic, instead of only practicing this exercise when you see the possibility of bad situations and begin worrying about them, try to practice it in every situation and have a logical reaction prepared.

6. Everything Is the Same

Stoics such as Marcus Aurelius and Seneca reminded people that no matter when they were born, who they married, who they became, or what they did, they were people just like everyone else. What they meant was that people have been doing the same thing since the beginning of time. They have struggled, just like we are struggling. After we are gone, people will continue to struggle.

There is nothing we can do to change this system, so it's best for us to just understand that it's a part of our fate. The Stoics believed that its best we learn to accept this, so we can handle our situations with ease and be able to move on. They also believed that because of this, we shouldn't be surprised over situations. Because it's been the same for centuries, we should realize that it will remain the same. Nothing that happens to us has not happened to someone else - we are all one.

In a sense, we're supposed to take the situations we go through in life, from the bad to the good, and treat them as if nothing is new. As one generation leaves, a new generation comes, and the universe continues on regardless.

7. Imagine Your Death

For many people, death is something to be feared. However, death is inevitable. Just like we all took our first breath, we will all take our last. You can't avoid death, so why fear it? Furthermore, fear can become an irrational emotion when applied to situations that don't require it. Fear may save you in the jungle, but it will harm you if you can't bear to think of your dying day. By ignoring death, you cheat yourself out of the knowledge that your life is fleeting, and therefore precious.

It's important to remember that imagining your death isn't supposed to have a negative outcome. Stoics believe that through imagining your death, you can start to focus on the present and live your life to the fullest. As Marcus Aurelius said, "Think of yourself as dead. You have lived your life. Now, take what's left and live it properly. What doesn't transmit light creates its own darkness." Marcus Aurelius and other ancient Stoics referred to this technique as Memento Mori, which translates to "remember you must die."

This doesn't mean that you have to change what you're doing in your life or the goals you're trying to accomplish. Imagining your death means that you will start to focus on living your life as if today is your last day on earth. For instance, you might still complete the same activities, but your mindset might change. Instead of becoming anxious over your presentation for a meeting, you will focus on doing your best, because this could be your last presentation.

Many people struggle with imagining their death because they feel it's depressing, but this isn't what the technique is supposed to do. Instead, you're supposed to gain the most fulfillment out of your life daily. This exercise is supposed to help you achieve eudaimonia and your greatest self by imagining what you would want to change if today were your last day.

Through this exercise, you can ask yourself what you truly want to accomplish in your life. You can ask yourself what type of people you want to be friends with, how you want people to remember you, and what is important. You stop taking things and people for granted and become more grateful for what and who you have in your life.

8. Use a Reserve Clause

You can never fully know what the result will be in any situation. A reserve clause gives you the mindset that you can achieve what you want to achieve, providing nothing prevents you. Seneca explained the reserve clause when he stated, "I will sail across the ocean, if nothing prevents me." To follow the reserve clause, you need to understand two parts. First, you will do everything in your power to succeed. Second, you must understand that the result isn't in your control.

In every situation, there is only so much that is in your control. For example, if you're preparing to present at a meeting, the factors which are in your control are the work you put into your presentation and how you present at the meeting. You do not control what other people think of your presentation, how they interpret your presentation, or any other outcome from your presentation. You accept the outcome, because it's not in your control.

The reserve clause helps you maintain your confidence. It helps you realize that not everything is going to go the way you want it to, but that shouldn't stop you from trying. Even if you put a lot of time and effort into your presentation, other people might not view your presentation as successful. Even if you deserve praise, you might not receive the praise. Instead of letting what other people think influence your confidence, you accept the result and move on.

9. Always Work on Self-Improvement

Self-improvement is one of the concepts which is at the heart of Stoicism. Through various exercises, you are constantly working towards becoming your best self. To do this, you have to continuously improve yourself. You do this by learning from your mistakes and through your mentor. You also work on self-improvement by having a clear idea of the person you want to become.

Stoics advise that you never stop working on trying to improve yourself, as there is no ending to self-growth. You work to improve yourself from the time you wake up with your morning reflection until the time you go to bed with your evening reflection. Every moment of every day, you strive to do better than the next moment. You remain mindful so you can continue to note the changes you need to make to improve yourself.

10. What You Own Is Borrowed from Nature

Seneca stated, "We have no grounds for self-admiration, as though we were surrounded by our own possessions; they have been loaned to us." Stoics ask themselves, "What do I truly own?" The truth is, you don't own anything but your own mind. You don't own any of your material possessions, such as your house, vehicle, computer, iPad, or televisions, as these items can be gone in a second.

They are simply borrowed from nature. You can't own something that can be taken away.

Seneca taught that instead of believing we own our possessions, we need to imagine what would happen if they were taken away. What would you have left? We live in a world where people lose their possessions every day, yet we never think it could happen to us. We don't believe that our house will catch fire or our dog will escape from the backyard. We believe these things only happen to other people. This mindset starts to make us take our possessions for granted, making us believe we will own them forever.

Ancient Stoics also taught that we should remember our possessions are temporary and have been loaned to us. If we do this, we will be able to handle these items disappearing rationally and we won't take these possessions for granted. As Seneca stated, "it is a sorry debtor who abuses his creditor."

11. Morning Reflection

Reflection is a huge part of Stoicism, and one of the best times to focus on reflection is after waking up in the morning. Many people believe it's best to take time to reflect in the morning because we already have our own morning routines. Morning reflection won't take too long, generally just a few minutes of your time.

Epictetus taught about morning reflection when he told his listeners that they should rehearse their day. During this reflection, you can ask yourself a variety of question such as, "What good should I do today?" or, "What do I need to work on to achieve eudaimonia?" Through these questions, you will be able to focus on achieving your goals and reaching your highest self. Every day that you reflect on the person you want to be, how you want to handle the situations you are given, and what you want to work on will bring you closer to eudaimonia.

Your morning reflection can be about more than just planning out your day. You could also meditate or take time for yourself. Often, our mornings can be chaotic as we get ourselves and our families ready for the day. Therefore, your morning reflection can become a great way to put your mindset on the right track so that you can handle any tough situations throughout your day. It will give you a sense of calmness and confidence that allows you to handle whatever life hands you.

The key to morning reflection is to make sure you accomplish this task every day. Make it a permanent part of your morning routine.

12. Evening Reflection

Evening reflection is similar to morning reflection. During your evening reflection, you can take time to think about your day. You could ask yourself if you accomplished the tasks you set out to do. You can ask yourself what you did well and what you could work on. Reflect on how you handled difficult situations and examine if there is anything that you should do differently in the future if a situation occurs again.

When Seneca discussed evening reflection, he told his listeners to be completely honest with themselves. "I examine my entire day, going through what I have done and said. I conceal nothing from myself." This advice is very important, because you won't be able to reach your highest self unless you're completely honest. Even if you feel your actions have caused you embarrassment or shame, reflect on these actions. Ask yourself how you can improve on these actions.

You can use this time to write in a journal. You can write about your day and how you can further improve yourself so that you can reach your best self. *Meditations* by Marcus Aurelius is an excellent example of evening reflections. He took time every day to reflect on his day through writing. Writing can also help you stay mindful as you become aware of your actions.

For example say you are working on remaining calm during chaotic situations. While at work, you found yourself in a chaotic situation. As you reflect on this situation, you realize that you didn't remain as calm as you want to be when you envision your highest self. Therefore, you take this reflection time to examine how you can change your behavior, so the next time you find yourself in a chaotic situation, you can be calmer.

Remember that in evening reflection, compassion is your friend. Just as you want to show others compassion, you also want to show yourself compassion. As you reflect on your day, keep in mind that you're allowed to make mistakes and you can learn from these mistakes so that you can reach your best self. It's also important to remember that as long as you did your best, you were successful.

13. Your Health Matters

Your health matters more than you might realize when it comes to practicing Stoicism. What you must remember is that you can't put your best effort forward if you health is left on the back burner. You not only need to take care of your body, but you also have to take care of your mind.

You will only be able to reach your greatest good if you remain healthy. Therefore, it's important to make sure that you follow a daily routine which will keep you calm and in a positive mindset. You also want to make sure that you're eating right, sleeping well, exercising, and continuing to strengthen your mind through knowledge.

Taking care of your health will help your energy level and keep you focused. You will be able to not only establish goals, but reach those goals. You will have a clearer version of your best self and continuously strive to become that person if your body and mind are healthy.

Musonius Rufus was one of the most outspoken Stoics when it came to health. He believed that the best source of self-control someone could possess came from what they drank and ate. He believed that people needed to be mindful of what and how much they ate, because too much food and drink could make people sluggish and unmotivated. Musonius Rufus taught that strength and health were more important than physical pleasure. He further stated that physical pleasure "weakens us and makes us the slaves of our stomachs."

14. Voluntary Discomfort

You can look at voluntary discomfort as the next step after negative visualization. Instead of imagining negative outcomes from events, you can practice placing yourself in an uncomfortable situation. This will allow you to practice various Stoic exercises and reach your best self. Voluntary discomfort is a technique used to help you gain self-control in situations that make you uncomfortable. Through this exercise, you will train yourself to become comfortable.

Cato the younger, a Stoic from Ancient Rome, practiced voluntary discomfort. As a senator in the Roman Republic, Cato had to dress in certain attire. However, he would sometimes be seen in clothing that didn't fit his role as a senator. At first, this made Cato extremely uncomfortable because of how the Romans would react to his outfit. But as Cato continued to dress in clothing not suited for his role, he started to become more comfortable. Seneca preached that people should practice voluntary discomfort by living in poverty.

Today, there are many ways you can practice voluntary discomfort. If you are uncomfortable speaking in front of a large crowd, find an event where you have to develop a speech to present. You could follow what Seneca taught and find ways to live well below your means, such as buying cheaper food than you typically purchase or wearing rough and dirty clothing.

When you place yourself in uncomfortable situations, you want to make sure to ask yourself what you feared about this situation. As Seneca taught, people should ask themselves, "Is this the condition that I feared?" This exercise isn't about erasing all the comforts from your life; it's about helping you reach your highest self. It helps you learn self-control by overcoming situations you fear. Voluntary discomfort also helps you prepare for difficult situations by making you branch out of your comfort zone, gain confidence, and become resilient.

15. Speak and Act Wisely

Marcus Aurelius taught aspiring Stoics to speak and act wisely. There are many things people can say and do that are not important. Marcus Aurelius stated that if it's not essential, it should not be done. "Most of what we say and do is not essential. If you can eliminate it, you'll have more time, and more tranquility."

Acting and speaking out of habit rather than necessity can bring you into a cycle that's hard to get away from. If it's not essential, the cycle will make you miserable. You will continue to want to say more or want to do more. You will never find your eudaimonia and you will never be able to reach your highest self when you get trapped in this cycle.

As Marcus Aurelius taught, the only way to keep yourself out of this cycle is by choosing your words and actions wisely. You want to focus on what matters instead of what is trivial. Marcus Aurelius told aspiring Stoics to, "Ask yourself at every moment, 'Is this necessary?'"

16. Remember Moderation

When you start to practice Stoicism, you might feel overwhelmed by everything you need to do. Every Stoic starting with Zeno knew that reaching their best self would take a lot of time and a lot of work. However, they also knew that the journey would be possible if they remembered moderation.

Seneca spoke of keeping things in moderation when he stated, "So-called pleasures, when they go beyond a certain limit, are but punishments."

You want to focus on moderation in every part of your life, as this will help you maintain balance. You will also be able to focus on the tasks you need to perform and remain devoted to reaching your highest self. You should strive to not only live in moderation when it comes to your work, but also your eating habits, relaxation techniques, education, and daily routine.

17. Manage Your Time Wisely

Marcus Aurelius, Seneca, and other ancient Stoics taught that time needed to be managed wisely, because you can never take it back. They believed that because of this, time was very valuable and you should only spend your time doing what is worth your time. This is another reason why you should only focus on what is truly important. If you focus on the non-essentials in life, you're wasting time.

Seneca stated that people "think too little of wasting time, the one thing about which we should all be the toughest of ministers." Seneca taught that people focus on things that aren't important. These things included everything that wasn't part of their control, such as what other people thought, what other people had, wanting more in life, and other nonessentials. Seneca asked aspiring Stoics why they would spend so much time worrying about the things they cannot control instead of worrying about the person they want to become.

"It's not that we have a short time to live, but that we waste a lot of it," Seneca stated as he spoke of why people should manage their time better. Marcus Aurelius also spoke of managing time wisely because our life is short. Therefore, Aurelius advised, you want to make sure you fit as much as you can into every hour. Because we will one day take our last breath, we should remember to appreciate every breath we have. We will not always be here to perform the essential duties we need to perform in order to reach our highest self. Therefore, we need to take the time we are given without wasting it.

Marcus Aurelius wrote in his book *Meditations*, "You only have limited time. Use it then to advance your enlightenment. Or it will be gone, and you will have no power over it." In his book, Marcus wrote about how you must appreciate the time the gods give you, especially if they give you more time than you were originally given. He further stated that you must thank the gods for your time because, without them, your time wouldn't exist.

18. Become an Eternal Scholar

Musonius Rufus, Marcus Aurelius, Seneca, and all other Stoic leaders spent their days continuing to learn. They all taught people to learn as much as they could and become a seeker of wisdom. Wisdom will help you become closer to your highest self as you learn and live what you learn.

Take these Stoic exercises and practice them daily. Epictetus told his students that their knowledge was one of their greatest values, and they should make sure to learn something new every day. Marcus Aurelius told his students the same thing, but added that they should not only practice everything, they should also remain modest about their wisdom.

Marcus Aurelius believed that in order to learn, you had to realize that you didn't know everything and be willing to learn. Furthermore, he told his students that they had to seek the truth to learn.

Modern-day Stoics also follow the path of becoming eternal scholars. Ryan Holiday states that people should "take a day off from work...but not a day off from learning." Holiday knows that we live in a fast-paced and busy world. Therefore, we might need to make time for learning. He believes that we should not feel bad for taking this time, as our wisdom is one of the most important pieces of our lives.

19. Learn That Pain and Challenge Are Virtues

Today, we live in a society where we try to limit any type of pain as much as possible. While we often refer to pain as a body ailment or a broken bone, ancient

Stoics thought of pain as more than just how you're physically feeling. To Stoics such as Epictetus, pain could also be seen in the form of challenges.

No matter what type of pain you have, you need to be able to cope with it. Today, this often means that you head to the medicine cabinet to grab some Tylenol or Ibuprofen. However, when it came to the days of Seneca and Marcus Aurelius, you learned to cope with pain through other means, because pain made you stronger. Stoics taught that pain would bring you closer to your highest self.

Epictetus told aspiring Stoics that when you're "faced with pain, you will discover the power of endurance." This means that you will realize your true strength and be able to build on this strength. You will realize what you can achieve and you will become the best you can be through this strength.

In other words, Stoicism teaches us to turn the negative of pain and challenges into positives which can help us reach our highest self. We can use our challenges to help teach us the value of patience and hard work, become economical, learn independence and compassion, and anything else we need to work on.

20. Live Simply

"Wealth consists not in having great possessions, but in having few wants." - Epictetus

Ancient Stoics such as Musonius Rufus and Seneca taught that people should live as minimalists. A minimalist is someone who only lives with the items they absolutely need. They don't strive to have a bigger house, the newest car, or many material items. Instead, they live within their needs and focus on their happiness.

Materialism can drag you into the same cycle that Marcus Aurelius discussed when we speak or act out of turn. In this cycle, you will let yourself become influenced by outside forces. You will constantly strive to become a person that someone else wants you to become, whether this is through society's expectations or another person's. You won't be who you want to be; you will be what they want you to be. You might find yourself trying to keep up with your neighbors, friends, or family. In this cycle, you will lose sight of your ideal self.

When spreading the philosophy of Stoicism, Musonius Rufus discussed the way people dressed. He wanted people to not focus on dressing to impress other people but simply to protect our bodies. The lifestyle the Stoics lived was very simply. They didn't seek out riches, wealth, or fame, and they preached to others to do the same.

Epictetus stated, "Freedom is not achieved by satisfying desire, but by eliminating it." Epictetus and Seneca believed that living simply would allow everyone to become free of the chains of materialism which often hold us back from reaching our highest self. To be completely free, we need to value our goals, happiness, and our ideal self instead of placing this value on wealth and fame.

Wealth doesn't come from the riches and materials we receive in life. Wealth comes from reaching our highest self. Modern-day Stoic William Irvine believes that Stoicism doesn't ask anyone to reject wealth; the philosophy simply asks people to think wisely when it comes to wealth and remember where our true wealth lies.

21. Courage and Calmness over Anger

Anger is one of the most common negative emotions which Stoics discuss in their writings. Stoics focused on learning to release their negative emotions by focusing on positive emotions. Marcus Aurelius wrote that a true man would not become angry. Instead, he will focus on his gentle nature. He will rise to find his courage which will help him overcome his anger.

Seneca wrote a whole essay on anger. In this essay, Seneca discusses how you need to catch your anger and overcome it immediately. The sooner you stop your anger, the easier it will be to overcome. He further discusses how once you let your anger consume you, it's harder for you to reach a healthy mindset, as anger clouds your thoughts and emotions.

This happens because anger is a passionate emotion. As Seneca stated, "it carries us away" with its force. Furthermore, anger is an emotion that we can fully control. However, we have to choose to control our anger. We have to want to overcome our anger and focus on remaining calm. The calmer we are, the more likely we are to make rational decisions, as anger can drive us to act quickly and without thinking.

The damage that anger can cause is huge and can not only affect ourselves, but those around us as well. In a sense, anger is a form of judgment upon us and other people. We become angry over something because we allow our judgement of the situation to bring out anger. Furthermore, we tend to justify this anger with our judgement. When this happens, you must ask yourself what good the anger you hold will do. Seneca asked his students what good anger would do when they could reach the same conclusion through reasoning.

22. Your Strength Is Compassion

One of the biggest strength Stoics say you can possess is compassion. When you're a compassionate human being, you feel concern for other people and you understand what they are going through. You take the time to help anyone, whether they are less fortunate than you or exactly like you. Compassion has no boundaries when it comes to helping other people.

Seneca wrote, "Wherever there is a human being, there is an opportunity for kindness." Of course, your compassion should expand to animals and not just people. However, no matter what living being you run into, you need to strive to be as compassionate as you can. Even when you're faced with a difficult situation or are feeling bullied, you need to react with compassion.

Marcus Aurelius wrote that we need to remain compassionate because our compassion can attach itself to other people. He taught that people who treat your harshly will learn the ways of compassion as long as you continue to show compassion. He further believed that it was human nature to be compassionate, as we are all brothers and sisters in the bigger picture.

Stoics such as Seneca and Marcus Aurelius believed that you should work on your compassion everyday, because it will be at the center of your highest self. One of the best ways to work on this is through your morning or evening reflections. As you reflect about your day, ask yourself in what areas of your life can you focus on becoming more compassionate. You can even ask yourself who you would like to make smile or who you would like to help.

23. Pick a Role Model

Seneca taught his students to always have a role model for two reasons. First, they can ask this person for advice and ask themselves what their role model would do if they were faced with a certain situation. Second, they can use their role model to measure themselves as they work towards reaching their full potential. Furthermore, the role model would help guide them down their path of enlightenment.

Stoics often refer to their role model as a Sage. The Stoic Sage was known to be one of the greatest models for Stoics who were still trying to reach their highest self. The Sage was incredibly wise, patient, and honorable. Ancient Stoics often felt that Socrates or Zeus were examples of ideal Sages.

However, perfection as a human being doesn't exist. While we strive to reach our best self and we have a vision of our perfect self, this doesn't mean that we will become completely perfect and without flaws or mistakes. Instead, it means that we will accept and learn from our mistakes.

When you look to pick a role model, you can look towards anyone. You can choose a family member, friend, celebrity, or even your favorite superhero to become your role model. The key is to learn about your role model. You want to know what good your chosen role model has done and strive to do the same. You want to not only focus on the best characteristics of your role model, but also on your model's flaws. You can take this time to learn from your role model's flaws so that you can better yourself as a human being.

Not only do you want to learn about your role model, but you also want to make sure to remind yourself of your role model. When you are faced with a difficult situation, stop and ask yourself what your role model would do in this situation.

24. Act Good, Don't Just Avoid Acting Evil

Stoics taught that you needed to act good instead of simply not acting evil. Marcus Aurelius talked about this when he told his students that they could find injustices both in what they were and were not doing.

We can act as kind as we want towards others. However, if we stand around and watch someone suffering, we're not living up to our full potential. When we allow other people to be mean, we are simply avoiding the negative action instead of trying to create something positive out of it.

Marcus Aurelius felt that if you stood back and allowed evil to happen, you are just as guilty and a coward. It takes strength for someone to stand up and tell another person that how they act isn't right. However, Marcus Aurelius also understood that stepping in cannot only be dangerous but also difficult. Therefore, he stated that we should start with the smaller negative actions that occur daily. By doing this, you will be able to build your confidence and train yourself to act out of good instead of just avoiding evil.

25. Don't Worry About Fame

Forget about fame, because fame will not lead you to the person you want to become. When you seek fame, you're seeking the approval of people around you and not your highest self. Furthermore, fame is temporary. Marcus Aurelius spoke about how fame doesn't last, because everyone dies, which means you will one day be forgotten.

Fame is also not within our control. Stoics focus their energies on the parts of their lives which are in their control. Therefore, instead of focusing on becoming famous, you should be focusing on reaching your highest self. As Marcus Aurelius believed, it's not fame that will leave a mark on the world, but reaching your highest self. What truly matters is the person you were, how you acted and behaved during your lifetime.

Marcus Aurelius wanted us to look at fame as a bonus for being the best person we can be. He wrote in *Meditations,* "When you've done well and another has benefited by it, why like a fool do you look for a third thing on top— credit for the good deed or a favor in return?" Marcus wanted people to make sure that if they became famous, it was for the right reasons, like being a good person, as this is where our power sits.

26. Beat Your Fear

People's fears often come from their own imagination. Take a moment to think about what you fear. Do you have a fear of speaking in front of a large crowd? You might have a fear of failing, or you might fear getting fired from your job. No matter what your fears are, take a moment to rationalize your fears. Ask yourself why you have this fear. Ask yourself how rational your fear is.

Even though we imagine our fears, they cause us real anguish. Our fears often paralyze us, so we don't take the chance to find out if our fears are real. Seneca, Marcus Aurelius, and other Stoics understood the dangers that fear created. They understood how paralyzing fear could be for people. They also understood how difficult it could be to overcome fear. However, they also knew that everyone could beat their fear.

Like every other emotion, we are in total control of our fear. Epictetus taught that one way to overcome fear was to ask yourself what is causing this fear. Ask yourself why you fear something which is not even in your power.

Seneca explained to people that they often fear what they believe they can't have because it's not in their power. We fear our dreams and our desires for the future. We fear that they will not happen or fear what might happen, because we see these moments as outside of our control. However, we can control parts of these situations once we are faced with the situation. Seneca stated that if we wait for the situation that we fear, we will be able to control the situation when it happens. But, if we continue to fear the situation, we will not be in control when it happens.

Stoics believed that another reason we fear things is that we become attached. For example, we fear the death of a loved one because we're attached to the loved one. We can overcome this fear if we let go of our attachments. If our fear deals with death, we can let go of this fear by understanding that death is a part of nature - Memento Mori.

27. Life Is a Challenge

How many times have you heard that life is unfair or life is a challenge? Life was the same for ancient Stoics. However, they took these challenges and learned to overcome them, as the Stoics knew that it would help them in their journey.

Epictetus taught that a person's character was developed by the challenges they overcame. He also said that in order to overcome these challenges, we need to remember that God, or whatever higher power you believe in, is on our side. Epictetus continued by teaching that these challenges are a natural part of life, and they are not around to harm you. In fact, they are around to help you.

Challenges make you work harder. They make you critically think. They teach you to solve problems. Stoics believed that these challenges were created for us so that we could further reach our highest self. Epictetus and other Stoics stated that if we didn't have these challenges, we would not be able to reach our best self. They further stated that we should thank nature for our challenges.

Epictetus also taught that everyone has their own challenges, even gods such as Hercules. The only way to handle your challenges is to face them. However, how you face them is up to you. The way you face your challenges is completely in your control. While you cannot always control what challenges come your way, you can control how you handle and react to them.

Seneca told people that if they never faced a challenge in their lives, they were considered unfortunate. He felt that people without challenge didn't understand their powers and wouldn't learn what they could truly do and handle. Instead, everything would be a guess. Seneca also believed that a lack of challenges could cause fear and anxiety, because people would never learn how to handle difficult situations.

28. Judging Is Harmful

Whether we judge ourselves or someone else judges us, we can become harmed by these judgments. Marcus Aurelius wrote about how our judgments often cloud our actions. He felt that the only reason people became upset over judgements is because they are focused on their thoughts or another person's words instead of the action. However, it's the action that we should focus on because it's the action which created the judgment.

For example, you worked hard on a presentation only to find out that your boss believes you could have put more effort into it. You become hurt by your boss's statements. Even though you know how much time and effort you put into your presentation, this is overclouded by your boss' harsh reaction. In response, you give yourself a harmful judgment.

Marcus Aurelius taught that we should "wipe out" these harmful judgments. These judgments will only build negative emotions, which will keep us from working towards reaching our highest selves. You're letting go of your power over the situation and allowing negativity to fuel your interpretation and reactions. You're allowing the harmful judgments to take away your focus on the situation. Furthermore, we might turn to blaming those who harm us with their judgements for our failures.

Stoicism teaches us to take responsibility for our own decisions. Therefore, if you allow yourself to blame someone else for what you feel is a failure, you're not taking responsibility.

29. Remember Your Blessings

When we count our blessings, we focus on the things we have, whether we own them or not. Remember, Stoics don't believe they own their possession; they believe they are borrowed from nature. However, Stoics also believe that you should count these possessions among the things you are grateful.

This is a great exercise to focus on when you're faced with challenges or are struggling in your life. You can focus on this exercise when you start to wonder why you don't have certain things in your life. Simply reflect on the things you do have. Take time to remember that you have a sound and creative mind, that you have it within your power to receive an education, that you are able to continue learning, that you have a home, and food on the table.

Epictetus wanted us to make sure that we appreciate the things we have, even if they were borrowed from nature. To Epictetus, this was known as a divine law and one that every person should follow. He further stated that you should always be ready to give your blessings back, as this will help you appreciate what you have.

Seneca focused more on the mind than anything else when he discussed blessings. He taught that the greatest blessing anyone could receive is what is inside of them. Seneca was not only talking about the mind, but also about the person we become. He was talking about our compassion, understanding, and every other piece of us that connects us to our highest selves.

30. Look at the Bigger Picture

It's easy for us to see the smaller picture of things. Our view is often distorted by what we want to see, which is only a piece of the bigger puzzle. Marcus Aurelius discussed that people need to take a bird's-eye view of everything. Whether you're talking about a person, family gathering, death, or birth, you need to look at the larger picture.

When you look at the bigger picture, you will find that your problems become smaller. Compared to the world and the universe, your problem is a little speck in time. Marcus Aurelius taught that we should make sure to look at the bigger picture, so we can realize that the problems we see as major aren't that grandiose at all.

Marcus Aurelius further stated that through looking at the larger picture, you will forget about all the minor things that bother you. This will allow you to focus on the more important factors in your life and in the world. He advised people to "continually picture to yourself time and space as a whole, and every individual thing, in terms of space, a tiny seed, in terms of time the mere turn of a screw."

31. Find the Best People for Your Company

Stoics such as Epictetus and Seneca believed that the best people for us to become friends with are the people who think like us. In other words, if you want to become a Stoic, you should find other people who are aspiring Stoics. Epictetus explained the reason for this best when he stated, "if a companion is dirty, his friends cannot help but get a little dirty too, no matter how clean they started out."

While we can't always decide who we work with or who we have to converse with, we can always decide who our friends are and who we want to spend time with. Therefore, it's best to pick people who are going to help us instead of harm us and our progress. We should associate with people who will help us reach our highest self instead of hold us back. According to Epictetus, this meant that you need to find people who are going to make you feel good about your life and yourself.

You want to find people who are willing to change for the better, because you are working on changing for the better. You also want to find people that will help you learn and people who make you feel comfortable. Seneca taught that you should stay away from people who are always complaining and harming your self-improvement. Of course, this doesn't mean you completely avoid them. It simply means that you spend less time with them.

Stoics also stated that while it's important to find like-minded people, you also need to remember that you are not perfect. Just like anyone else, you can also become annoying and you can make mistakes. We all have our flaws.

32. Walk in Someone Else's Shoes

Stoics taught that in order to understand people better, we needed to put ourselves in their situation. As Marcus Aurelius believed, you need to take the time to get inside the person's mind and soul. You need to try to find out what type of person he or she is. Only by becoming them, in a way, can we truly understand them.

Walking in someone else's shoes ties into not allowing yourself to judge another human being. In fact, this exercise can help you stop and think before you start to judge someone else. Through this exercise, you try to find out why the person is acting a certain way. Marcus Aurelius tells us that we should "imagine their souls stripped bare," as this will help us understand their situation.

33. Learn How to Handle Insults

Insults happen often in our lives. We can receive insults on a daily basis from a variety of people, such as a supervisor, client, family, or friends. Some insults tend to bother us more than others. However, Stoics advise us that we need to move away from becoming emotional over insults. While we cannot control who insults us, we can control how we respond to the insults.

For example, you can control whether you let an insult ruin your whole day. You can also control how you react to the insult. It's easy to get hurt and defensive when you're insulted, however, this doesn't mean it's the best way to react.

Some Stoics state that you should use the insult to become closer to your highest self. You can do this through a variety of ways. For example, you could treat the person who insulted you with compassion. You could also analyze the insult to see if it's something you can improve on. Seneca looked at insults a bit differently by asking if you can consider truth to be an insult.

Marcus Aurelius looked at insults differently than Seneca. He stated that we shouldn't become angry over insults, because the people who insult us are showing flaws within their character. Stoics are aware of their flaws and continue to work towards overcoming these flaws. Therefore, Marcus Aurelius believed, insults about our flaws shouldn't bother us, because we are already aware.

Musonius Rufus taught that the best way to handle insults was to not respond. He told people that the best response was just to handle the insult internally as calmly as possible and then to work through it rationally. He believed that the people who insulted you wanted a reaction, therefore, giving them no reaction was the best choice.

34. Don't Expect

Stoics are meant to realize the truth. They are meant to see the world for how it truly is and not what they expect it to be. They aren't meant to see the world how they want to see it. Ancient Stoics such as Seneca discussed how expectations could lead us down a dangerous path, because what we expect isn't reality.

Furthermore, expectations can bring about fear, anger, and other negative emotions. We become frustrated when situations don't match up to our expectations. We might feel angry with ourselves or others because our expectations fell through. However, what we don't realize is how unrealistic our expectations are. Once we learn not to expect, we will start to realize the reality of every situation, which will help us accept the situation and keep our emotions in check. Overall, when we don't expect anything, we become happier people.

Stoics felt that if we remembered that nothing would last forever, then we would be able to let go of our expectations. If we let go of our expectations, we won't let society tell us how to be or how to act; we will just be ourselves. If we let go of our expectations, we won't become demanding in trying to reach our expectations and we won't feel disappointed when we find we can't reach our expectations.

Marcus Aurelius further commented on expectations by telling his students not to be surprised by anything. Aurelius told his followers that things unexpected do happen, and when these things happen, we should realize that they are possibilities of the situation, which will help us feel less surprised. Even when disasters happen, we shouldn't allow ourselves to feel surprised, because disasters are a part of nature.

35. Recognize Your Daily Bad Habits and Establish Good Habits

We all have bad habits that are part of our everyday lives. Sometimes we know our habits are bad or not good for us, and other times we don't realize this. Take a look at your daily habits and when you do this, recognize your bad habits. Do you tend to hit the snooze button in the morning and make yourself rush to get ready? Are you a smoker? Do you skip your exercise routine? You don't have to focus on changing the big habits right away. It might help you to start small.

Breaking your bad habits might not seem like a big deal, however this is one of the best ways to make yourself feel free. When you break your bad habits, you can find yourself closer to your highest self.

Once you recognize your bad habits, it's important to begin to establish good habits. Often, one way you can break your bad habits is by turning them into good habits. Good habits will make you feel physically and mentally better about yourself. You will begin to gain more confidence and might even feel healthier and more energized.

36. Don't Live in the Past

It's important to remember that your past is just that - your past. Stoics such as Marcus Aurelius and Seneca focused on learning from the past, but not dwelling on it. Marcus Aurelius often wrote about the past. He taught that only your present has power; your past does not. However, if you allow yourself to live in the past, you allow your past to have power over you. Stoics asked how you can reach your highest self if you agonize over your past mistakes?

Marcus Aurelius wrote, "If you separate . . . everything you have done in the past . . . and apply yourself to...the present-you can live...until your death in calm, benevolence, and serenity." Aurelius taught that in order to reach eudaimonia, you need to realize that you can't focus on your past. You have to keep your mind on the situations you're in and focus on reaching your highest self in each present situation.

Seneca taught that you shouldn't live in the past, because your life is short and the past is certain. Seneca asked why we would focus on what we cannot change when we only have a short period of time on this earth.

37. Recognize Your Faults, but Not Faults of Other People

Marcus Aurelius wrote in *Meditations* that you will be better at handling other people's faults when you understand that nature gives you ways to cope with their faults. Aurelius discussed how nature can help you realize that everyone on this earth has a purpose for their existence. When you begin to understand this, you are able to cope with the faults of other people. This understanding will help you act compassionately towards them, giving you a coping mechanism for their faults.

When it comes to your own faults, Marcus Aurelius stated that you should not look unnecessarily for them but also not flee from them. You have the power to change your faults. If you ignore or flee from your faults, you're not making the effort become one with your highest self, and you are not being honest about who you are.

38. Don't Blame Others

Marcus Aurelius wrote that "it is pointless to blame other people and best to blame no one." He stated that this is because you can only control your actions and thoughts. You cannot control the thoughts or actions of others. While you have the right to gently correct something, if you can, you're to accept the situation if you can't correct anything.

Aurelius didn't understand why anyone would focus their energy or time on blaming other people when both time and energy are valuable. He taught aspiring Stoics that life is short and time is one of the most valuable pieces of your life. Therefore, Aurelius wondered why anyone would waste it on blaming a person when you can't correct or change what happened.

Epictetus believed that only ignorant people would blame other people. He believed it was never our place to put blame on someone else, as this was a form of judgement. When it comes to blaming ourselves, Epictetus felt it showed a person was making progress, as he could learn from his actions. It also showed that he took responsibility. However, Epictetus stated that the smartest person will never blame themselves or anyone else.

39. Only Say What Needs to be Said

Epictetus taught that people should only talk when they felt it was necessary. Furthermore, he believed that people should speak briefly and be kind with their words. Stoics believed that you need to think before you speak. You don't want to harm someone with your words. Therefore, you should never gossip or speak in anger.

Stoics taught that if you took the time to observe the conversation and speak only when necessary, you won't talk out of turn. Stoics were firm in their belief that people should not gossip, complain, blame each other, or talk too often. Epictetus took this belief a step further when he told aspiring Stoics that they shouldn't tell excessive stories. He felt that people who told their own stories were doing so for attention and greed. Just because the story makes you happy or excited, that doesn't mean other people will feel the same way.

Marcus Aurelius further discussed this point by writing about how people should speak. He felt that always speaking with the correct tone and in a kindly way is important. You don't want to speak with the goal of impressing others, but you do want to speak with authority.

40. Solve Every Problem

Problems are a big part of life. Therefore, Stoics taught that you should look for the best possible solutions when you find a problem. They believed that every problem had a solution, however, you also need to make sure you are thinking wisely about the problem at hand. People tend to overthink or worry about problems too much. Stoics advised that if you start feeling anxious about the problem, you need to take a step back. Worrying about the problem won't help you look for a solution. By letting go of control, you let go of worry. Worry comes from not knowing what will happen, but by letting go of the outcome, you can instead focus on solutions.

41. Forgive Those Who Harm You

Stoics spoke often about forgiving other people and ourselves. They taught that no one is perfect, which means everyone will make mistakes. Whether someone said or did something to hurt you or forgot to help you with a task, it's important to remember the person is only human. Stoics believed if you remember this, forgiveness would become easier.

Stoics advised that we observe the situation when someone does something we perceive as wrong. Instead of getting angry over the situation, we need to understand that the person doesn't know better. Some Stoics further advised that it's fine to correct others, as long as you do so gently. Stoics believed that part of their role was to help other people reach their best self. Let the person know that what they did or said isn't helpful or kind, but let go of any anger or judgement attached to the action.

Seneca believed that the only way you could ever be truly forgiven in life was to learn to forgive other people. Epictetus taught that you should forgive your enemies because they feel that their actions were right. There are two sides to every story, and even if you feel you are on the side of the "right," the other person more than likely thinks they are, too. Epictetus believed that people who wronged others didn't understand that their actions were wrong.

42. Understand That People Stumble

Understanding that people stumble ties into forgiving yourself and other people. Marcus Aurelius wanted us to show compassion for the people who stumble. He taught people to remember four important principles so we can better understand people who stumble. First, we are all related through a higher power. Second, we must remember that life is short and we will all die one day. Third, people don't always realize what they do or say is wrong. Fourth, it's our choice to feel hurt by people who have harmed us.

Stoics believed that your job was to help people who stumble because they are misguided. They are not naturally bad people, they are just lacking the wisdom which you hold. Therefore, Stoics taught that you should guide those who stumble. However, Stoics also realized that trying to guide people who stumble might not be in your best interest. Marcus Aurelius believed that the best action you could take is simply to show compassion and forgive them because they don't see the wrong in their ways.

At the same time we note that other people are in the wrong, we always need to keep in mind that we might be in the wrong. We must always remember that we are all human and we all stumble. In fact, Stoics taught that it was a part of nature for us to stumble.

43. Listen to People so You Understand

Stoics wanted us to do more than just hear people who are talking - they wanted us to truly listen to them. Stoics taught that we should say little but pay close attention to the speaker so we can fully understand what the person is saying. This exercise is important because it helps us learn how to understand and accept another person's values, especially if we don't agree with the person. Zeno believed that listening was more important than talking. He stated that it is "better to trip with the feet than with the tongue."

However, Stoics felt that observing the speaker's emotions was another part of listening. Understanding the person's emotions can help you make a further connection with the person's words. Zeno taught his students that they should only speak when they know they can contribute information which will advance the discussion.

44. Establish goals

Goals are important to have in our lives because they make us determined to complete a task. Establishing goals can also make us focus on acting a certain way. For example, one of the main goals every Stoic has is to reach their highest self. To do this, Stoics establish a series of goals which they can fulfill through various exercises. You can even use this exercise, establishing goals, as a goal!

45. Recognize Your Body Language

Body language is the way we move when we are talking or listening. Stoics believe it's important for us to recognize the body language we are using. Our body language can give people a lot of information about what we're thinking or how we're feeling. However, our body language isn't always obvious to us, which means we could give the wrong impression to someone without realizing it.

Another reason to recognize our body language is because it will help keep us mindful in situations. We not only need to remain mindful of our environment, but also of ourselves.

46. Be a Good Role Model

Just as a previous exercise involved finding a good role model, you need to learn to lead by example. As Marcus Aurelius stated, "Waste no more time arguing about what a good man should be. Be one." Stoics believe that actions are more important than words. You to be a good role model, you must act like one.

When you're a good role model, you take the time to show what you've learned instead of lecture about it. For instance, if someone is disrespectful, you forgive them and understand that everyone stumbles. Instead of being disrespectful towards the person, you show compassion or move on from the situation. This teaches the other person the proper reaction.

47. Seek Guidance

Part of learning is seeking guidance. There are many different avenues for you to choose from when you're looking for guidance. For example, you could read Marcus Aurelius' book *Meditations*. You could also expand on the ideas stated here by reading a more modern-day self-help book, such as Ryan Holiday and Stephen Hanselman's book, *The Daily Stoic: 366 Meditations on Wisdom, Perseverance, and the Art of Living*.

Another avenue to seek guidance is through looking beyond the physical realm and into the spiritual realm. When you feel like you've lost control or you're struggling, you can always turn to prayer in order to help guide you. You could ask the universe to direct you down the right path.

48. Learn from Your Mistakes

No one is perfect. Therefore, everyone makes mistakes. Even the smartest people make mistakes. Marcus Aurelius stated, "If someone can prove me wrong and show me my mistake in any thought or action, I shall gladly change. I seek the truth, which never harmed anyone: the harm is to persist in one's own self-deception and ignorance."

Marcus Aurelius understood that even he would make mistakes. But he also knew that the important part about making mistakes is that you can learned from your mistake. No matter what type of mistake you make, as long as you realized your mistake and you learned from it, you will continue to move towards your highest self.

49. Writing Meditation

Writing meditations is a great technique which can help people focus on the positives of their life in a different way. One of the best writing meditation techniques is keeping a journal. At the end of the day, you can take 15 minutes to write about what you did, how you feel, what mistakes you made, and what your accomplishments were. This ties into and can become part of your Evening Routine. You could also use your journal to write about the negatives in your life and focus on turning them into positives.

50. Don't Take Things Personally

Stoics taught that people were not to take anything personally, because nothing is meant to be personal. For example, Marcus Aurelius taught himself not to worry about the way some people smell, because it had nothing to do with him personally. He focused on not letting the smells bother him and instead learned to accept how other people smelled. This sounds like an old world problem, but the concept is still applicable today.

Epictetus discussed how we should not take things personally through the following example. He stated that people protect their bodies more than they protect their mind. While they would not let someone take their body, they will allow anyone to take their mind. Epictetus believed that when you take something personally, you allow it to control your mind.

Furthermore, Stoics state that people aren't saying or doing anything on purpose. Therefore, why should you take it personally? Marcus Aurelius wrote that whenever he encountered someone who said something shameful, he would ask himself if it's possible to live in a place where no one says anything shameful. Of course, he knew the answer was no. There will always be someone who says something that is shameful. The key is to not take what the person said personally.

51. Don't Respond to Rudeness

There is no way to ignore rude people. You're going to encounter them nearly every day of your life. Just as people are rude today, they were rude back in Marcus Aurelius's and Seneca's time. Marcus Aurelius believed that one way to respond to rude people was to simply not respond at all. Of course, you don't want to be rude back. Therefore, if they are asking you a question, answer them politely.

Marcus Aurelius also knew that no matter what you say or do, a rude person is going to continue to be rude. He discussed that no matter how much you try to talk to them, they will continue to be rude because this is their way. Therefore, it is important for us not to fall into this same cycle of rudeness giving way to rudeness.

52. Devil's Advocate

A devil's advocate is someone who disagrees with you, often to make you think of situations or factors that you didn't think of previously. They want to create a debate with you through their opinions. While these types of debates can sometimes become heated, many Stoics believe that the opinions of a devil's advocate can help you.

Stoics believe that you can become your own devil's advocate. You can debate with yourself by coming up with questions that go against your initial thoughts. You can use the devil's advocate exercise to make you think of situations that you hadn't thought of before. You can also use this exercise to make sure your ideas are rational. It's also helps boost your brain activity, as you are taking part in critical thinking and problem-solving.

53. It's Okay to Say No

Sometimes we struggle with saying no, especially when it's to ourselves. However, it's important to master the skill of saying no to yourself because it can help you hold off on immediate gratification. When you do this, you are helping yourself learn self-discipline, because you are not allowing yourself to get what you want when you want it.

Practicing Stoicism is not always an easy task. You have a lot of pieces of the philosophy to remember. Plus, it's not always easy to make sure you are doing your best constantly. Sometimes, you might feel like you want to procrastinate or slack off on your work. You might not always feel like you want to work towards establishing your highest self. These feelings happen because we're human.

One technique which can help you overcome these feelings is by telling yourself no. If you find yourself procrastinating, tell yourself that you are not allowed to do so. If you feel that you don't want to focus your energy and time on reaching your best self one day, tell yourself no, you have to focus on what's important. This also works the other way - if someone else wants you to commit to something that doesn't resonate with your highest self, you can so no. You owe no one but yourself any obligation.

54. Do I Feel Better?

You can try this technique on yourself or someone else. It's a question you can ask someone if they are crying or yelling because they are frustrated or angry. You simply ask them "Is your behavior making you feel better?" Chances are pretty good that their reaction to their situation is not making them feel better - in fact, generally, negative reactions over negative situations always makes us feel worse. Instead, it's best to focus on finding a solution to your problem in a positive way. If you're angry because your computer is running slow, you can stop focusing on how slowly your computer is running and take a break or go for a quick walk. Then come back and try to figure out why your computer is having problems. In any situation that brings up negative emotions, ask if the emotions are making you feel better. If not, they serve no purpose.

55. Remember to Relax

It's hard to remember to relax when your world seems to be so busy. However, Stoics realize the importance of relaxation and how it can help our mind. For a Stoic, the mind is one of the most important pieces of a person, because the mind is how you learn and where you store information. Stoics know that in order to keep working towards your best self, you need to have a clear and healthy mind. Therefore, it's important to take time out of your day to relax.

There are many ways you can relax. For example, you could relax through mindful meditation. For an aspiring Stoic, this is a great way to relax because it covers other exercises. Through mindful meditation, you learn to become more calm and to become more mindful of your environment. Another perk of mindful meditation is it doesn't take very long. You could set aside a few minutes in your morning when you find a quiet place to focus on your meditation.

Another way you can relax is through reading. Stoics spend a large part of their day learning as much information as they can. Reading is a great way to help you learn new pieces of information. You don't have to read a very thought-provoking book, but you could sit down and read Marcus Aurelius's *Meditations*.

56. Protect Your Peace of Mind

You're going to work hard to gain your peace of mind. There are going to be dozens of exercises from this book that you will use to help establish it. When you do, you need to protect it. Think of it this way - when you work hard to achieve something, you want to protect it because of all the hard work you put into it. You want to treat your peace of mind the same way, and protect it because you will work hard reaching this state.

You should always want to protect what's positive in your life. You will be able to achieve your ultimate potential by protecting your valuable and positive personality traits. If in any situation you find yourself slipping back into negativity, remember how hard you worked to bring positivity and peace into your life. Hold onto that hard-earned peace.

57. Failure Happens But Life Carries On

While you strive to be the best person you can be, it's important for you to remember that no one perfect. You can work hard at a task and still fail. In Stoicism, you will learn that failure happens, but life carries on.

Stoicism teaches that you don't have to continue to think about the task you did poorly as this will welcome negative thoughts and emotions, which are counterproductive. The reality is, no matter how hard you try, you're not going to do great in every task. Sometimes you work hard and you still do poorly. It's going to happen and when it does, you need to remember that it's okay. Learn from your mistakes, see what you can do to improve, and move on.

Fear is one of the strongest emotions that we feel. It's also an emotion that can keep us from accomplishing tasks which we want to accomplish. Fear of failure can cause people to not even try to focus on and accomplish a task. When you practice Stoicism, you will work on controlling emotions, which means you can work on controlling your fear of failure.

It's important to remember that failure is okay if you learn from it. So, don't let the fear of failure hold you back from accomplishing any goals and dreams you have in your life. If you let fear hold you back, you're going to miss dozens of opportunities. Instead of becoming fearful of the opportunity, you should look at the situations that can come with the opportunity. For example, if you think "What if I fail?" Trying thinking instead, "What if I succeed?" You can ask yourself what the worst possible situation is if you do fail, and come up with a plan of action instead of trying to stay away from the situation because you're afraid of failure.

58. Know Your Freedom

Epictetus once wrote, "The person is free who lives as they wish, neither compelled, nor hindered, nor limited— whose choices aren't hampered, whose desires succeed, and who don't fall into what repels them..." This is an important exercise to take on, because our lives are busier than the lives of Epictetus and the other early Stoics. On top of this, they didn't live in the technologically advanced times as we do now. Therefore, it's extremely important to understand your freedom with regards to your time.

Of course, I'm not just talking about jobs, personal responsibilities, or family obligations. I am talking about the time we spend trying to impress people that we don't need to impress. For example, when you find out that company is coming over, you decide to focus on cleaning your house as well as you can. You want to impress your visitor with a clean house and don't want them to feel like you live in a messy house. When you believe you have to make sure your house is spotless, you are limiting your freedom by spending all your time making it so. Even after that time is gone, you may still not get the result you desire - the admiration of the person entering your home. You have the choice - the freedom - to decide not to put too much time into controlling the reactions of another.

59. Pay Attention to Yourself

In order to reach your highest self, you need to pay attention to yourself. This exercise is similar to mindfulness, however, it's meant to help you achieve a higher sense of self through positivity. Of course, the Stoics realized that we will not be able to remain positive 100% of the time. This is why Stoics such as Seneca and Musonius Rufus spent time talking about mistakes. As a Stoic, it's a mistake to think negatively, whether it's about a person or yourself.

When you pay attention to yourself, you become self-aware. You notice every thought and action you make. You also start to question why you are thinking about a certain situation or why you are acting a certain way. When you start to question yourself, continue to answer yourself. Your answers will help you become more self-aware.

Not only do you want to pay attention to the way you look, your thoughts, and your actions, but you also want to pay attention your self-talk. As humans, we tend to be our own worst critics. We say things to ourselves, especially when we make a mistake, that other people wouldn't even say to us. These things tend to be very negative, which is something Stoics stay away from. Marcus Aurelius and

Seneca discussed how we shouldn't talk about another person in a negative way, so why should we talk about ourselves in a negative fashion? Just as you want to give others positivity, you want to make sure that you're being positive to yourself as well.

In order to keep yourself more aware of your actions, thoughts, and self-talk, you could take time to journal your self-awareness. You could also use some of your morning or evening reflection time to focus on your self-awareness. Ask yourself how you spoke to yourself. Did you say anything negative to yourself over a mistake you made? You could also rate your self-awareness. How well aware were you of your actions and thoughts towards yourself?

60. You Can Avoid Harm

In *Meditations*, Marcus Aurelius discussed how there are a lot of things we can focus on avoiding if we put forth the effort. For example, Aurelius stated, "In everything you say and think, remember this. It is in your hands when you want to leave this life." Marcus Aurelius was a true believer that we control everything about ourselves. We not only control our actions and thoughts, but we also can control how we let others treat us.

In his book, Aurelius discusses how we should not fear death because the gods will not harm us once we die. They will not put us in harm's way. Therefore, hr wondered, why would we let anyone else put us in harm's way? If God won't even subject us to harm, why would we let our friends, family, or anyone else on this earth subject us to harm?

While you won't always be able to avoid harm, as the Stoics also taught that pain can make us stronger, you can limit the harm you face from other people. It's as simple as doing what you can to stay away from the person who brings harm to you. Remember, Marcus Aurelius didn't just mean people who physically harm you. He also meant the people who harm your soul. The people who talk negatively towards you, are rude, and hurt your feelings. Staying away from emotional and mental harm is just as important as staying away from physically harm.

61. Don't Let Your Soul Harm Itself

Marcus Aurelius was one of the ancient Stoics who spoke the most about harm. When he talked about harm, he talked about any type of harm, whether it was physical, mental, or emotional. He talked about how you can avoid some harm, but avoiding all harm is not possible. Even though nature doesn't want us harmed, it is still part of life's process.

Meditations is filled with dozens of Stoic exercises you can incorporate into your everyday life. One of these exercises is to not let your soul harm itself. Marcus Aurelius explained this by stating "The soul inflicts on itself the greatest harm when it becomes a tumour on the universe."

Aurelius laid out five ways the soul can harm itself. First, this can happen when you decide to steer off the path nature has laid out for you. You don't listen to nature or you become rebellious towards nature. Marcus Aurelius believed that nature would never put you in the way of harm, therefore, when you don't listen to nature, you are putting yourself in the way of it.

The second way is when you lose your sense of compassion and treat another human being with hate or harm them. This is one of the biggest reasons, Aurelius believed, that we need to stay away from anger. The angrier we are towards someone, the more likely we are to end up harming our soul.

Allowing yourself to feel pain or pleasure is the third way your soul can harm itself. Of course, Marcus Aurelius was aware that this isn't always avoidable, however, he felt that staying out of harm's way as much as possible was in our control. Furthermore, allowing ourselves too much pleasure will end up harming our soul, because it could lead us to pain. When we strive for pleasure, we are going to find ourselves disappointed because we cannot always have the pleasure we strive for. We could also lose sight of our highest self, which would lead us to lose eudaimonia.

A fourth way that our souls can harm themselves is by lying. Marcus Aurelius stated that it didn't matter if we were lying to ourselves, someone else, or through an action. A lie is not being honest, and as Stoics, we need to strive to be 100% honest in everything we say and do.

The final way our soul can come to harm is by wasting time and energy. Many Stoics, such as Aurelius, discussed how short our lives are, which makes our time more precious. Therefore, as Aurelius discussed in *Meditations*, the smallest act that wastes our time or energy can harm our soul. We always need to think before we speak or act. We need to ask ourselves if what we are about to do or say is necessary. Then, we only need to perform the action or speak if we deem it to be necessary. If it's unnecessary, then we have not only wasted our time and energy, but we have also put our soul in harm's way.

62. Notice When You Are Off Balance

Life is unpredictable. No matter how hard we try or how many exercises we incorporate into our daily lives, we are going to get caught off guard by situations. No matter how often you tell yourself that you can't control these unpredictable moments, you will find times when these moments start to bring you down. They might make you feel frustrated, anxious, or angry.

When this happens, or as Marcus Aurelius stated, "When force of circumstance upsets your equanimity," you want to do whatever you can to find your balance. You need to use the various Stoic exercises and techniques in order to notice that you're off balance, and then waste no time in working to rebalance yourself.

The first step to take when you find that you have lost your balance is to calm yourself. Whether you are feeling scared, angry, or sad, you need to focus on calming your mind. You need to remember that obstacles are going to happen and these factors are not in your control. You need to tell yourself that you can only change what factors are in your control. Once you start to regain your sense of control over yourself, you will be able to create a better balance within your mind.

You can also take this time to remember that nature gives you these obstacles to increase your strength. You can use obstacle as an advantage for yourself in your journey to reach your highest self. However, in order to do this, you have to return to your balance.

63. Your Mind Is Important

Meditations contains a lot of information about the importance of the mind. Aurelius felt that before we do or say anything, we have to have the best regard for our mind. Remember, Stoics believe that our mind is one of the few things that we can truly control. Therefore, it's extremely important, as Aurelius noted, to make sure that we have the best intentions for our mind.

If we have the opportunity to harm someone, whether it's physically or emotionally, we should not do so, because this is not in tune with having the highest regard for our mind. We should never do something that will cause us to betray ourselves in any way. This means that we should always remain honest and never lie. We should always have self-respect and never speak negatively about ourselves. We should always strive to treat ourselves with the highest good, just as we would want to treat anyone else with the highest good. By doing this, we will always have the highest regard for our mind.

In his book, Aurelius states that when you keep the best regard for your mind, "you will be free of fear and desire." Furthermore, you will not worry about how much time you have on this earth or whether you want to be alone or have company, because you will be at your highest peace. Marcus Aurelius believed that having the best regard for your mind would help you achieve your highest self.

Chapter 7: What to Do If You're Struggling to Implement

When you first read some of the exercises in Chapter 6, you might have wondered how you can complete some of the exercises. It's understandable, and many people can struggle with some of the exercises in the beginning. Sometimes, it's just a matter of not understanding why Stoics used these exercises to help them achieve their purpose in life. And that's okay! These are all things we can work on overcoming in our own time. Stoicism teaches us to be patient and when it comes to learning the practical exercises, you will have to have patience. If you are struggling to implement some of them, you shouldn't be ashamed. Learning the exercises and practicing Stoicism takes time.

Continue to Read Stoic Books and Articles

Stoics taught that we should never stop learning. They wanted us to take time to read every day. If you're struggling to implement Stoicism into your life, simply take a step back and continue to learn about the philosophy. Marcus Aurelius's book *Meditations* is readily available online or easily purchased. *Meditations* is a great book to start reading if you're struggling to implement. Throughout his book, Aurelius focuses on many thoughts and practical exercises that he wanted every aspiring Stoic to follow. You can start your journey by picking a few of the exercises in Aurelius's book and implementing them into your daily life.

Join an Online Forum or Class

The internet is a great resource for anyone who is struggling with implementing Stoic exercises. There are a variety of online websites that offer forums and discussion groups. These forums are filled with Stoics who are available to help you. Stoicfellowship.com is a great website that can help you find a community close to your area. You could also look into any online courses about Stoicism.

Live the Stoic Way of Life Everyday

Even when you find yourself struggling, one of the best ways to implement the exercises is to continue to practice the exercises everyday. Remember, some exercises are easier than others. Therefore, if one of the exercises doesn't work for you, simply try a different exercise. The key is to do your best to practice the Stoic way of life throughout your day.

Stoicism Is a Habit, Not a Job

You might struggle implementing Stoic exercises because you feel that they are something you have to do and not something you want to do. You might feel that the exercises are more like a job. Remember, no one is forcing you to practice Stoicism - you have chosen to do so on your own for one of a number of reasons. You might want to improve your life by thinking positively. Maybe you are afraid of death, and practicing Stoicism is the way to help you overcome your fear. You might be working to overcome your anxiety.

Remembering that Stoicism is a lifestyle choice will help you treat Stoicism as a habit and not a job. At first, you're going to have to work harder to make sure you're using the practical exercises in situations. However, as time goes on, you will start to find that you're automatically using the exercises. This is when Stoicism has become a habit. For those who regularly practice Stoicism, it naturally becomes a habit in life, as long as you work on it regularly and stick to your routine.

Before Epictetus, Seneca, and Marcus Aurelius practiced Stoicism, they were angry and struggled to control their emotions. They didn't always know what factors of their lives they could control and what factors they couldn't. They started practicing Stoicism because they wanted to learn how to live better. They weren't born Stoics - they worked, used previously formulated exercises, and developed their own exercises to help themselves live the Stoic way of life. Through their dedication, Stoicism became a habit for them.

Remember, You Can Do This

We all have bad days. Even the ancient Stoics had bad days. This is why they established practical exercises to help them through these bad days. Sometimes we struggle to remember to implement Stoic exercises. Sometimes we catch ourselves not implementing an exercise when we know we could. These situations can make us feel like we have failed. They can make us feel like we can't do this. In these moments, it's important for you to remember that you can do this. You can implement Stoic exercises into your everyday life.

Just as you wouldn't allow someone else's negativity to burst your positive bubble, don't let your own negativity bring you down. Take a moment to collect yourself, collect your thoughts, realize that you have made a mistake, and take a moment to see how you can learn from this mistake. Then, move on from the situation. Don't dwell on the mistake you made. Don't dwell on the fact that you didn't implement an exercise when you should have. Learn from your mistake and move on. Tell yourself that you will do better next time, because you can reach your best self.

Consequences If You Don't Implement

Unfortunately, there are consequences if you don't implement Stoic exercise. No one will punish you, but you will miss out on all the benefits already discussed, and you will not live your best life. That may seem consequence enough, but a few additional ramifications of falling out of the practice of Stoicism include the following.

You Will Continue to Struggle Implementing Stoic Exercises

The ancient Stoics spent every moment of their time growing Stoicism. From the time they woke up in the morning until the time they fell asleep, they used exercises and made observations to establish new exercises for other Stoics. Every Stoic discussed in this book, from Zeno to Marcus Aurelius, knew that one of the most important steps a person could take was to practice Stoic exercises and teachings on a daily basis. This is because they knew that if they didn't follow through, they were more likely to struggle with implementing the practices.

You Won't Put Your Best Foot Forward

Stoicism is about putting your best foot forward. All the practical exercises seen in this book are there to help you accomplish this so you can reach your highest self. If you don't implement these exercises, you're not going to be able to reach your best self because you're not putting your best foot forward. This basically means, without doing the work, you won't be able to accomplish the main goal of Stoicism.

Sometimes we struggle with being our best selves because of those around us. Like Marcus Aurelius stated in *Meditations*, "When you wake up in the morning, tell yourself: The people I deal with today will be meddling, ungrateful, arrogant, dishonest, jealous, and surly. They are like this because they can't tell good from evil. But I have seen the beauty of good, and the ugliness of evil, and have recognized that the wrongdoer has a nature related to my own…" Marcus Aurelius understood that sometimes, treating others with positivity is difficult when you're faced with negativity. However, he knew that implementing Stoic exercises, such as morning reflection, could get you through these moments so you can put your best foot forward. If you don't implement the exercises, you will find yourself giving off negativity instead of positivity.

You Will Not Reach Eudaimonia

In Stoicism, you implement practical exercises in your daily life so you can work to reach eudaimonia, which will help you reach your highest self. Therefore, if you don't implement the exercises, you're not going to reach eudaimonia. This isn't saying you won't be happy at all, it's just that you won't reach your ultimate happiness.

Once you reach your highest eudaimonia, you will find that you make peace in nearly every situation you face. You will find that you become less angry, less hurt by other people, and less likely to feel like you're worthless. You'll realize that there are things in your environment that you can control and things you cannot. You'll learn to let go of the things that aren't in your control, because your time is precious. There are several exercises which allow you to reach this level of eudaimonia, however, it's only possible if you continue to implement the exercises.

You Won't Reach Your Highest Self

Before you start learning Stoic exercises and teachings, you need to have a sense of your highest self. You have to imagine the person you want to be for yourself and other people. You want to imagine your perfect self, the one who doesn't make mistakes, is always in a state of eudaimonia, and the one who is able and willing to help anyone in any situation. While you're practicing Stoicism, this is the person you are striving to be every day.

If you don't implement the dozens of Stoic exercises, you won't be able to focus on reaching your ideal self. You will find that one day you feel more in harmony with your best self and the next day you feel farther away. This inconsistency will start driving a wedge between you, Stoicism, and your highest self. Soon, you might start to feel that reaching your highest self is impossible. You might find yourself following your old, negative ways as you become less positive towards yourself and other people.

No, perfection is never going to happen, but this doesn't mean that you can't become one with your version of your highest self. This doesn't mean that you can't strive to be the best person you can be. Every day, you can focus on handling situations the best you can, learning from your mistakes, and becoming the best person you can be.

Conclusion

"Virtue is not simply theoretical knowledge, but it is practical application as well...So a man who wishes to become good not only must be thoroughly familiar with the precepts which are conducive to virtue but must also be earnest and zealous in applying these principles." – Musonius Rufus

Everyone wants to reach their full potential, live a balanced life, and become the best person they can be. One of the ways to do this is by learning and implementing the practices of Stoicism. Not only can Stoicism help keep you calm during difficult situations, but it can also help you achieve goals in your life that you never imagined you could accomplish.

This book discussed several benefits of Stoicism, such as learning how to control your emotions, accepting what you can and cannot change, and letting go of greed. These benefits prove that Stoicism can help turn your life around. Once you start practicing Stoicism, you will start to gain a sense of freedom. You will start to become happier with your life and you will be on your way to reaching your true eudaimonia.

You will find that your problems are not as big as you originally thought they were. Through Stoicism, you will come to find that your problems are just a small piece of a larger picture. This realization will help you learn how to problem-solve and remain calm in chaotic and stressful situations.

Through its many exercises, values, and principles, Stoicism teaches you that you can overcome any obstacles in your life, have peace of mind, and reach your highest potential. Even if you think you can't do this right now, start to work on some of the exercises in this book. You can start by choosing whatever five exercises you feel most comfortable doing. For instance, start off by thinking about what your ideal self is. How do you want people to remember you? Do you want to be remembered as kind, generous, and determined? Write down the things you want to be remembered as and then go through the exercises and pick a few that you feel you can start with that will help you become the person you want to be.

Maybe you want to focus on overcoming your anxiety by creating peace of mind. You want to be able to overcome your anxiety at any moment, including out in public. Once you establish the obstacle in your life you want to move past so you can feel more balanced and reach your full potential, focus on some exercises to help you accomplish this. Remember, it's important to work on building your confidence, which you can complete through a number of Stoic exercises.

There is a lot of information in this book to help you learn Stoicism; it's teachings, exercises, and what it can do to help you reach your full potential. Whether you have learned and studied Stoicism previously or you are just learning about the Stoic philosophy, you can gain insight from this book to help yourself grow. On top of this, you can also gain insight into how to help other people achieve their ultimate potential.

Stoicism has been a way of life for thousands of years. It is a great way to help you overcome your fears, understand ways to control your negative emotions, overcome obstacles, reach your highest potential. No matter where you are in life or who you feel you are, you're capable of learning Stoicism, accomplishing its exercises, and reaching your highest potential. Every human being is capable of reaching their highest potential and becoming the best person they can be. Stoicism can help you achieve these goals in many ways.

I want to thank you for taking the time to read this book! I am honored you chose this book to help you better understand and implement Stoicism in your life. If you enjoyed this book, I would appreciate it if you could leave a review, as it helps my work and it helps to get the message of Stoicism out to more people. Thank you!

Bibliography

A brief history of stoicism. (2016). Retrieved from https://stoicjourney.org/2016/07/28/a-brief-history-of-stoicism/.

A Stoic Response to Grief. Retrieved from https://dailystoic.com/stoic-response-grief/.

A Struggle With One Of The Stoic Psychological Techniques. (2018). Retrieved from http://whatisstoicism.com/stoicism-resources/a-struggle-with-the-stoic-psychological-techniques/.

About Stoicism Today. Retrieved from https://modernstoicism.com/about-stoicism-today/.

Allan, P. (2017). Honesty Is Not a Tool for Your Personal Gain. Retrieved from https://lifehacker.com/honesty-is-not-a-tool-for-your-personal-gain-1797680959.

Anderson, K. (2012). Five Reasons Why Stoicism Matters Today. Retrieved from https://www.forbes.com/sites/kareanderson/2012/09/28/five-reasons-why-stoicism-matthttps://www.forbes.com/sites/kareanderson/2012/09/28/five-reasons-why-stoicism-matters-today/#17b0d8047a64ers-today/#17b0d8047a64.

Aurelius, Marcus | Internet Encyclopedia of Philosophy. Retrieved from https://www.iep.utm.edu/marcus/.

Aurelius, M. (2019). Meditations. Kindle Edition.

Babin, J., & Manson, R. (2019). Stoicism: The Complete Guide for Beginners to Apply Stoicism to Everyday Life, Gain Wisdom, Confidence, and Resilience with Philosophy from the Greats...Extreme Mindset and Leadership. Kindle Edition.

Ben Martin, P. (2018). In-Depth: Cognitive Behavioral Therapy. Retrieved from https://psychcentral.com/lib/in-depth-cognitive-behavioral-therapy/.

Cardus, M. (2016). 7 Life Lessons from Marcus Aurelius. Retrieved from https://mercecardus.com/7-life-lessons-from-marcus-aurelius/.

Chakrapani, C. (2018). Stoic Lessons: Musonius Rufus' Complete Works (Stoicism in Plain English Book 6). Stoic Gym Publications. Kindle Edition.

Chakrapani, C. (2018). Stoic Meditations: Marcus Aurelius Complete Works 1 (Stoicism in Plain English Book 7). Stoic Gym Publications. Kindle Edition.

Christ, S. 8 Important Lessons Stoic Philosophy Will Teach You About Being Happy. Retrieved from https://www.lifehack.org/articles/lifestyle/8-important-lessons-stoic-philosophy-will-teach-you-about-being-happy.html.

Daily Stoic Exercises for Beginners. (2017). Retrieved from https://astoicremedy.com/2017/04/17/daily-stoic-exercises-for-beginners/.

Donnelly, K. (2019). 12 Time Management Apps to Organize Your Life and Keep You on Track. Retrieved from https://www.shopify.com/blog/time-management-apps.

Donovan, J. How Stoicism Works. Retrieved from https://people.howstuffworks.com/stoicism1.htm.

Don't Take It Personally | Philosofina. Retrieved from https://www.philosofina.com/dont-take-it-personally/.

Earp, B. (2019). Do Not weep for Dour Dead: How to Mourn as the Stoics Did. Retrieved from https://aeon.co/essays/do-not-weep-for-your-dead-how-to-mourn-as-the-stoics-did.

Eliason, N. Discourses by Epictetus: Summary, Notes and Lessons. Retrieved from https://www.nateliason.com/notes/discourses-epictetus.

Epictetus and Marcus on dealing with other people: Stoicism: the Very Basics. Retrieved from https://canvas.instructure.com/courses/1054798/pages/epictetus-and-marcus-on-dealing-with-other-people.

Faja, E. (2016). 10 Insanely Useful Stoic Exercises. Retrieved from https://observer.com/2016/02/ten-insanely-useful-stoic-exercises/.

Garratt, G. (2012). Introducing Cognitive Behavioural Therapy (CBT) for Work. Retrieved from https://books.google.com/books?id=5SBfz2Xyv2sC&pg=PT16&lpg=PT16&dq=A+consciousness+of+wrongdoing+is+the+first+step+to+salvation...you+have+to+catch+yourself+doing+it+before+you+can+correct+it&source=bl&ots=frFCZWZ45R&sig=ACfU3U1-azXcB2owEpu-Xuxdgu2Ce96Gw&hl=en&sa=X&ved=2ahUKEwjSo9jKuqPhAhVI4YMKHQg2C5kQ6AEwAnoECAcQAQ#v=onepage&q=A%20consciousness%20of%20wrongdoing%20is%20the%20first%20step%20to%20salvation...you%20have%20to%20catch%20yourself%20doing%20it%20before%20you%20can%20correct%20it&f=false.

Garnett, K. (2018). Stoicism For Beginners: Master the Art of Happiness. Learn Modern, Practical Stoicism to Create Your Own Daily Stoic Routine. Kindle Edition.

Gill, N. (2019). Does the Serenity Prayer Echo the Greco-Roman Notion of Stoicism?. Retrieved from https://www.thoughtco.com/stoics-and-moral-philosophy-4068536.

Gollberg, K. 10 Lessons Stoics Can Teach Us About Living A Good Life. Retrieved from https://www.smartliving365.com/10-lessons-stoics-can-teach-us-living-good-life/.

Guaderrama, R. (2018). Honesty. Retrieved from https://stoicanswers.com/2018/02/05/honesty/.

Hamm, T. (2016). How the Principles of Stoicism Can Help Your Personal and Financial Life. Retrieved from https://lifehacker.com/how-the-principles-of-stoicism-can-help-your-personal-a-1783277251.

Holiday, R. (2017). 7 insights from the ancient philosophy of Marcus Aurelius that will change the way you think about life, death, and time. Retrieved from https://www.businessinsider.com/stoicism-lessons-life-death-2017-6#you-could-leave-life-right-now-5.

Holiday, R. (2016). 37 Wise & Life-Changing Lessons From The Ancient Stoics. Retrieved from https://thoughtcatalog.com/ryan-holiday/2016/10/37-wise-life-changing-lessons-from-the-ancient-stoics/.

Holiday, R., & Hanselman, S. (2016). The Daily Stoic. New York: Penguin Random House LLC.

Irvine, W. (2014). What Stoicism Isn't. Retrieved from https://www.huffpost.com/entry/what-stoicism-isnt_n_5346269.

Johnson, E. "Happiness is a smoothly flowing life.". Retrieved from https://excellentjourney.net/2015/04/04/happiness-is-a-smoothly-flowing-life/.

Jun, P. (2016). Seneca on Using Philosophy to Overcome Grief. Retrieved from http://motivatedmastery.com/seneca-philosophy-overcome-grief/.

Kreiss, T. Stoicism 101: An introduction to Stoicism, Stoic Philosophy and the Stoics. Retrieved from https://www.holstee.com/blogs/mindful-matter/stoicism-101-everything-you-wanted-to-know-about-stoicism-stoic-philosophy-and-the-stoics.

Loren, G. (2018). Stoicism: Apply Stoicism to Your Everyday Life and Overcome Destructive Emotions (Learn Self Control, Become Free from Anger, Greed, Jealousy and Take On Negativity in Your Life). Kindle Edition.

Lucius Annaeus Seneca Quotes. Retrieved from https://www.brainyquote.com/quotes/lucius_annaeus_seneca_155016.

Marcus Aurelius' Meditations: On Stoicism – Part II - Investing in the Classics. (2015). Retrieved from http://www.investingintheclassics.com/archives/497.

Mayor, N. (2019). Practical Stoicism: Your Step-By-Step Guide to Create a Life of Wisdom, Perseverance, and Joy: Ancient Philosophy for Modern Life. Kindle Edition.

Meah, A. 40 Inspirational Seneca Quotes On Success. Retrieved from https://awakenthegreatnesswithin.com/40-inspirational-seneca-quotes-on-success/.

Meditations by Marcus Aurelius: Book Summary, Key Lessons and Best Quotes. Retrieved from https://dailystoic.com/meditations-marcus-aurelius/.

Memento mori – Art Term. Retrieved from https://www.tate.org.uk/art/art-terms/m/memento-mori.

Modern Stoicism. Retrieved from https://modernstoicism.com/.

Monk, H. (2017). 5 Stoic Principles for Modern Living. Retrieved from https://medium.com/pocketstoic/5-stoic-principles-for-modern-living-applying-an-ancient-philosophy-to-the-21st-century-2a8e10f31887.

Morin, A. 4 Ways Emotions Can Screw Up Your Decisions. Retrieved from https://www.psychologytoday.com/us/blog/what-mentally-strong-people-dont-do/201602/4-ways-emotions-can-screw-your-decisions.

Pigliucci, M. (2017). How to Be a Stoic. Retrieved from https://books.google.com/books?id=pUh_DQAAQBAJ&pg=PT178&lpg=PT178&dq=faced+with+pain,+you+will+discover+the+power+of+endurance&source=bl&ots=1RNMKbxxwO&sig=ACfU3U2lYqmRc2HsjQw-96lUsfAhaucGtQ&hl=en&sa=X&ved=2ahUKEwiqssu06KDhAhWD94MKHXp-DR8Q6AEwAXoECAgQAQ#v=onepage&q=faced%20with%20pain%2C%20you%20will%20discover%20the%20power%20of%20endurance&f=false.

Popova, M. Seneca on Overcoming Fear and the Surest Strategy for Protecting Yourself from Misfortune. Retrieved from https://www.brainpickings.org/2016/02/15/seneca-letter-18/.

Posidonius (135 BC-51 BC). Retrieved from http://www-groups.dcs.st-and.ac.uk/history/Biographies/Posidonius.html.

Robertson, D. (2018). What do the Stoic Virtues Mean?. Retrieved from https://donaldrobertson.name/2018/01/18/what-do-the-stoic-virtues-mean/.

Robertson, D. (2013). Stoicism and the Art of Happiness: Practical Wisdom for Everyday Life (Teach Yourself). Retrieved from https://books.google.com/books?id=MhYtDwAAQBAJ&pg=PT224&lpg=PT224 &dq=Continually+picture+to+yourself+time+and+space+as+a+whole,+and+eve ry+individual+thing,+in+terms+of+space,+a+tiny+seed,+in+terms+of+time+th e+mere+turn+of+a+screw&source=bl&ots=8mfludMRgB&sig=ACfU3U3HvNEs QL133dyZv1m1GN-EwIj86w&hl=en&sa=X&ved=2ahUKEwi71PH2oqHhAhUsuVkKHdiLDQIQ6AEw AHoECAkQAQ#v=onepage&q=Continually%20picture%20to%20yourself%20ti me%20and%20space%20as%20a%20whole%2C%20and%20every%20individual %20thing%2C%20in%20terms%20of%20space%2C%20a%20tiny%20seed%2C %20in%20terms%20of%20time%20the%20mere%20turn%20of%20a%20screw &f=false.

Rosser, C. Meditations by Marcus Aurelius: Summary & Notes. Retrieved from https://calvinrosser.com/notes/meditations-marcus-aurelius/.

Rosenberg, E. (2019). The 8 Best Expense Tracker Apps of 2019. Retrieved from https://www.thebalance.com/best-expense-tracker-apps-4158958.

Sadler, G. (2017). Hadot's "Active" Stoic Exercises by Anitra Russell. Retrieved from https://modernstoicism.com/hadots-active-stoic-exercises-by-anitra-russell/.

Salzgeber, J. (2017). 13 Reasons Why Modern Stoics Should Live a Minimalist Lifestyle. Retrieved from https://www.njlifehacks.com/13-reasons-why-modern-stoics-should-live-a-minimalist-lifestyle/.

Salzgeber, J. (2019). The Little Book of Stoicism: Timeless Wisdom to Gain Resilience, Confidence, and Calmness. Amazon Digital Services LLC.

Smith, M. (2018). Stoicism: Stoic Philosophy Made Easy. Kindle Edition.

Stoic Communities. Retrieved from https://stoicfellowship.com/stoic-groups.html#communities.

Stoicism. Retrieved from https://www.iep.utm.edu/stoicism/.

Stoicism - By Branch / Doctrine - The Basics of Philosophy. Retrieved from https://www.philosophybasics.com/branch_stoicism.html.

Stoicism | Definition, History, & Influence. Retrieved from https://www.britannica.com/topic/Stoicism.

The Definitive List of Stoicism in History & Pop Culture. Retrieved from https://dailystoic.com/stoicism-pop-culture/.

Seneca, Lucius Annaeus | Internet Encyclopedia of Philosophy. Retrieved from https://www.iep.utm.edu/seneca/.

Stoic Ethics | Internet Encyclopedia of Philosophy. Retrieved from https://www.iep.utm.edu/stoiceth/

Stoic Philosophy of Mind | Internet Encyclopedia of Philosophy. Retrieved from https://www.iep.utm.edu/stoicmind/.

Stoic Quotes: The Best Quotes From The Stoics. Retrieved from https://dailystoic.com/stoic-quotes/.

The Stoic Range of Virtue: In Defense of Moderation. Retrieved from https://dailystoic.com/stoic-range-virtue-defense-moderation/.

Stoicism | Internet Encyclopedia of Philosophy. Retrieved from https://www.iep.utm.edu/stoicism/.

The Stoics. Retrieved from https://www.theschooloflife.com/thebookoflife/the-great-philosophers-the-stoics/.

What Is Stoicism? A Definition & 9 Stoic Exercises To Get You Started. Retrieved from https://dailystoic.com/what-is-stoicism-a-definition-3-stoic-exercises-to-get-you-started/.

What Is Stoicism? A Simple Definition & 10 Stoic Core Principles. Retrieved from https://www.njlifehacks.com/what-is-stoicism-overview-definition-10-stoic-principles

Stoicism Reveals 4 Rituals That Will Make You Confident - Barking Up The Wrong Tree. Retrieved from https://www.bakadesuyo.com/2017/12/make-you-confident/.

Tanner, G. (2017). Stoicism: A Detailed Breakdown of Stoicism Philosophy and Wisdom from the Greats: A Complete Guide To Stoicism. Kindle Edition.

Toren, A. (2015). 5 Epic Leaders Who Studied Stoicism -- and Why You Should Too. Retrieved from https://www.entrepreneur.com/article/252625.

What the Stoic Philosophers Can Teach Us About Health and Nutrition. (2016). Retrieved from http://www.cavemandoctor.com/2016/02/28/4954/.

Who is Gaius Musonius Rufus? Getting to Know "The Roman Socrates."
Retrieved from https://dailystoic.com/gaius-musonius-rufus-the-roman-socrates/.

Stoicism

The Art Of Being Calm And Centred In

A Manic World

Author

Conrad Miller

Table Of Contents

Introduction

Most people want to live the best life possible. There are many who are constantly looking for ways to make themselves happier, more successful, or more positive. There are also many who struggle with creating this type of life for various reasons. Some of these reasons can stem from childhood trauma or problems while other reasons stem from situations in adult life. No matter what the reason is that you feel is keeping you from reaching your best life, you need to know that it's possible to overcome it and this book is one way that can help you.

Stoicism is a word you might have heard of in the past, whether it was in school or because you ran into it online or somewhere else. It's often a word that makes people think of statues or ancient Greece. But Stoicism is so much more than that. Stoicism is a way of life that can help you achieve happiness and freedom from your emotions that control you. Through Stoicism, you will learn how to control your emotions so when you make decisions, YOU'RE making the decisions and not your emotions.

This book is laid out with seven main chapters. The first chapter is going to describe what Stoicism is. This chapter will not only look into Stoicism as a belief, but it will also give you principles which will help you throughout the rest of this book. Through these principles, you will learn a little more about Stoicism, how to achieve your ultimate happiness, best self, and how to achieve in life as a Stoic. Everything we discuss in this book will focus on the ways you can make your life more positive and fulfilling. This chapter is the first step into your more positive life.

The second chapter of this book is going to give you a bit of history on Stoicism. While Stoicism has been around for centuries and includes more history than what can fit in this book, I will give you the best historical outline of Stoicism. I believe that in order for you to really grasp the Stoic life, you need to understand where the beliefs came from. In this chapter, we will also talk about various historical people who followed Stoicism. Of course, we will talk about the founder of Stoicism, but we will also discuss Epictetus, Marcus Aurelius, Musonius Rufus, and a couple of others.

Chapter three is going to look a bit more on the history of Stoicism as we go through the ages. Because Stoicism has been around for so many centuries, it's developed over time from when the ancient Greeks started to preach Stoicism in the streets. Of course, Stoicism started to fall on the sidelines for a few centuries but then skyrocketed back into the mainstream during the 1970s. Since then, Stoicism has continued to grow into the self-help community and into the lives of celebrities. This chapter will look at this growth.

Chapter four is going to focus on why you should become a Stoic and what the benefits are of Stoicism. Everyone wants to know the whys of a new way of life before they start digging into any changes they want to make. The benefits we will discuss will help lead you grow and become the best version of you.

Chapter five will focus on death and grief. Death of a loved one is something that everyone has to go through in their lives, and grief only follows. This is often some of the toughest times in a person's life and can make emotions go crazy. This chapter will help you learn how to deal with death and grief through Stoic teachings and philosophy.

Chapter six is probably a chapter you will find re-reading many times as you are learning more about the Stoic way of life. This chapter is going to go over the techniques and exercises of Stoicism. In this chapter, there will be well over 50 different exercises to help you grow in Stoicism.

Chapter seven will help you if you're struggling with implementing any of the exercises and practices of Stoicism. One important factor I want to mention about this now is, if you ever find yourself struggling, it's ok. You're learning a new valuable tool to help you to grow. You're going to focus on controlling your emotions so you can learn to be the best that you can be. You're going to have to have patience and realize that it's ok to struggle. As long as you continue to work on your exercises and practices of Stoicism, you will gain the insight needed to be the best that you can be. It's also important to remember that no one is ever perfect and we all need help when learning new techniques to better our lives.

Remember, trying to learn new ways of being in the World is a very honorable trait and you should be proud of yourself. Be proud of yourself; even if you make a mistake because you're doing your best and you will succeed.

It's also important to remember that you will not be perfect because nobody is perfect. You will make mistakes and sometimes you will feel as if you failed. At this moment, it's important to rise above the negative thoughts and focus on positive thoughts. You will also want to take this time to make sure you can control your energy. You can rise above your negative thoughts and control your emotions in many ways. This book will discuss 60 exercises which you can use to help rise above your negative thoughts. Of course, there are many other exercises that will help you which you might not find in this book. In fact, some exercises you might create yourself.

Finally, I want to thank you for choosing to read this book to help you along your journey of learning Stoicism so you can become more balanced, productive and reach your full potential. I am honored to be a part of your journey and know that you will succeed in becoming the best person you can be.

Chapter 1: What Is Stoicism?

Stoicism is a philosophy that teaches people to remain calm and keep a rational mind no matter what their situation is. They focus on using techniques and exercises so people can control themselves during times of crisis. Stoicism maintains that you can do this by focusing on what matters. If you can't control a situation, then you don't need to worry about the situation. Instead, you focus on the factors you can control which are your thoughts and actions. Stoicism sticks to the belief that our negative reactions to situations are caused by impulsive emotions. When you practice Stoicism, you're able to accept the situations that we can't change, change the behaviors we can change, and overcome the impulsive emotions. Because of this, Stoicism has helped many people overcome their worries, anxieties, and fears. When people start to practice Stoicism, they find their inner peace and strive to become the best person they can be.

Stoicism is focused on the word action. The core belief of Stoicism from its beginning is that we can only lead meaningful lives if we overcome our impulsive behaviors and focus on good and positive behaviors. For example, you work in customer service at a Deli and are getting ready to close up. You have fifteen minutes left before the Deli closes. Just as you're about to shut off the pizza oven and the fryer, a couple of customers walk in. They come up and order a couple of large pizzas. You try to keep your cool on the outside because you don't want to be rude to the customer, but you start to think angry thoughts as you take their order and start to make their pizza. You know they are regular customers, so they are well aware of when you close the Deli. You've had a long day, and all you want to do is go home. The more and more you think these negative thoughts, the angrier you become.

A person who practices Stoicism would not react in this way. Someone who practices Stoicism would understand that there are still fifteen minutes of their shift and that it only takes ten minutes to make a couple of pizzas. A person who practices Stoicism would focus on the positives of the situation, such as she will only be a few minutes later getting home, these pizzas will increase the revenue of the business, and the customers will be happy. A person who practices Stoicism realizes that they can't change the fact that people walk in to place an order as they are closing, but the person does realize their actions are a choice. In this example, a person who practices Stoicism uses logic to realize there is still 15 minutes before the Deli closes and pleasant customer service skills is their top priority in the job. Therefore, a person who practices Stoicism won't focus on the frustration and impulsive negative emotions but on the positive and logical emotions and actions.

At this point, I feel it's important for me to discuss how the word understanding is an important part of a Stoic's beliefs. When a person is understanding of situations, they are more likely to remain in control of their emotions during situations, even when the situations become chaotic. On top of this, you're more likely to think clearly, or logically, when you are understanding. In terms, understanding means that you can comprehend the situation and you're sympathetic to the way other people feel. Once you are able to reach the level of understanding situations or how a person feels, you'll be able to control your emotions, which will allow you to remain calm. If you don't understand the situation, you're going to have a harder time controlling your emotions and remaining calm. This often happens because people have unanswered questions or the misunderstanding makes them feel frustrated, angry, or negatively in another way.

Through the exercises and the techniques you will learn when you practice Stoicism, you will be able to satisfy your hunger for happiness. While people are generally happy, they often feel the need for more to completely satisfy their happiness. For example, when someone increases their income with a new job or raise, they will be happy and content with this income for a while but will feel a hunger for a larger income later. People who practice Stoicism won't feel this hunger as they are happy with what they have. Stoics don't have a list of desires that they feel will satisfy their happiness. This is because one of the many factors that Stoicism gives a person in their life is seeing the truth of situations, emotions, and life in general.

While Stoicism has a great definition, it's also very complex and goes way beyond any definition you will find on the Internet. For example, let's look at a can of soda. Soda is something that can be good or bad, depending on how you look at it. For someone who doesn't practice Stoicism, they will see the can of soda through their beliefs. In a sense, they will be either supportive or critics of the soda, depending on how they feel. If they love the taste, have a caffeine addiction, and don't pay attention to their health, they will be supportive of soda. However, someone who is focused on their health will be a critic of soda because of its health effects, such as high blood sugar levels and gaining weight. Someone who practices Stoicism, while they might have internal emotions towards soda, they would be able to control these emotions. Therefore, when the person decides to drink the soda or not, they make the decision in a logical way and not based on emotions.

Principles of Stoicism

Discussing the principles of Stoicism is a great way to explain what Stoicism is. There are several key principles to discuss, such as finding a mentor, acknowledging your emotions, how life goes on when you fail, be honest, reflecting on your time, and being present in every moment.

Rational Life is the Greatest Virtue

Emotions and irrational thoughts tend to cloud our mind. They make our mind foggy so we can't think in the ways we should when situations arise. When our minds become cloudy, we don't always think before we act or speak. Instead, we act irrationally and sometimes quickly, which could easily make the situation worse. We don't see the long-term benefits which can come from acting rationally instead of irrationally. Instead, we're looking at short-term gratification. This isn't what Stoicism is about. With Stoicism, you look at the long-term benefits over the short-term gratification.

Of course, people aren't perfect. No matter how well you practice Stoicism every day, you're not going to be perfect at thinking rationally with every situation. However, it is something you strive to do. Therefore, you will always strive to make the best possible decision. You will always strive to do what you can in these situations to remain calm. This is going to be harder when you first start focusing on the Stoic way of life. But over time, you will find that you start to think rationally in most situations and you're able to remain calmer when certain situations, such as emergencies, arise.

For Stoics, the grand purpose is to live a rational life. Therefore, Stoicism will help you achieve this purpose through your daily exercises and beliefs. Of course, you will need to have patience and understand that achieving a rational life will take time. It's not something that can happen overnight because we can't change our behaviors overnight. Changing behaviors is a process, but if you remain determined and focus on keeping a positive mindset, along with working to remain calm in situations, you will be able to reach the rational life.

Mindfulness

Mindfulness means to live in the moment. You're aware of your surroundings and pay attention to what's going on. For example, if you're driving to work on your regular route, you don't tend to let your thoughts drift you away from your task. This usually happens when people are repeating tasks every day. They become so used to their tasks that they tend to let their thoughts wander them away. Of course, they are able to accomplish the task, but they often wonder how because they don't remember completing all the actions. Think about a route you drive often. Have you ever gotten to your destination and wondered when you passed the lake or the grove of trees because you don't remember seeing these landmarks? This is an example of being mindless in a task, which is the opposite of mindfulness. If you were mindful, you'd remember all the landmarks you passed as you remained in the moment.

It's important for Stoics to remain mindful or in the moment at all times. This is because when you're mindful, you're more likely to think rationally and make the right decisions. People who are mindful are better equipped to control their emotions and actions. When people take themselves out of the moment, or they are mindless, they will run on instinct. Instead of making decisions logically, they will make decisions based on their emotions and might not be able to control their instincts.

One of the best ways to be mindful is to continue to focus on the task you are working on. For example, if you're writing a book, you will be able to get more writing done if you're mindful of your task and you focus on writing the book. If you let yourself become mindless of your task, you're less likely to get your book finished. We will discuss several exercises and practices which will help you work on mindfulness later in this book.

Purpose Reflection

We all want to know our purposes in life, and often this isn't a quick and easy answer. This can often take years to realize. No matter how long it takes you to try to figure out your main purposes, once you do, you want to reflect on those to make sure you're truly following your purposes. For example, you might feel that one purpose in your life is to help others. You decide to take time where you can volunteer at a food pantry. Here, you're given the task to check people in who are requesting to use the food pantry. You have to make sure they fill out the forms and prove their identity. It's your job to make sure that they are under the income guidelines and location restrictions before they can use the food pantry. While you know you're helping in the lives of many people, including the nonprofit you volunteer for, you also feel like you're not living your full purpose. Therefore, you decide to reflect and try to find out what your real purpose is while you're helping others.

Through this reflection, you know that you're on the right path, but you don't like the restrictions and guidelines you need to follow. You feel that anyone who needs food in their home should be able to receive that food. As you do some digging to further find your right direction, you notice the need your community has for food pantries. You then decide to go around and talk to executive directors of nonprofits who are in charge of food pantries. You realize that the main reason these guidelines and restrictions are in place are thatthere is so much need for food pantries that they have to focus on their target location. Because of the need and trouble securing enough food for their target location, they can't help people outside of it.

After you've completed your research, you decide that the best way to fulfill your purpose is to establish another food pantry. You learn there is an area in your community that no other food pantry targets. Through talking with members of this area, you find out they are often the clients turned away at other food pantries because they are outside of the pantry's target area. With this research, you find a couple of grants to help you establish a food pantry in the area. You also secure other funding, which helps you secure a building where you can build the food pantry. As you open the food pantry, you realize that you're fulfilling your purpose the way you want to. Even though you also need to be cautious of how much food is given out to people, you're able to focus on helping the community members who were being turned away by others as they didn't live in the correct area. You understood why the food pantries limited their clients and that you need to remain aware of this. But you continue to feel your purpose is fulfilled through helping your target community.

Ask Yourself Why

While you want to learn to control your emotions in Stoicism, you don't want to learn to ignore or try to become emotionless. Instead, Stoicism tries to make you understand your emotions, so you know why you're reacting the way you are. No matter how many practices and exercises you complete throughout your day, you will still find yourself responding emotionally to situations. In a sense, this is regular human behavior and something that you will learn to accept and work through.

One of the best ways to try to figure out why you're reacting out of emotion is to ask yourself why you're feeling the way you're feeling. For example, you're watching television, and you see a commercial about politics. You're not a person who pays attention to politics, but as you're watching this commercial, you start to become angry and frustrated. In order to understand why you reacted this way to a commercial, you ask yourself why. In your answer, you might realize that what made you angry is the way the candidates of the political parties treat one another in their commercials. As you thought about the commercial, you felt fine when the candidate was talking about what they would do in order to help the country. However, once the candidate spoke negatively about their opponent, you became angry.

However, you don't want to stop with this answer. You want to ask yourself furtherwhy you get angry when the candidates speak negatively about each other. Remember, as a Stoic, you want to try to dig as deep as you can in trying to figure out your emotional reactions. As you ask yourself the second why you realize you feel this way is because you see the behavior as disrespectful. Through digging some more, you realize that you feel the candidate should be respectful towards everyone, including their opponent as, to you, this makes the person seem like the ideal candidate and someone you can trust in their position of power.

You can ask yourself as many whys as you feel necessary. The point is to dig as deep as you need to so you can find out why you reacted so emotionally and so you can work on your control when the situation comes up again.

Procrastination Is Your Enemy

Stoicism focuses on time management. You use your time to help you live your purpose in life. Therefore, you don't want to waste your time. For example, if your purpose in life is to open a food pantry, you want to focus on finding ways to make sure people get the food they need in their homes and not waste time. If you waste time, you won't be able to help feed the families you need to help feed. This means you're not living your purpose to its full potential.

When you waste time, you're basically procrastinating. While we all procrastinate at one time or another, you will focus on your important life tasks which will help you fulfill your purpose. Through techniques and exercises, and you will learn later in this book, you will learn how to focus which will decrease any procrastination. Over time, you will realize that you're not able to fulfill your purpose through procrastination and will soon see procrastination as an emotion. This means you will realize that you can control it. Once you gain control of your procrastination tendencies, you will find yourself being mindful of your time and tasks.

Find a Mentor

A mentor is a trusted guide. They are someone that we go to when we need advice about certain situations in our lives. When we start to focus on staying mindful and controlling our emotions so we can make the right decision, we can struggle. When we behave a certain way for so long, they become habits, which are hard to break. This is especially true for people who are younger as they tend to lack self-discipline.

Self-discipline is the ability to control your feelings and gain determination to accomplish your tasks and dreams so you can be successful. This is a part of Stoicism which you will build during the techniques and exercise you learn later in this book. The younger we are, the harder it will be to learn self-discipline or change or behaviors, especially with emotions. One of the reasons for this is because people who are younger still deal with hormones, which can often change their emotions and make it harder for them to control these. On top of this, a person's mind doesn't stop developing until your 20s and into your 30s. These are some reasons it's important to find a mentor.

A mentor can help you, no matter what age, and learn the exercise, techniques, and the meaning of Stoicism. They can give you insight when you need it and help you through the consequences of your actions. A mentor can be anyone you trust to go to when you have a concern or problem. For example, you could find a mentor in a grandparent or other older relative, a teacher, pastor, or a friend's parent. The key points being able to trust this person and being comfortable enough to go to this person if you ever need help with something.

One of the biggest reasons mentors are so helpful is because they won't be affected by your choice. Therefore, they are able to look at your choices in a different way. They will also be an influence that can help you look at all sides of a situation, including pieces of the situation you don't see or understand. For instance, your mentor might be able to see that your mind is cloudy when you feel it's clear. Through discussing your options and concerns about a situation, they will be able to show you the right path.

Keep in mind that while your mentor can help lead you down the right path, it's up to you to follow your mentor's advice. Your mentor can't make you make one decision over the other. They are there to help you through the process, but they will let you make your own decision in the end. Therefore, you need to make sure you're listening to your mentor when you're trying to make the right decision.

Remember Failure Happens and Life Carries On

While you strive to be the best person you can be, it's important for you to remember that no one is perfect. You can work hard at a task and still fail. In Stoicism, you will learn that failure happens and life goes on. You don't want to continue to think about the task you did poorly on as you will welcome those negative thoughts and emotions back. The reality is, no matter how hard you try, you're not going to do great in every task. Sometimes you work hard and still do poorly. It's going to happen, and when it does, you need to remember that it's okay. Learn from your mistakes, see what you can do to improve, and move on.

A great way to think about this is that we learn from our mistakes. If you don't make mistakes, you're not going to learn what you need to do to change things. For example, you're given three tests during your math class for the whole semester. The first test you take during the first quarter, the second test is scheduled for the second quarter, and then you will have the final test. Your teacher informs you that your final test will be cumulative, which means it will be a combination of both your quarterly test. When you take the first quarter test, you get a D. When you look at the problems you got wrong; you realized they were all in one section. As you dig more into the reason why all these problems are wrong, you learn that it was because you missed a step in the formula. When this happens, you realize that you missed a step because you went too fast and didn't double check your work. Therefore, for the rest of the semester, you slow down and double check your work. For your next two tests, you receive a higher grade.

Fear is one of the strongest emotions that we feel. It's also an emotion that can keep us from accomplishing tasks which we want to accomplish. Therefore, you can have a fear of failure, which can cause people to not even try to focus and accomplish a task. When you practice Stoicism, you will work on controlling emotions, which means you can work on controlling your fear of failure.

It's important to remember that failure is okay as long as you learn from it. So don't let the fear of failure hold you back from accomplishing any goals and dreams you have in your life. If you let fear hold you back, you're going to miss dozens of opportunities. Instead of becoming fearful of the opportunity, you should look at the situations that can come with the opportunity. For example, if you think "What if I fail?", Try thinking of "But what if I succeed?". You can ask yourself what the worst possible situation is if you do fail and come up with a plan of action instead of trying to stay away from the situation because you're afraid of failure.

Money Reflection

Stoicism is a lot about reflection. You'll not only reflect on your purpose in life, but you will also reflect on other situations in your life, such as the way you spend money. When you focus on Stoicism, you're trying to be the best person you can be, and for many of us, money has a lot to do with this. The biggest reason money can be such an influence over us is because of the emotions associated with money.

If you have ever struggled to pay bills, you understand the feelings associated with money more than other people. Some people are lucky in that they don't have to worry about if they will have enough money for rent, food, or other necessities. However, this doesn't mean money doesn't cause stress in their lives. People might become stressed about money when they invest in something, such as the stock market.

Of course, Stoicism will help you separate the emotions you have and money as much as possible. This is one of the first steps in money reflection. You will start to separate your emotions attached to money. After you focus on separating your emotions and money, you will want to work on reflection. During this reflection, you will focus on how much money you spend. You will look at your income, your bills, and the amount you spend on groceries.

To help you reflect on your spending, you could download a money tracker on your phone. There are a variety of different money trackers that you could look at using.

- Mint is one of the most popular money trackers. Mint will connect to your account and help you track your spending. On top of this, it is free to use and also supports a great list of banking institutions.

- Penny is a money tracker who many people love because this app uses artificial intelligence to help you manage your money. People who don't like having to figure out spreadsheets and graphs are the people who like Penny. When you log onto the app, you will talk to Penny through a series of questions. It will analyze these questions and let you know where you sit on your spending. Through it, you can learn how you can change some of your spending habits to help you manage your money better. Another expense tracker similar to Penny is known as Wally.

- Clarity Money is an app which is topping the charts in the financial app category. It will help you manage your spending in comparison to your monthly income. It's an app which will help make sure that you're living within your means and not overspending.

Of course, you're not just going to want to focus on managing your money with apps. You're going to want to make sure you reflect on your spending as it's this reflection which will help you notice where you can change your spending and how you can make money less stressful in your life. You want to make sure you take emotions out of the money situation and focus on living within your means.

Time Reflection

Time is another big area you want to focus on when you're reflecting. When you can reflect on your time, you will take some of the same steps you do when you reflect on your money. You will focus on your time management aspect of your life and how you can improve this so you can have the best experience with your time and help yourself reach your main purposes in life.

Just like how you can manage your money with apps, you can also learn to manage your time apps.

- Toggl is a time management app which allows you to learn how much time you're spending on what task. You can keep your tasks organized with a way that's easiest for you and add notes, which can allow you to see what you were doing at a later date. You can also use it if you want to focus on time management for your team. While there is a free version of Toggl, to gain the best benefits, they suggest you pay a monthly fee.

- Timely is an app which is similar to Toggl. However, Timely will show you what work you have coming up over the next week and allow you to see how much time you will need to spend on what projects.

- Focus@will is an app which not only helps you manage your time but will also play music which is guaranteed to help you focus on your tasks. It is a newer app which has been through a series of scientific studies for confirmation that it will help people focus on their tasks and manage their time better. Unfortunately, there is no free version of Focus@will.

Of course, you can find your own ways to manage your time instead of using any type of app. The trick is for you to also reflect on your time management and find areas where you can improve your focus so you can gain the best focus for your purposes in life.

Always Be Honest with Yourself

While we know it's important, to be honest with the people around us, we also need to remember it's important, to be honest with ourselves. However, the difference is, when we are honest with others, we want to be honest in a way that's not brutal. With ourselves, it's often easier to be brutally honest. However, there is also a fine line with this as you don't want to be hard on yourself. You want to be honest with yourself.

If you're hard on yourself, you could easily gain low self-esteem. You want to be honest with yourself, so you can help improve factors of your life which could use improvement, not the opposite. The reality is, no one is perfect, and we sometimes like to make ourselves seem better than the next person. This is what you don't want to do. While you want to know your strengths so you can help those around you, you also want to be aware of your weaknesses, so you can improve yourself. This is a factor which will help you become the best person you can be.

One idea you can use is to see how you manage the same tasks compared to your peers. For example, if you notice within your college courses that your classmates tend to start their assignments before you do, you might want to think about managing your time better with your assignments. While you might be a good student, you might find that your grades will improve if you focus more on your assignments over the course of a number of days instead of working on an assignment in one day.

You want to be honest with yourself to help you benefit from the techniques and exercises you will learn later in this book. On top of this, being honest with yourself is a way to keep you more level. You don't want your ego to become too big.

Purposely Learn and Apply Your Knowledge

One of the best ways to think about learning is that you will never stop learning. However, on top of learning, you also want to make sure you're applying what you're learning. You can learn a lot of new things throughout the day, but if you don't start applying what you've learned, then what's the point?

As a Stoic, you want to take what you learn and apply it so you can not only better your life but you can also better the lives of others. You want to create a purpose for what you learn and your new knowledge and helping others is one of the best ways to do this.

For example, if you're worried about your finances but want to do more than just reflect on your spending habits, you can learn more about financing. There are dozens of books and websites available to you where you can learn how to manage your money better, invest, and how to save your money. If you have money lying around you want to invest in, you can look into the different ways of investing from a savings account to the stock market. Then, once you've learned what you need to learn, you can bring your knowledge to the world and help others. For example, you could create a self-help book. so other people can learn about saving and investing their money through you.

This is similar to a lot of the self-help books which focus on Stoicism and other ways that help people boost their self-esteem and happiness in life. People are focusing on ways to help improve their lives and then once they reach their highest potential, they decide they want to help other people do the same thing. Therefore, they write a self-help book so they can help guide others in a path to better their own lives. This is applying what they learned and using it to better the world.

Four Cardinal Virtues

Now that I've discussed several principles of Stoicism, I want to look at four virtues that tie into Stoicism. Like the principles, these virtues will not only help you gain a better understanding of Stoicism as a whole, but you will also be able to apply these virtues throughout this book and your life. They are a main part of Stoicism, so it's important to take a moment to discuss them. The four virtues are prudence or wisdom, justice or morality, fortitude or courage, and temperance or moderation.

Prudence / Wisdom

The first virtue I want to discuss is considered to be the most important, prudence or wisdom. Whether you want to refer to the virtue as prudence or wisdom is simply up to you. When you grasp the virtue of wisdom, you understand what is good, what is not good, and what is indifferent. Stoics use this virtue to help guide them in finding their ultimate good and using this good to help better the world. If you feel something is bad or indifferent, then you don't believe it's good, and you shouldn't focus your time on it. You also want to make sure you understand the good you're grasping rationally, as Stoics think in a rational manner.

Justice / Morality

When you think of justice, you don't just want to focus in the legal sense. You want to look at what is morally right or wrong, which is why some Stoics refer to justice as morality. It's the way we treat others. For example, if you want to teach someone the golden rule, which is to treat others the way you want to be treated, you would discuss this in terms of justice or morality.

Another great way to explain this is to show that this is the area where you think about kindness and compassion. Stoics not only believe that they should become the best person they can be, but they also feel that anyone can and should strive to become the best person.

Fortitude / Courage

The virtue of fortitude or courage simply states that you won't let fear control you. Remember, fear is a powerful emotion which is often negative in nature. Instead, you want to face the situations and factors in life that make you fearful.

Temperance / Moderation

No matter who we are, there are things we are going to enjoy more than others. These things we often want to do as much as possible. For example, we might enjoy the taste of alcohol and the bar scene. However, the virtue of temperance and moderations shows that we need to make sure to keep the things we enjoy in moderation. Therefore, you wouldn't want to focus on drinking so much every weekend that you get drunk. Instead, you might just go and have a drink and then drink some water or a regular soda.

Common Misconceptions of Stoicism

Because there is so much information in this chapter, I'm going to take a moment to recap some of the most important factors. First, you want to remember that Stoicism is not meant to teach you how to be unfeeling. You are still going to have your emotions, and you're still going to feel these emotions. Stoicism doesn't want to take away emotions from you. Stoicism is here to help you better handle your emotions so you can make a rational decision instead of decisions based on emotions.

Stoicism wants to help you learn how to process your emotions before you make a decision. If you don't learn to process your emotions, then you will make an irrational decision, which can harm you and those around you in various ways. For example, if you're excited, you might feel that you can accomplish more than what you truly can. Then, when you realize that you can't handle what you told yourself and others you can handle, you start to feel like a failure. But, this doesn't make you a failure; it just makes you a person that overestimated what they could do because of emotions. Remember, Stoicism also teaches us to learn from our mistakes. If you find yourself in this position, you can learn from the mistake so you can better estimate your task the next time.

Another reason it's important to take your emotions out of any decision you make is that other emotions can creep in when you realize you can't accomplish the task in time. For example, you could start to feel anxious, stressed, and embarrassed. These emotions aren't going to help you when you need to focus on a task. Stoicism wants to teach people how to focus on positive emotions and be able to better handle their negative emotions so people can achieve their purposes in life and become successful.

Stoicism focuses on giving you exercises and a mindset so you can become the best person you can be, not so you can become better than anyone else. This is often a common misconception among people who don't understand Stoicism. People who don't understand Stoicism often feel that those who practice are trying to be better than anyone else. But, the only thing a Stoic wants to do is focus on becoming the best person they can be so they can bring this good out to the world and help others.

To truly and honestly help another person, you have to be able to understand how to help the person. For example, if you want to help someone find their happiness, you have to make sure you're happy. If you want to help someone find their self-worth and gain high self-esteem, you have to make sure you understand your self-worth and have a good amount of self-esteem. Stoics not only want to help themselves find their highest happiness and self-worth so they can focus on their purposes in life, but they want to help others achieve their purposes as well.

Stoicism isn't a religion; it's a philosophy. Many people view Stoicism as a religion because many of the early Stoics discussed Greek gods in their writings. However, Stoicism is meant to be a philosophy. Think of it this way - religions tend to be concerned with how you act in this world because you want to reach Heaven. While this is a great way to think, it's not the purpose of Stoicism.

Stoicism wants people to achieve their ultimate good, so they can live the best life on earth. Stoicism doesn't focus on getting to an afterlife; it focuses on what you can do to make the world a better place for you and other people now. Of course, Stoics have nothing against any religion, and most Stoics follow their chosen religion. But, it's important to remember that it isn't a religion. It's a philosophy to help you learn the best way of life you can live.

Chapter 2: The History of Stoicism

In 300 B.C., Zeno of Citium founded the School of Stoicism in Greece. After this, Greeks started practicing the life of Stoicism, which focused on logic, personal ethics, and the natural world. At first, this school of thought was referred to as Zenonism. After being shipwrecked in Athens, Zeno started looking around the city. Over time, he came across a philosophy known as Cynicism and started to take part in its teachings. However, Zeno wasn't completely fulfilled by Cynicism. This was when Zeno started to his own teaching, which was influenced by Cynicism.

When people focused on teaching Stoicism, they brought their words to the streets. They wanted everyone to be able to hear their teachings. Because of this, people started to refer to Stoicism as the "philosophy of the street." People started to refer to Zenonism as Stoicism because of where Zeno taught his philosophy. He would stand at the Stoa Poikile, which means painted porch when teaching. Stoicism became the philosophy to follow in the Hellenistic world. In fact, Stoicism became so popular that several Roman Empires became Stoics. Chrysippus became one of Zeno's major followers and is credited for many Stoic beliefs today. Along with Chrysippus, many Roman Emperors helped shape Stoicism to what it is today.

Because the history of Stoicism is so large due to its lengthy timeline, historians like to break the history of Stoicism down into three phases.

- Early Stoa (300 - 100 B.C.) starts with Zeno and continues to Chrysippus, who became the third head of the School of Stoicism.

- Middle Stoa (100 - 0 B.C.) starts in the late second century and into the first century B.C. A couple of the most famous Stoics during Middle Stoa is Posidonius and Panaetius.

- Late Stoa (0 - 200 A.D.) finishes the first century and goes into the second century C.E. Many famous Stoics lived in this period, such as Musonius Rufus, Marcus Aurelius, Seneca, and Epictetus.

Unfortunately, no written texts from the Early and Middle Stoa timeframe survive today. However, there are some texts which survived from the Late Stoa Era. This doesn't mean the history of Stoicism is lost. We know that during the early days of Stoicism, many famous Stoics helped mold the philosophy, such as Cato, Seneca, Cleanthes, Epictetus, and Marcus Aurelius. These Stoics would take the teachings of Zeno and put their own beliefs in it. They would sometimes add to the previous teachings or debate the teachings of Stoicism. For example, Epictetus was a slave when he first started to listen to the Stoic teachings. Then once he gained his freedom, he started to teach Stoicism himself. While he taught the original teachings of the philosophy, he also added his own beliefs, which he wrote down in "The Enchiridion."

When people think of the days of Early Stoicism, they think of Zeno and how he started the school of thought because he didn't like the materialistic world. Another reason Zeno started Stoicism was that he didn't believe that the people had to experience pain in order to get to pleasure. Zeno started many of the beliefs that Stoics still teach today, and that you will learn in this book, but he also looked at the basics of Stoicism in three main ways.

- Logic

- Physics

- Ethics

Today, people tend to focus more on ethics than any of the other basics. However, logic and physics are still important pieces of Stoicism.

After Zeno, the next leader of Stoicism became Cleanthes, who followed Zeno's teaching very closely but did add some of his own beliefs. After Cleanthes, Chrysippus took over the school and focused mainly on logic, though he did take time to teach physics and ethics as well. Historians often credit Chrysippus with bringing Stoicism into the mainstream as after his time as leader. Stoicism became the most popular philosophy of the time. Zeno of Tarsus took over as leader of Stoicism after Chrysippus, and he was followed by a man named Diogenes. The last leader under the Early Stoa Era was Antipater.

Middle Stoa Era starts with Stoicism becoming popular in Rome. Panaetius was one of the first leaders under this Era. While he was less interested in teaching logic, he focused a lot on physics. Next, Posidonius took over as the leader and focused on building the school of thought in Rome. It was here that Cato the Younger and Cicero would join in on the Stoic teachings and way of life. Out of the two, Cato has become the most popular Stoic, who also changed a bit of the belief as he focused on several previous Stoic leaders such as Zeno, Chrysippus, Panaetius, and Posidonius.

The Late Stoa Era held many famous Stoics, such as Epictetus, Seneca, and Marcus Aurelius. The leaders of this era tended to focus on ethics more than logic or physics. Because this is the era where original writings survive, historians know the most about the Late Stoa Era compared to the first two eras. *Epistulae Morales ad Lucilium* by Seneca and *Ta eis heauton* or *Meditations* by Marcus Aurelius are a couple of the most notable works of this era. However, there is also *Discourses and the Enchiridion* by Epictetus, which is basically a handbook. To this day, people say that this handbook is one of the best ways to start learning about Stoicism. However, *Meditations* is probably the work that is easiest to find today. This work focuses on self-discipline and how you can improve yourself in the ways of a Stoic.

Chapter 3: Stoicism Through the Ages

Along with the history of Stoicism, it's important to understand how Stoicism has changed over the centuries. With the birth of Stoicism, many people started to view Stoics as passive, cold, and stone-faced. However, the Stoics were very different from the way they were perceived in society. They were active members of society, trying to spread their teachings so people can reach their highest potential and good. They wanted people to find their everlasting peace and happiness.

For about five centuries, Stoicism remained one of the most popular schools of philosophy. This is the pieces of Stoicism we discussed in the previous chapter, which included the Early Stoa, Middle Stoa, and Late Stoa eras. However, over time, Stoicism started to die down. In fact, the philosophy was almost completely forgotten. It wasn't until the 1970s when Stoicism started to find itself in the lives of many people again. The main reason for the revival of Stoicism was because of Cognitive Behavioral Therapy.

Cognitive Behavioral Therapy is a hands-on psychotherapy treatment which focuses on goals and problem-solving. It's a short-term therapy which wants to change the way people think and solve their problems so they can overcome difficulties and reach their goals. On top of this, Cognitive Behavioral Therapy is used to help change the negative way people think in a positive way. For example, if someone came in because of their anxiety, a therapist who focused on Cognitive Behavioral Therapy would figure out the negative thought patterns of the person. These negative thought patterns would be the reason for the person's anxiety. Therefore, the therapist would use techniques to help the person think more positively, which in return would reduce the person's anxiety.

Since Stoicism has started to make a comeback during the 1970s, many famous people have turned to Stoicism. If you're a football fan, you may be happy to learn that coach Pete Carroll uses Stoicism in his football tactics. A famous historical figure who followed Stoicism was President Theodore Roosevelt. Warren Buffett, an investor, and Bill Gates have also used techniques of Stoicism to help them succeed in their careers.

A couple of Founding Fathers of the United States were also known to have studied Stoicism in their time. One of the Founding Fathers was George Washington, who became the first official President of the United States. The other Founding Father was Thomas Jefferson, who was the author of the Declaration of Independence and third President of the United States.

There are many famous singers and actors/actresses which are also followers of Stoicism. LL Cool J is one singer who has been known to follow Stoicism. Actress Brie Larson has quoted from Marcus Aurelius's *Meditations* along with actress Anna Kendrick. JK Rowling, Ralph Waldo Emerson, and John Steinbeck are just a few famous authors who were known to follow the ways of Stoicism.

Because Stoicism is so helpful for many people, it has become a stable in the self-help area. Many books with a self-help focus have started to take exercises and principles from the Stoic philosophy and use them to help people overcome obstacles and find ways to better their lives.

Through the ages, Stoicism has developed, became almost forgotten, and found itself into people's lives in a way that its early leaders would have never imagined. Throughout the ages, Stoicism has focused on turning the bad into the good. Reframing negatives into positives has been at the heart of Stoicism. However, this doesn't mean we should avoid our shadows, and the necessary inner work should always be done to help us become a more whole and balanced human being. To just focus on one aspect means you're potentially missing out of something.

Chapter 4: Benefits to You as a Practicing Stoic

Once people start to practice Stoicism, they begin to realize some of the benefits of the philosophy are immediate. While there are dozen of benefits of practicing Stoicism, we will discuss several in this chapter. You might also realize other benefits as you practice Stoicism. It's important to remember that because we're all individuals, Stoicism is going to benefit us in many ways. Some of the ways will be conditional, meaning these are benefits that most people who practice Stoicism notice. Other benefits will be more individual, which are the benefits you might realize that aren't found in this chapter.

Controlling Your Emotions

Through the many teachings of Stoicism, you will learn to control your emotions. While Stoicism teaches you to control your emotions so you can focus on making rational decisions, you'll also learn that controlling your emotions is a huge benefit of Stoicism. Of course, the older you are, the more you will benefit from Stoicism when it comes to controlling your emotions. People who are younger are going to have a harder time due to hormones which are raging in their bodies. Therefore, if you're in your late teens or early 20s, it's important to note that you will naturally have a harder time controlling your emotions. This is okay. You will still be able to learn how to; you're just going to struggle with it a bit more than someone who is in their 40s or 50s. With this stated, it's important to remember that you need to be kind to yourself. If you find yourself making decisions because of your emotions, just take a step back and breathe. Don't lose patience with yourself or talk negatively about letting your emotions take control. Mistakes are a part of the process.

Understand You Can't Control Everything

One of the greatest benefits you will learn through Stoicism is that you can't control everything, and how to let go of what you can't control. Often, when we can't control situations, we start to feel stressed and worthless. Stoics refer to knowing what you can and can't control as the Stoic dichotomy of control. Once you understand what you can control and what you can't, your mind becomes free of the situations you realize you have no control over. This freedom releases a bunch of negative emotions which comes with being unable to control situations. Once you realize that you can control your thoughts, judgments, and actions, your mind becomes more clear, and you can focus on your ultimate happiness.

Live In the Present

Another benefit of learning Stoicism is you learn to live in the moment. When you live in the moment, you become mindful of your thoughts, actions, and judgments. Living in the present will help you achieve your tasks successfully.

Don't Care What Others Think or Say About You

Through Stoic exercises, you will learn that you don't care what people think or say about you. This happens because you know that you're doing well in your life. You focus on the exercises and your mentor to help guide you in the path you're supposed to take in life. You know that as long as you work hard to achieve your purposes in life, you're doing well.

Focus On the Positives

One of the best ways you can focus on establishing a better life for yourself and the people around you is by focusing on the positives. Stoics don't tend to focus on negative emotions because they often bring out other problems in a person's life. For example, if you focus on the negatives, you won't be able to be the best person you can be because you're not truly happy. If you don't have the right mindset, you can't focus on the factors you need to change in your life so you can achieve your greatest potential.

Strengthen Your Mind

Through their teachings, exercises, and principles, Stoics focus on strengthening their mind. When you strengthen your mind, you gain great knowledge which you can use to create a better world for you and the people around you.

You're Thankful

Through the techniques and exercises of reflection, Stoics focus on remaining thankful for what they have in their lives. They don't focus on the things they don't have or don't need. Instead, they spend their time focusing on their purposes in life and reminding themselves how thankful they are for the gifts God, nature, and whoever else has given them. This type of thinking gives people peace of mind which helps them lead a happy and healthy life. On top of that, they are able to focus easier on the positives of life and learn to handle their negative emotions easier.

You Focus On Helping Others

Stoics are not people who strive to ignore feelings and try to keep to themselves. They are people that focus on creating the best life and mindset they can for themselves so they can help other people. When they are able to help others, Stoics feel that they have accomplished one of their greatest accomplishments in life. No matter who you are, when you help someone else, you feel good about yourself, and this gives you a positive mindset.

Live Simply

Another benefit of Stoicism is that you live to live a simple life. This doesn't just mean that you learn to live without all the wants you have, such as a bigger television, nicer phone, or bigger house. It also means that you learn to live without the stress of feeling you're not good enough or you're not on the same financial level as your friend or neighbor. Instead, you focus on where you are in life and how you can change the things you need to change so you can fulfill your life's purpose.

Become the Best Person You Can Be

Most people live their lives trying to be the best person they can be. However, through this process, they often put too much pressure on themselves as they try to become perfect. Stoicism doesn't teach you that you're perfect. In fact, it teaches you that no one is perfect and the only way you can become the best person you can be is through Stoic exercises, principles, and teachings.

Stoicism teaches that instead of dwelling on the mistakes you make in your life, you learn from them. These mistakes will help you grow as a person, and they will help you reach your ultimate potential. You will also reach this potential when you focus on making the right decisions, which you will do when you realize you can control your thoughts, emotions, and actions.

Improve Your Mental Health

Another great benefit of Stoicism is it improves your mental health. There are a lot of factors in this world which can worsen a person's mental health. When your mental health worsens, you often deal with things such as anxiety, depression, and other mental illnesses. Through Stoicism, you learn to understand your emotions so you can make rational decisions. You also learn that you can't control everything and in turn, you learn to accept fate and move on.

There are many Stoic exercises and teachings that can help improve your mental health. Once you start practicing Stoicism, you will find yourself becoming happier and feeling better mentally and emotionally. You will start to realize that you have an important purpose in this world and through Stoic teachings, you will be able to reach your full potential.

Live Freely

Of course, you're still going to have situations and tasks that you have to do, such as going to your job and accomplishing your responsibilities, but Stoicism can also teach you how to live freely. There are a few exercises which will help you live freely, such as time reflection and deciding whether a task is worth your time or not. While we will go through both of these exercises in chapter 6, one of the greatest benefits of following Stoic teachings is that you will live more freely because you will manage your time better and complete tasks which are worth your time.

Chapter 5: Stoicism and Dealing with Death and Grief

Death is a common theme in Stoic texts because it's a common theme in our lives. No matter who you are, where you live, or what you do, you're going to know and love someone who is going to die. We all die, and there is nothing anyone can do about it. Therefore, instead of stressing over death and grief, Stoics find a way to handle the situation with a rational, calm, and peaceful manner.

When you read about death and grief in Stoicism, you will often run into the phrase "Memento Mori." This phrase is simply a reminder of death. It's a phrase to help Stoics remember that death is going to occur in their lives, that they can prepare for death, and that one day, they too will die. Once you reach this mindset, being able to handle death and grief will become easier. Of course, you will have to go through the seven stages of grief just like everyone else, after all these are stages that you go through as a human. For example, no matter how someone dies, there is a part of you which will feel shocked because you will always go through that phase of grief. It's hard to realize that you will never be able to talk, to give the person who passed away a hug or ask them how they're doing. While you will still go through the stages of grief, following the teaching of Stoicism will help you handle the stages of grief in the best way possible.

There are many ways Stoics focus on conquering death and grief. Of course, remembering that it's all around them is one way. However, other ways are through the many exercises and techniques you learn throughout this book. For example, death is something that we don't often control. Of course, there are ways in which we can control ourselves or someone else dying, but for the most part, death isn't controllable. Therefore, Stoics don't focus on death as something they control. They focus on death as a part of life, a fate, that they have to accept.

Because Stoics focus on processing their emotions in a logical way, they are able to process all the emotions that accompany death. For example, they won't fear death by focusing on exercises and techniques to help them overcome their fear. Along with this, they will learn to process the other emotions that are part of grief, such as anger, sadness, regret, and any other emotions we feel with it. Through their processes, Stoics will be able to handle grief in a more rational way. They won't suppress their emotions as this isn't what Stoicism teaches. By doing certain exercises or techniques, Stoics gain a better understanding of death and grief, which helps them overcome the situation.

Cherishing the memories of the loved one you lost is another way Seneca taught people to work through death and grief. This is a step that most people tend to do when a loved one dies. They will often share their memories and post pictures of their loved one.

Stoics also work through death by accepting it as fate and thinking about what they will do when it happens. For example, a Stoic might one day think "What would I do if I was told I have terminal cancer?" This technique helps a Stoic remember that one day they will die as one day everyone will die. This also helps a Stoic remember to treasure each and every moment of the day as if it was their last moment.

In his teachings, Seneca stated, "It's better to conquer grief than to deceive it." This ties in with fear and not letting death and grief control your life. Because grief is an emotion, you want to conquer it like you would conquer any other emotion. For a Stoic, letting yourself fall into self-pity over death isn't productive. A Stoic always wants to remain productive with their time, no matter what is going on or what has happened. A Stoic uses every situation as a teaching tool, and they do the same with death and grief.

Chapter 6: Practical Exercises of Stoicism

There are dozens of practical exercises of Stoicism. Some of these exercises you will find more useful than others. Some of them you might find a little silly at first - or at least the names - but it's important to follow through with the exercises as they will help teach you.

Don't just read through this list and pick out a few exercises that you think you want to focus on. Because it's so important to make sure you find the right exercises for you, try to practice all of these over a period of time. Maybe you want to do one exercise a day. Over the course of two weeks, you might find that you have time to focus on more than one exercise a day so then you start to focus on one exercise in the morning and one before you go to bed. You also might find that you use a few exercises when you start feeling stressed or find yourself thinking negatively.

These exercises are here to help you. They're not only here to help you find the best exercises for yourself and your lifestyle, but they're also here to help you learn more about the Stoic way of living.

This chapter is full of dozens of exercises. I wanted to try to fit as many exercises as I could inside of this book because I understand how everyone is different. I wanted to give you a place where you could find your favorite exercises to help you grow mentally and emotionally and didn't have to worry about doing your own research to find what exercises can help become the happiest and best person you can be.

1. What Would Batman Do?

Batman is a popular figure in today's world. When we think of Batman, we think of someone who spends his time trying to help people and make the world a better place. While this exercise might sound a little silly when you first read the title, it's a great simple exercise to help you think rationally. It's also a great way to help kids develop the knowledge for Stoicism as kids tend to really like the character known as Batman. Therefore, this exercise will be easy for them to remember.

The exercise is simple. All you need to do is ask yourself "What would Batman do?" or someone else you admire, whenever you are struggling to find a solution to a problem. It's the same thing as asking what your mom, grandpa, grandma, friend, or dad would do in a certain situation. Seneca said it best himself when he discussed this exercise:

"Choose someone whose way of life as well as words… have won your approval. Be always pointing him out to yourself either as your guardian or as your model. There is a need, in my view, for someone as a standard against which our characters can measure themselves. Without a ruler to do it against you won't make crooked straight."

While this exercise is titled "What would Batman do" doesn't mean you literally have to ask yourself what Batman would do. You could ask yourself "What would Jesus do?" or "What would Buddha do?" It really all depends on who your role model is.

Exercise Practice

You will want to use this exercise when you're facing a tough situation or decision. It could be any type of situation, such as wondering if you should change jobs or what to do when you're running out of time to finish a task. For example, if you're close to the deadline for a homework assignment and you wonder if you should ask for an extension or work all night on your assignment. You might ask yourself "What would my mom do?"

2. Imagine You're Dead

Before you ask yourself "What?" take time to read about what this exercise means. Marcus Aurelius was one who practiced this exercise when he said, "Think of yourself as dead. You have lived your life. Now take what's left and live it properly." So, what this exercise really means is that you want to focus on the dream and goals you want to accomplish. This exercise will help you put your focus on the things you still want to do that you haven't been able to complete yet. For example, you might think if you were to die today, what weren't you able to accomplish? Maybe you weren't able to establish the homeless center you want to open, or you weren't able to finish a project that you've been working on. On top of this, it can also make you think of what the most important factors of your life are, from your family to your career.

Exercise Practice

Take a moment to think that you passed away in your sleep last night but were given another chance at life. Now that you're on your second chance, you want to make sure you're focusing on the best parts of your life and the tasks you want to accomplish. You can do this by making three lists. In the first list, write down the goals that you still want to accomplish in your life. In the second list, write down what things are the most important in your life. In the third list, you can write down what you actually spend your time doing. Over the next few weeks or so, work on these lists and take notice of the changes you make in your life.

3. Voluntarily Make Yourself Uncomfortable

This exercise is supposed to help you learn how to handle fearful situations. You want to do something that you fear doing so you can work through your emotions and start to separate your emotions from the task at hand. The trick is you want to perform the uncomfortable action for a series of days as this will make you more comfortable. Another way to look at this exercise is it will get you out of your comfort zone.

Practice Exercise

Of course, what comfortable situation you put yourself in is up to you. However, here are some ideas to think about: lay on the floor in a public place, sleep on the floor, park your car in a public parking lot and sing with the music, go a period of time without caffeine.

4. Acknowledge Your Emotions

When you find yourself getting emotional over a situation, or you find yourself making a decision with your emotions, acknowledge these emotions. You can do this in many different ways from sitting down and thinking about your emotions to writing down what you were feeling and why. Remember, one of the techniques you can use to help you with this exercise is to ask yourself why as many times as you need to so you really grasp your emotions.

Practice Exercise

The next time you feel emotional whether it's in a situation or while you're making a decision, take time to write down the emotions you felt. You could do this by keeping a journal or simply writing your emotions in a Word document. Ask yourself why you felt these emotions during the situation. Work on really getting a hold of your emotions. You could even use a combination of exercises in this situation. After you write down your emotions, you could then ask yourself "what would Batman (or whoever) do?" You can then write down your answer to this question.

Try to do this every time you find yourself becoming overwhelmed with your emotions. Over time, you will really grasp your emotions and why they happen. This will help you in learning how to control your emotions as well as possible.

5. If Nothing Prevents Me

Stoicism isn't about learning to control everything you can; it's about learning to control what you can and learning to let go of what you can't control. The exercise "if nothing prevents me" will help you realize what you can and can't control.

Practice Exercise

Over the next few mornings, write down the tasks you want to accomplish that day. For example, you might want to accomplish reading a book. When you write down the tasks you want to accomplish, you also want to write down "if nothing prevents me" after the task. Therefore, your first task would say "I want to finish reading my book if nothing prevents me." This is basically adding a reserve clause to your task to let you know that sometimes we don't finish a task because of situations beyond our control. For example, you might not be able to finish reading that book because your basement might flood. This is a situation you couldn't control, and it prevented you from completing your task.

6. Love Your Fate

Love your fate is another exercise that helps you understand that you can't control everything, but you can accept what you can't control. In other words, instead of disliking or hating your fate, you learn to love it.

Practice Exercise

The best way to practice this exercise is to ask yourself if you can control the situation. If you can't, then just accept fate. If you can, then change the fate as you're in control.

7. Don't Gossip

Stoics don't focus on gossipping or conversations where they say things they shouldn't. While this isn't always easy to control, you can do your best to control what you say and what you don't say.

Practice Exercise

Whenever you find yourself in a crowd, think about the conversation going on around you. If you feel it's a conversation filled with gossip or negative talk, remove yourself from the conversation. You can do this by excusing yourself or by simply not taking part in the conversation. If you can't or don't want to leave the conversation, listen closely to see what helpful advice you can give those around you. In a sense, you want to turn the negative talk into a positive talk.

8. Choose a Person Who Will Keep You Honest

This exercise will help you in being honest with yourself and with others. It fits into the role model exercise, which we will discuss later. When you pick a person who will help keep you honest, you want to pick someone you know you can trust. This person will not only help in keeping you honest with yourself, but they will also help in keeping you humble by being honest about you.

Practice Exercise

Pick someone that you not only look up to but that you feel will be 100% honest with you. This can be a parent, best friend, or sibling. Once you pick the person, talk to them about what you want them to help you with. Let them know that you want to focus on being honest with yourself so this person's task is also to behonest with you and help you stay humble. Make sure they understand that they are to help you grow so you can not only accomplish your tasks but become the best person you want to be.

9. Find a Role Model

Everyone needs a role model or a few in their life. In this exercise, you will find a role model that you trust. You will want to pick this person carefully as you will use this person for several exercises to help you become Stoic. Therefore, this person will not only need to be honest with you but need to understand or be willing to learn Stoicism.

Practice Exercise

You might already have someone in mind who is going to become your role model in this journey. However, you might also be considering a few others. It will help you to create a list of the people you are thinking of and reflect on how they can help you reach your full potential through Stoicism. Some questions to ask yourself are: Will this person be willing to learn Stoicism? Does this person already know Stoicism? Do I trust this person 100%?

10. Early Morning Reflection

This exercise is about being thankful for the gifts of your life and reflecting on what you are about to accomplish that day. This is the time where you can write down your "if nothing prevents me" task list or simply take time to reflect on the positives of your life.

Practice Exercise

First, allow yourself time to accomplish this exercise every morning. If you're often rushed in the mornings, this means you will want to work on getting up earlier. Maybe set your alarm clock for 10 minutes earlier. Reflection is really as much time as you want to devote to it. During this time, you want to make sure you're in a quiet area of your home, and you want to focus on the positives of your life. For example, you could be thankful that you woke up healthy, your kids are healthy, or anything you feel is positive. You can be thankful for your career, home, wisdom, and strength.

11. Bedtime Reflection

This is similar to early morning reflection, but you do it before you go to bed.

Practice Exercise

Find time before you head to bed each night to find a quiet spot in your home where you can reflect on your day and be thankful for all the positives of your day. You can also use this time to reflect on your mistakes, but you don't want to dwell on them. Instead, be thankful for your mistakes and find ways to learn from them. Accept your mistakes, learn, and move on. Go to bed with a peace of mind.

12. Mirror Reflection

In Stoicism, you focus a lot on reflection, so there will be a lot of exercises where you reflect on situations and decisions in your life. Mirror reflection is done in front of the mirror. This type of reflection is helpful for people who are working on building up their self-confidence.

Practice Exercise

Stand in front of a mirror and think or have a conversation with yourself. Tell yourself what you're thankful for and what positives happened in your day. Similar to bedtime and morning reflection, discuss the mistakes you made, how you can learn from them, and be thankful for these mistakes because they will help you grow.

13. Practice Life Goes On

One of the principles of Stoicism is that life goes on after you make a mistake or fail at a task. In order to fully grasp this principle, it's important to practice it.

Practice Exercise

The next time you feel you've failed at a task or made a mistake, don't dwell on it. Instead, focus on accepting fate and simply move on with your life. You can do this by reflecting or telling yourself "It's okay. I will do better next time." Through practicing this exercise, you can find your way to make sure you understand that life goes on.

14. Think Before You Act

Thinking before you act is an important exercise for everyone to try. It will help you learn to react with logic over emotions. We often find ourselves in situations where we act without thinking. For example, you might yell at the car in front of you if you are prone to road rage or you might throw your pen on the floor when you're frustrated with a math calculation you're trying to solve.

Prac...tice Exercise

The ... time you feel yourself get angry or frustrated, find a way to calm down.
You ... do this by taking a few deep breaths or counting to ten. Once you feel
calm, reflect on the situation by asking yourself if getting angry or frustrated
make... sense. If it doesn't, find a logical way to act when put in that situation
again

15. Put Your Phone Away

We often find ourselves in situations which are uncomfortable or boring. When
these situations occur, one of the first things people do is take out their phone.
However, this takes you out of the present moment, which is not something you
practice as a Stoic. You want to remain present.

Practice Exercise

The next time you're out in public or visiting friends, keep your phone in your
bag, purse, or pocket. There is no need to take it out. Put your phone on silent, so
you don't even have to try to ignore it if you hear a notification or your ringer.
Focus on keeping present at the moment. Even if other people are on their phone,
focus on staying off your phone.

16. Time Is Precious

One of the main principles of Stoicism is time reflection. There are exercises
which can help you reflect on your time management. You can use this exercise
with the use of time management apps or without the use of apps.

Practice Exercise

One way to practice this exercise is to take time throughout your day and reflect. You can do this when you're at a stoplight or taking a break at work. Just stop and think about what you're doing and how helpful you are in this world. Think about all the time you put in to helping other people and working on your tasks successfully. Help yourself remember that your time is precious so you will continue to use your time wisely.

17. Pain Is in the Body, Not the Mind

Stoicism even trains you with exercises to help you handle pain. The philosophy does this by telling you the pain you feel is your body and not your mind. This thought also goes with sickness.

Practice Exercise

The next time you feel you have a headache, don't head to take Tylenol or Aspirin; instead, use this opportunity to gain strength. Power through the headache or lay down and take time to reflect on your day. If you're stressed, taking time to reflect might help your headache go away. If you start to feel sick, take a break. Take time to relax instead of continuing work.

18. Everything Is Borrowed - You Own Nothing

Stoics believe that everything is borrowed and they truly own nothing in this world. In fact, the only thing Stoics believe they really own is their mind. Because of this, Stoics believe that we don't want to get too attached to things, including our vehicles, pets, family, and friends. Stoics believe that people and things can leave as quickly as they come; therefore, it's important to value our time with them.

Practice Exercise

Take time to write down some of your favorite possessions, such as your laptop, television, Xbox, etc. Once you have your list, tell yourself that you do not own the item and reflect on how grateful you are that you can borrow the item from nature, God, or your fortune. You can say something like "Thank you a fortune for letting me borrow the laptop I use for work."

19. Remember Your Resources When Faced with a Challenge

We will always be faced with challenges in our life. It's important to remember the techniques, exercises, principles, and teaching of Stoicism when you're faced with these challenges as you can use these things to get through the challenge.

Practice Exercise

The next time you're faced with a challenge, ask yourself a series of questions to help you find the right exercise, principle, or technique from this book so you can overcome the challenge. For instance, you can ask yourself "What exercise will help me overcome this challenge?"

20. Count Your Blessings

Stoics are always very grateful for what they have in life, from the possessions they are borrowing to the gifts God has given them.

Practice Exercise

Take time every day to count your blessings. You could do this at any time during your day. You might do this while heading to work or when you're struggling with a task. You could even write down your blessings.

21. Worst Case Scenario

While the worst-case scenario isn't something people often want to think of, Stoics do. They reflect on worst case scenarios for situations because it helps them react in a calm manner if the situation arises.

Practice Exercise

You can take part in this exercise throughout the day. All you need to do is think about something you're going to do and imagine the worst case situation that could arise from your actions. You can do this by asking yourself questions like "What if this happens?" Then, you want to think of the best course of action to take. Remember, Stoics train themselves to stay calm in all situations, so you want to make sure your plan of action keeps you calm.

22. Only Buy What You Need

Stoics are minimalists. This means that they live with whatever they absolutely need. They usually don't go out and buy extra pairs of shoes, knick-knacks, or other items that are not necessary.

Practice Exercise

The next time you're out shopping and wondering if you're buying items you don't need, you can ask yourself questions like "Do I need this?"

23. Forgive Others

Stoics are quick to forgive others because they believe people always try to do what's right. Therefore, if someone makes a mistake, they deserve to be forgiven. On top of this, Stoicism focuses on remaining calm and happy. If you are focused on getting revenge or being angry at someone, you're only hurting yourself and wasting your time.

Practice Exercise

If you ever find yourself in a situation where you're being bullied, you can use this as a training exercise. Instead of focusing on what the person said, you can tell yourself that everyone has bad days and life goes on. Another way to work on forgiving others is to tell yourself that the person who did wrong didn't know any better.

24. Peace of Mind

Stoicism teaches people to find ways to remain calm in every situation. Telling yourself that you're going to focus on peace of mind is one exercise to help you remain calm. Epictetus said it the best when he stated, "Starting with things of little value – a bit of spilled oil, a little stolen wine – repeat to yourself: 'For such a small price I buy tranquility and peace of mind.'"

Practice Exercise

You can practice this exercise by repeating "I choose peace of mind" whenever you're angry or frustrated about a situation. For example, if someone cuts in front of you when you're driving, instead of getting angry just tell yourself "It's okay, things happen. I choose peace of mind."

25. Observe What's Around You

This is an exercise which can help you stay grounded, which is important teaching is Stoicism. This exercise ties into the principle where you're honest with yourself and also ties into time reflection.

Practice Exercise

Take time out of your day to go outside. Find a peace spot in the grass where you can lay down and stare at the sky, the clouds, and listen to the sounds of nature. During this time, reflect on the good you're doing and how well you spend your time focusing on your purposes in life. You can also take this time to be thankful for nature and your health. If you want, you can even write down your observations as this can help you grasp the teachings of Stoicism.

26. Meditation

Meditation is similar to reflection and can help you remain mindful throughout your day.

Practice Exercise

One meditation technique that can help you become mindful of your surroundings and stay in the moment is called mindful meditation. First, you need to find a quiet spot where you won't be interrupted. Then, you need to lay down or sit in a comfortable position. After that, you can close your eyes and start focusing on your breathing. You want to breathe normally as you start to clear your mind. After breathing normally for a bit, you want to focus on deep breaths. Breathe in slow and exhale slowly as you let your mind clear. Focus on your clothing as it's touching your body or lay one hand on your stomach and the other hand on your chest. Notice how the hand on your stomach goes up and down with your breaths while the hand on your chest barely moves. Once you've been able to clear your mind and you feel refreshed, you can get up and continue on with your day. While this technique might take a while, over time you will come to realize that you're paying more attention to what's going on around you.

At this point, it's important to say that if you start to notice your mind wander while you're meditating, be kind to yourself. Don't get angry because of it. Instead, just focus on clearing your mind and continue with your meditation.

27. Hang out with the Right People

Stoics believe that you're going to act like the people you hang out with. Therefore, it's important that you hang out with the right crowd if you want to focus on becoming the best person you can. If you hang out with people who make fun of you for practicing Stoicism, then you might stop practicing. You don't need to stop being friends or talking to them, just keep your distance so you can focus on establishing a better environment for yourself. Of course, you can always try to get them to listen to Stoic teachings, but you can't force anyone.

Practice Exercise

The next time you're out with your friends, pay attention to how they act and if you agree with the way they act. If you don't, be honest with them and let them know your feelings. However, you will want to remember to remain calm and be as kind as possible when you're honest with them. If they don't care about how you feel or ignore you; you might want to reflect on the type of people you want to associate with. Don't get angry or frustrated at them; try to understand where they are coming from. However, remember that people often act like the people they hang out with.

28. Don't Do Anything Because of Habit

While you won't always be able to ignore your habits, especially the route you take to and from work, the most you keep yourself from doing things out of habit, the easier it will be to remain mindful.

Practice Exercise

There are many techniques you can use to remain mindful when you have to do things out of habit. For example, you can look for landmarks that you will pass on your way to work. If you change something within your habit, you're more likely to remain mindful while performing your habit.

29. Ideal Human Being

This exercise focuses on helping you to become the best person you can be. To do this, you need to imagine what type of person you believe is the ideal person. Don't focus on who the perfect person is because perfectionism doesn't exist when it comes to people. You want to focus on your ideal self.

Practice Exercise

One of the best ways to focus on who you want to become is to think of how you want people to remember you. You could even ask yourself "If I die today, how would I want people to remember me?" Would you want people to remember how thoughtful, compassionate, and determined you are? You can take time to write down the traits you would want people to remember you by and then focus on improving those traits in your life.

30. Become a Philanthropist

Many people feel you need to have money or be rich in order to be a philanthropist, which is someone who promotes the welfare of other people. However, philanthropy has nothing to do with money. It has to do with helping others to make sure they are taken care of and given the necessities they need in life. Therefore, anyone can become a philanthropist as it just requires the right attitude when it comes to people.

Practice Exercise

The next time you're in line at the grocery store and someone is behind you, start talking to them. No, you won't know this person, but that's the point. You want to talk to a stranger. You could ask the person how they are doing, talk about the weather, or anything else you can think of. If you notice something about the person, for example, they are a veteran, you could thank them for their service.

31. Self-Retreat

In talking about a self-retreat, I don't mean actually going on vacation or traveling to a spa. I am talking about finding peace of mind inside your own home. It doesn't matter if someone is watching a movie next to you or your kids are playing a game in the background. Challenge yourself to find peace of mind amongst the noise in your own home.

Practice Exercise

The next time you're feeling a bit overwhelmed by the noise of your home, your job, or anywhere, take a moment to go into a self-retreat mode. You can do this by working on some meditation techniques or reflecting on the positives inside your mind. You want to focus on calming yourself so you can reach your peace of mind.

32. Imagine Bad Things Happening

Usually, people want to focus on good things happening as they believe this will boost their self-esteem. However, Stoics believe that if you imagine negative things happening, you're going to be able to focus on the positive parts of your life easier. For example, you could imagine where you would be if you never met your spouse or what would happen if your house burned down.

Practice Exercise

If you're more comfortable starting out small with this exercise, that's what you do. You don't have to imagine someone dying, but you could imagine something like failing a course in college or failing out of college. Once you imagine the negative happening, turn around and focus on the positives. For example, you're still in school and will not be more thankful that you're still a college student. You will probably start studying harder because you don't want to fail a course or flunk out. If you continue on with this exercise, you can start imagining other negative situations, including national disasters. You could also add a plan of action as an additional exercise. For instance, what would you do if your community was flooding?

33. Post-It Notes

Post-it notes seem to be everywhere in the homes of people. It's on these notes that we write daily reminders to ourselves, such as 'pick up soap' or 'get help from Skye.' However, we can also use Post-it notes to give ourselves positive reminders or help us to reflect on our lives.

Practice Exercise

If you don't have Post-it notes, you can go out and buy some. Or you can create your own notes with the paper you have around the house. The trick is to place these notes in areas where you will see them often. For example, the mirror in your bedroom, on a table by your bed, next to your purse, etc. If you want to focus on reflecting throughout your day, you could write a note about a reflection. For instance, you could write "Reflect on my job responsibilities" which can help you reflect on your job that day. If you want to focus on the positives of your life, you could write "What is one great thing that happened today?" You could also use this as a way to focus on the positives by thinking of a negative by writing "What bad thing happened today and what good thing happened today?" What you write is up to you.

34. Visualization Board

This is a newer exercise that often helps you focus on your goals and makes you determined to overcome your obstacles to reach your greatest potential. A vision board is basically a board you create with what you want to accomplish over a certain period, for example, six months or a year. Vision boards are easy to make. All you need is cardboard, images from magazines or online which you cut out to place on the board, scissors, glue, and then a place to set up your board which will allow you to see it every day.

Once you have all the supplies, you can rearrange your vision board however you like. You want to focus on what goals you want to accomplish over the year. For example, you might want to meditate every day, make sure you do your morning and evening reflections, and you might want to focus on eating healthier. Whatever you want to do in order to reach your ideal potential and behavior as a person, this is what you put on your vision board. Once you've completed your vision board, place it in an area where you can view it often. For instance, you could place it in your bedroom and reflect on where you are every evening. You can reflect on what steps you took that day to reach the goals on your vision board.

35. Self-Help Books

As I've discussed before, Stoicism is a popular philosophy in self-help books. One of the best ways to learn more about Stoicism is to look at other materials that will help you grow in philosophy.

Practice Exercise

You can start this exercise by seeing what type of information is out there. You could actually go to the end of this book and check out the references I used to help me create this book. You could also go on Amazon and see what type of books are available to help you. Remember, Stoics are here to help you so you can reach your potential good just as anyone else can.

36. Giving Up Your Addictions

There are many things people get addicted to, while the most common addictions people think of are alcohol and drugs; these aren't the only addictions. People can also be addicted to coffee, energy drinks, checking their email, and checking their phone. Most of our addictions that take over our lives, we don't even realize because we automatically do them every day.

Practice Exercise

For this exercise, you want to start by thinking about your addictions. You could create a list of the things you believe you're addicted to, such as caffeine, your phone, your iPad, laptop, gossiping, or biting your nails. Once you have your list, you can start working on overcoming your addiction. Of course, you might add to your list as time goes on and that's okay. The point is to get yourself to a place where you don't let your addictions control your life. Instead, you control your addictions. For example, if you want to not depend on your cell phone so much, you might only check it a couple of times a day.

37. Cut the Ties

Cutting the ties will help you focus on limiting what you buy and becoming a minimalist. There are tons of advertisements for us to view on a daily basis. Usually, these advertisements will give us a good deal on the things they want us to buy. It seems that no matter where you go, there is someone that wants to dig in your pocketbook.

Practice Exercise

Cut the ties for the advertisements and people who want to dig into your pocketbook. Don't buy into the deals that a restaurant or store has on their products; it's just a way to get you to buy their items, along with other stuff you don't need. Only focus on the items that you need. If you notice a bunch of advertisements on your Facebook page, disregard them. In fact, sometimes you are able to tell Facebook to stop showing certain advertisements. Otherwise, just scroll past them. Tell yourself you don't need what they are selling.

38. Calm Your Anxiety

Epictetus stated, "When I see an anxious person, I ask myself, what do they want? For if a person didn´t want something outside of their own control, why would they be stricken by anxiety?" There is really no other way to figure out what is causing your anxiety so you can focus on calming it than to follow Epictetus' advice.

Practice Exercise

The next time you start to feel anxious, ask yourself what you want that is outside of your control. Then you can focus on finding out why you want this and using other exercises to help you overcome your anxiety and reach a calm state.

39. Just Start Living

Some people can jump right into things while others need to take their time. This exercise might be more for people who can just jump head first into things. What this exercise does is literally tell people just to start living. Don't worry about the things you can't change, focus on what you can, do what you want, and live your life the best you can.

Practice Exercise

Before you just jump in and start living, you want to ask yourself what are you living for? You want to ask yourself, why do you spend time fearing death when death is going to happen to every single one of us? What are you trying to do when you're trying to remain in your comfort zone? For example, are you spending hours watching television, gossiping, or surfing the Internet? Instead of keeping yourself tied down because you're afraid of dying, go out into the world and do whatever you want to do because you want to live your life to the fullest. Remember, no matter what you do, you're going to die one day. Therefore, you want to make sure to live while you can.

40. You're Not Breakable

Yes, our feelings can be fragile, but you're not breakable. This is an important piece of information to remember when you are faced against a bully or someone who is trying to bring you down. You need to remember that the person can say mean things about you or to you, but they can't break you. The only thing you can do is allow them to bring you down emotionally. However, you don't have to allow this to happen either. It's your choice to allow the person to bring you down emotionally.

Practice Exercise

Because you're human and you have emotions, you might take time to feel down when someone says something mean to you. However, it's your choice to allow yourself to feel hurt by the person's words. In order to move on from what the person says and not allow yourself to fall, victim of a negative mindset, you can tell yourself "I am not breakable. No one can break me. I am as strong as a chain." Of course, you can find your own way to tell yourself that you're not breakable, but you want to tell yourself in a way that will make your mind believe your words. While people can break your bones, they can't break your mind or your spirit. It's your choice to let them break your spirit. Your mind can never be broken.

41. Stop and Be Grateful

One of the biggest things that you can learn from Stoicism is to be grateful for what you have in life. There are many exercises which focus on being grateful through various points throughout your day. One of these exercises is to take a moment throughout your day and literally thank God or whoever you want for what you've been blessed with in your life. You can even stop and think to yourself (or say out loud) "I am grateful for everything I have."

Practice Exercise

In order to get into the swing of taking a moment throughout your day to be grateful, you might want to schedule times. You can do this mentally or by setting some type of alarm on your cell phone or your watch. For example, you can decide that on every even hour of the day (12:00, 2:00, 4:00, etc.) you're going to stop and tell yourself that you're grateful for everything in your life. You can also mentally decide to do this while you're struggling with a task or each time you sit down to eat a meal.

42. Don't Overbook Yourself

Seneca stated, "The mind must be given relaxation—it will rise improved and sharper after a good break." Since then, no one has said it better. In order to be able to reach your full potential, you need to make sure that you're not doing more than what you should be doing. After all, if you're overstressed or feeling overwhelmed by all your tasks, you're not going to be able to find the peace of mind or focus on the exercises you need to reach your ultimate potential.

Practice Exercise

Take a moment to reflect on all the responsibilities you assign yourself, and others assign you. Then, take a moment to reflect on your time and not what time you have for what tasks and what time you need to take for your mental health. Establish a time to make sure that you're able to focus on yourself so you can find your peace of mind. If you need to get rid of some responsibilities, see which ones you can weed out of your schedule.

43. Get to Know Yourself Better

To reach your full potential, you have to get to know yourself the best you can. Dig deep within yourself so you can start to learn what you are capable of and what good you have in your heart. You can do this in several ways, such as through reflection or even writing. You can focus on asking yourself questions, such as what are your goals, dreams, and desires in life? You can ask yourself where you want to be in five years. For example, do you want to graduate from college, get married, start a family, or start a new career?

Practice Exercise

You can do start this process by asking yourself a variety of questions. For example, you could ask yourself what you would do in certain situations or to help people. You could even ask yourself what your real feelings are about things going out in the world. This is a conversation with yourself, so there is no need to worry about other people judging you. Get to know yourself, be honest with yourself, learn about what great talents you hold, and learn about your own kindness and love.

44. Be Kind to Everyone

There will always be people in your life that you feel don't treat you or someone else right. While most people often feel the mean person should be given the same treatment, Stoics have a different take on how to handle people who are mean. Stoics state that you should be kind to this person. The thing to remember here is people who are kind when other people are mean, rude, and disrespectful are the people who have amazing internal strength. A big part of Stoicism is building and using your strength. You're able to do this when you're placed in a situation with a mean individual.

Practice Exercise

The next time someone says something mean to you, you can start to be kind by smiling at the person or saying something nice to the person. While this person might not know how to react, you will feel better about yourself because you just showed how much internal strength you have when someone is disrespectful to you.

45. Don't Judge People

Stoicism teaches us not to judge. This philosophy states that everyone has their flaws and no one is perfect. Therefore, there is never any need or time to judge.

On top of this, judging is a negative action. It's similar to gossiping and goes against trying to find your positive balance in life to reach your ultimate best self.

Practice Exercise

This might be a difficult exercise because you might not even realize how much you actually judge people. This isn't your fault, but it is your choice. The reality is, we live in a world where people judge one another constantly. When this happens, we become so used to it that we don't even realize we are taking a part of it. Therefore, in order to work on this exercise, you want to make yourself very aware of your thoughts and your actions.

You can start by writing down statements that you feel are a judgment towards someone. You can even carry this notebook with you or use the notepad on your cell phone. Every time you hear someone say something in a judgemental way towards another person or you catch yourself saying something judgemental, write it down. Then you want to reflect on how you can change the behavior, so you don't continue to judge people; what you can say instead that wouldn't be judging the person. Or you might want to focus on just stopping the judgemental thoughts. Write them down and then note that you won't say something like that towards someone again.

46. Watch What You Say

This exercise can tie into not being judgemental. You want to focus on watching the words that come out of your mouth so you can make sure they are kind words that can help someone and not hurt someone's feelings.

Practice Exercise

The phrase "think before you speak" can be useful in this exercise. You can start to complete this exercise in different ways. If you're a writer, you can write down the types of things you should say and the types of things you shouldn't say. This can give you a visual example to make you more aware of what kind words are and what mean words are. You can also just start to focus on being mindful when you're about to speak and actually think before you say anything. Before you're about to tell someone something, you can ask yourself if what you're about to say is going to help the person. If it's not, then you might want to think twice about what you're about to say. You can always work on rephrasing words into a more positive and polite way.

47. Go for a Walk

Research has shown that going for a walk will not only help our mood, but it can also help to clear our mind so we can focus on tasks in front of us.

Practice Exercise

If you're struggling to implement some of these exercises or you feel that you can't concentrate on a task, then go for a walk. Take your iPod or phone so you can listen to music or just go for a walk and listen to the sounds of nature. You can walk however long you want. For example, go for a 20-minute walk and then come back and return to your task.

48. It's Okay to Ask for Help

No matter what the task is, it's always okay to ask for help. You can ask anywhere you're comfortable with. This is often another reason Stoics focus on finding a mentor or role model. It allows them to find someone they trust to go to if they have a question or concern.

Practice Exercise

If you haven't found a mentor yet, now is the step to take that action. Find someone that you can trust so you can ask them questions. You can also reach for help through any of the Stoic communities online. Of course, your friends and family are always ready and willing to help when you ask.

49. Look up at the Stars

Stoic Marcus Aurelius talked about looking up at the stars best when he stated, "Watch the stars in their courses and imagine yourself running alongside them." While many people already look up at the stars, it's a great way to help you reflect and focus on becoming the person you want to be. Looking up at the stars can help you realize that the struggles and obstacles you face in the world aren't that bad as there areso much beauty and a world beyond what we are living now that is so much greater.

Practice Exercise

Find a calm and quiet night where you can take a blanket, go outside, and observe the stars. Of course, you can always lay in the grass and forget the banket! When you're looking at the stars, imagine yourself walking or running alongside them. Notice the peace of mind you feel and how everything that's bothering you in this world doesn't compare to the bigger picture of the sky.

50. Trust Yourself

Sometimes we struggle completing tasks or even completing these exercises because we don't trust ourselves. There can be many reasons for this, such as lack of confidence in our abilities. In order to overcome your obstacles and take on the world as you want to, you're going to need to learn to trust yourself. Of course, this can take time just like many other exercises will. It's not easy to change your beliefs, but you will be able to overcome this one step at a time.

Practice Exercise

You can start to trust yourself by writing down tasks that you know you can accomplish. They can be large tasks, such as writing a book, or small tasks, such as making coffee every morning. The goal is to find a foundation of trust within yourself, so you can start to build that trust with other tasks. Once you've established your foundation, then you can write down tasks that you don't fully trust yourself completing. For example, this could be grilling hamburgers or learning how to drive. When you're writing down these tasks, you can write down the reasons why you don't trust yourself.

Once you have completed this list, start to mark things off your list by doing them. You will come to find that you can complete the tasks easier than you thought. You can start by the smaller tasks and work your way up to the larger tasks, or you can mix them. For example, you can work on a smaller task and then a larger task. You might even work on two tasks at the same time. However, when you start to build your trust with the first one or two tasks, you might want to start small as this will help you start to build your trust.

51. See Opinions as What They Are

Everyone has and can have their own opinion. People often get into a debate about opinions and often this debate makes someone, or both parties involved frustrated or angry. Sometimes people stop being kind to each other because of the difference of opinion and other times people become so angry they yell or cry because they feel so strongly. As someone who practices Stoicism, you don't want to fall into this heated debate with opinions. You want to respect everyone's opinions and just let them be what they are.

Practice Exercise

You can really practice this exercise at any moment because opinions are easy to find. For example, you can run across someone's opinion on social media that you don't agree with or you can hear someone's opinion that you don't agree with. Instead of stating your opinion and getting into a heated debate about your opinion and the other person's opinion, you can simply let the opinion go. While this might take some time, the more you realize that everyone has an opinion and this is okay, the more you will be able to let the opinions be as they are.

52. Focus on One Prize

The biggest thing that helped people like Bill Gates and Warren Buffett reach their ultimate potential in their career is by focusing on one prize. They decided to aim for one goal, and they did whatever they could to achieve this goal. For example, Warren Buffett is worth well more than $60 billion, but he has never purchased a new house. He still lives in the same small house that he and his wife bought in the late 1950s for a little over $31,000. Buffett, who is a Stoic follower, has never wanted to purchase more than what he and his family needed.

Practice Exercise

In this exercise, you're going to start by writing down all the goals you want to accomplish in your life. Then, you're going to look at your list and focus on one goal that you want to accomplish. This can be any goal from graduating from college to saving so you can purchase a newer vehicle. Once you pick your one goal, you're going to focus on that. This goal is going to become your prize. You will continue to strive towards completing this no matter how long it takes you. For example, if you want to purchase a newer car, you might have to save up money for a downpayment before you can look into other financial means to purchase the car.

53. Pick a Wise Person to Model

This exercise is similar to picking a role model or a mentor, but yet it can be done differently. We all find people that we look up to throughout our lives. Sometimes we know these people well, and sometimes these people don't even know we exist. It's okay to pick someone you believe is wise to help you overcome your obstacles and help you follow the right path for your life. But, it's important to note certain personality traits about the person you pick to be your model because you want to make sure you're looking up to a person who is going to help you overcome your obstacles, succeed, and become the best person you can be.

Practice Exercise

In this exercise, you're going to pick someone to model. You don't have to talk to this person, but you have to notice enough about this person's personality that you learn what you want to do and don't want to do. For example, you might pick a celebrity you really like. In order to learn as much as you can about this person's personality, you might watch interviews, movies, listen to their music, etc.

Through all this, you should be able to pick out traits that you will feel will help you become a better person. At the same time, you should also be able to pick out traits that you don't want to follow. For instance, if the model you decide is known to be very kind and generous, you will want to follow these traits. However, if you also read that your model has a temper, you won't want to follow this trait as it won't help you become the best person. Remember, a part of Stoicism is to remain calm and focus on positive feelings. Negative feelings won't help you become the best person you can be.

When you're picking a model, you don't need to worry about how many faults the person has. You need to worry about what behavioral traits you can learn from your model so you can reach your highest potential. Remember, Stoicism believes that every person makes mistakes, but the philosophy also believes that you can learn through these mistakes to help you become the best person you can be. On top of learning from your own mistakes, you can also learn from others'. Therefore, if your model makes a mistake, you can learn from it.

54. Let Go of a Few Things

There are a lot of things in this world that we feel we have to follow. For example, we often feel we need to keep up on politics because it's our civic duty to vote. However, this isn't true. If you are paying attention to things that frustrate or anger you, including politics, you can let them go. There is no law that states you have to follow politics as an American citizen. The great thing about being an American is you have the right to choose whether you take part in politics or not.

Practice Exercise

One of the best ways to practice this exercise is to let go of the media materials you come across in your daily life that bother you. For example, if you are following a couple of Facebook pages which often post comments about President Trump or political news, you can stop following the pages. If you get bothered by the local news because all you hear are the negative situations going on in the world, you don't have to listen to the news media reports. It's your choice whether you listen to these reports or not. If you want to reach your highest potential, you can find ways to overcome the obstacle of anger and frustration you feel with these. You can do this by simply letting go of the reports and not paying attention to them anymore or through another exercise in this chapter.

55. Do I Feel Better?

You can try this technique on yourself or someone else. It's a question you can ask someone if they are crying or yelling because they are frustrated or angry. You simply ask them "Is your behavior making you feel better?" Chances are pretty good that their reaction to their situation is not making them feel better; in fact, generally negative reactions over negative situations always makes us feel worse. Instead, it's best to focus on a solution to your problem in a positive way. For instance, if you're angry because your computer is running slow, you can stop focusing on how slow your computer is running and take a break or go for a quick walk. Then come back and try to figure out why your computer is running slow.

Practice Exercise

It's best to practice this technique on yourself before you start to help others with this exercise. In fact, it's always best to practice any of these exercises on yourself before you try to help other people. After all, if we practice the exercises ourselves, we will be more prepared to answer any questions that the other person might have. Plus, we will be better prepared to deal with the situation. Remember, you always want to be kind and gentle when you're trying to help someone else overcome their obstacles. Sometimes, we can't find kind and gentle ways to help people unless we are able to master the exercises of this book first.

To practice this exercise on yourself, all you have to do is ask yourself "Is my behavior/mood helping me feel better about the situation?" the next time you start to get angry or frustrated over something. For example, if you become so frustrated about all the work you need to do that you start to cry, ask yourself if crying is helping you feel better. You could also ask yourself if crying is helping you accomplish your tasks. The answer you give yourself will be no, which means that you need to focus on changing your behavior and reaction so you can accomplish the task you're frustrated about.

56. Protect Your Peace of Mind

You're going to work hard to gain your peace of mind. There are going to be dozens of exercises out of this book that you will use to help establish it. Once you have established your peace of mind, you need to protect it. Think of it this way - when you work hard to achieve something; you want to protect it because of all the hard work you put into it. You want to treat your peace of mind the same way and protect it because you will work hard reaching this state. On top of that, you should always want to protect what's positive in your life because all your positive personality traits will help you become the best person. You will be able to achieve your ultimate potential by protecting your valuable and positive personality traits.

Practice Exercise

No matter what situation you find yourself in, you want to make sure you're protecting your peace of mind. You want to keep this exercise in mind the next time you're in a stressful situation. You can work on protecting it by asking yourself "Is this really worth it?" or "Why am I allowing myself to go through this situation?" For example, if you're in a very stressful job and you find yourself asking these questions often, you might want to think about making a change. While it might seem like changing jobs is drastic, you want to ask yourself, is your stressful job worth losing your peace of mind?

57. Know Your Freedom

Epictetus once wrote, "The person is free who lives as they wish, neither compelled, nor hindered, nor limited— whose choices aren't hampered, whose desires succeed, and who don't fall into what repels them..." This is an important exercise to take in because our lives are so busier than the lives Epictetus and other early Stoics lived. On top of this, they didn't live in the technology advanced times as we do now. Therefore, it's extremely important to understand your freedom when it comes to your time.

Of course, I'm not talking about our jobs responsibilities or family obligations. I am talking about the time we spend trying to impress people that we don't need to impress. For example, when you find out that company is coming over, you decide to focus on cleaning your house as well as you can. You want to impress your visitor with a clean house and don't want them to feel like you live in a messy house. When you believe you have to make sure your house is spotless for your company, you are limiting your freedom by giving it to your company.

Practice Exercise

Before you decide to spend hours trying to make sure your house is perfect for your company, ask yourself if it's really necessary. How do you want your home to look for you? Your home should impress you because you live there. You pay the bills, and you take care of the family that lives inside of the home. Your company doesn't need to be impressed by your home.

You can practice this exercise with any obligations you have in your life. You can do this by creating a list where you write down your obligations. Then, you can go through each and ask yourself if the work you're doing is really necessary. Is the work you're doing for this obligation worth giving up some of your freedom?

58. Put Yourself in Someone Else's Shoes

You have probably heard a phrase like this a lot in your life. There are many phrases that tell us to put ourselves in someone else's shoes before we judge them. For example, we're often told to "walk a mile in their shoes." Stoics believe this is a very good exercise because it helps us so we don't judge another person and it helps us to understand the faults of another person. Remember, nobody's perfect, and everyone makes mistakes. When we put ourselves into someone else's shoes, we can learn to understand why the person behaves a certain way.

Practice Exercise

Socrates, who followed the Stoic belief, stated that no one means to do something wrong, meaning that everyone who does something wrong does so by accident. This is a great statement to remember when you are trying to think about why someone did something wrong. It's also a great statement to remember when you try to put yourself in the person's shoes so you can better understand why they did something wrong.

To put this exercise into practice, the next time someone does something you see as wrong, try to view it as they thought what they were doing was right. Go in with the mindset that no one means to do something wrong. This will help you become more understanding of the mistake the person made.

59. Beauty Is On the Inside

When Stoics think of beauty, they think of the person's actions and beliefs and not what they look like. Sure, you might be beautiful on the outside. You might work out and look fit, but if you're disrespectful to people, Stoics won't see your personality as beautiful. They will see you as someone who hasn't reached their highest potential. However, Stoics will also believe that you can reach your highest potential; you just have to follow the ways of Stoicism in order to reach your potential.

Practice Exercise

Focus on who you are on the inside and not what you look like on the outside. I realize that this can be tough in this world because people are always judging other people by the way they look. However, you can use other exercises from this book to overcome that obstacle. For example, you can look at listening to the media telling you how you should look if it is worth your time and freedom. Of course, it's not.

Spending your time and freedom working on achieving your ultimate potential is more important than listening to the media or someone telling you how to look beautiful. Instead, write down what you can do in order to focus on your inner beauty. For example, you can let people know that you treat them like family and they can always come to you for help. You can also talk to a stranger at the park or help someone carry their groceries to their vehicle. There are dozens of ways you can focus on your inner beauty. It won't be hard to come up with a list!

60. Give Your Thoughts Color

Just like our bodies can be molded a certain way, our mind can also be molded this way. For example, if you shove your feet into pointy-toed shoes, your feet are going to form a certain way, or if you slouch, your spine is going to show that your slouch. If we focus on negative thoughts, you're going to think negatively. However, if you focus on positive thoughts, you're going to think positively.

Practice Exercise

A good way to think about focusing on positive thoughts is by giving your thoughts color. When people see colors, especially bright colors, they start to feel good. For example, people often associate yellow to happy, or they associate green with nature. In this exercise, you want to practice keeping your thoughts bright and colorful, which mean positive. While you won't always be perfect as nobody is perfect, you can stop yourself from your negative thoughts and ask "Is this a colorful thought?" or "Is this thought positive?" If your answer is no, you want to change your thought to a more positive thought.

For example, you're a college student, and you're falling behind on your assignments. As you look at all the assignments you need to complete over the weekend to catch up, you start feeling like you're failing and you start telling yourself that there is no way you're going to complete all your assignments on time. When you think these type of thoughts, you need to stop and ask yourself if these thoughts are positive. Because these thoughts aren't positive, you need to focus on changing your negative thoughts into positive and colorful thoughts. For instance, instead of saying that there is no way you can complete all of your assignments on time, you can tell yourself that you will work hard to get as many assignments done as you can and then talk to your professors about getting an extension for the other assignments.

61. Start a Journal

Journaling is a great technique which can help people focus on the positives of their lives in different ways. Journaling about your day can help you reflect on your day. For example, at the end of the day, you could take 15 minutes to write about what you did, how you feel, what mistakes you made, and what your accomplishments were. You could also use your journal to write about the negatives in your life and focus on turning them into positives. You could also use your journal to create your lists to help you better focus your mind.

Practice Exercise

For your journal, you can go find paper lying around your home, use Microsoft Office on your computer, or purchase a journal which is inspiring to you. You can then set up a certain time every day where you write in your journal. You can reflect on your day, talk about any mistakes you made and how you can learn from them or discuss ways in which you can better yourself through your experiences and what you're learning.

Chapter 7: What to Do If You're Struggling to Implement

When you first read some of the exercises in chapter 6, you might have wondered how you could do some of those exercises. For example, many people struggle with imagining the death of a loved one or something bad happening in their lives. Instead of imagining the bad, they simply want to focus on the good. Sometimes people see thinking of the negative so you can reach your positive thoughts as an extra step is not necessary. Other people just can't wrap their head around why anyone would ask them to think negatively when they are supposed to focus on the positives of their lives so they can overcome their obstacles and reach their full potential.

It's understandable how people can struggle with some of the exercises. Sometimes, it's just a matter of not understanding why Stoics used these exercises to help them achieve their purposes in life. Other times, it's simply the individual. The person just can't bring themselves to think of certain negative thoughts. And that's okay. This is something the person can work on to overcome in their own time. There are a lot of other exercises that this person will find useful while they are overcoming a hurdle.

There are several avenues you can take if you find yourself struggling with an exercise. First, you can focus on an exercise you don't struggle with. While you don't want to ignore the exercise you do struggle with, you can continue to reach your full potential through another exercise as you're working on overcoming the exercise currently difficult for you. For example, if you find yourself creating a vision board but you can't focus on cutting the ties, complete the vision board and start using this as a reflection piece while you take time with cutting the ties.

People often state that patience is a virtue and this is very true when it comes to learning. Good things take time, and you will be able to overcome the obstacles of any exercise with patience and working through your emotions. You might surprise yourself with how much you can overcome by working through the exercises and implementing factors of Stoicism in your life. Therefore, it's important to be kind to yourself and have patience when you're struggling to implement a piece of Stoicism.

Sometimes you might find yourself thinking "I can't do this" when you read one of the exercises. If you find yourself struggling in this way, start to use an exercise to help you turn your "I can't do this" into an "I can do this" because you can, and you will complete the exercises, even the ones you struggle with. You are already a strong, smart, and amazing person who can overcome more than you can imagine. You might struggle with some exercises of Stoicism, but you will be able to overcome them because you are determined to become the best person you can be. You are determined to not only help yourself but be able to help others with the factors you learn about Stoicism.

It's important to remember that we all struggle with things from time to time. You might struggle with an exercise of Stoicism I've talked about in this book, or you might struggle with comprehending some of the ancient Stoic teachings from Zeno or Marcus Aurelius. Whatever you struggle with, it's important to remember to continue working towards understanding what you need to understand so you can reach your full potential. If you don't overcome the struggles you face, you won't be able to fully establish your balance to become the best person you want to be.

In other words, if you don't overcome the struggles you face in implementing Stoicism, you won't be able to reach your full potential. You will still be able to find a better balance and reach a higher potential, but you won't be able to reach the potential you can, and deserve to reach.

No matter how hard you feel implementing some of the Stoic exercises are, you don't want to give up. First, you can overcome the obstacles and continue on a well-balanced path that will lead you to your full potential. Millions of people have done this for centuries and you will be one of the people to reach your full potential.

One way you can work on overcoming your obstacles is to make sure you have a good structure in your life. Sometimes all we need to help us overcome challenges is not only a mindset but time to be able to focus on overcoming them. For example, you can start by seeing how you can manage your time better. You can do this by choosing one of the apps after you write down a list of the tasks you need to focus on, including the exercises of Stoicism you are struggling with.

You want to work on overcoming your challenges and creating a more balanced life, or you won't be able to reach your full potential. I'm not saying you won't be able to do well in life, or you won't be able to help other people; or that you won't be able to reach some of your goals, but you also won't be able to overcome all the obstacles that stand in your way. For example, you might not take part in certain activities because you're afraid of what could happen if you do. You don't want to live in fear. When you live in fear, you're allowing your emotions to control you. Stoicism works to help you manage your emotions so you control your emotions and can accomplish the tasks you want to accomplish.

Stoicism can also help you overcome mental illnesses that tend to take over your life from time to time, whether it's anxiety or depression. Mental illnesses are not only chemicals in the brain, but they also stick to a person due to their mindset. Therapists have been using Stoic exercises and techniques for decades with successful results. These exercises can help you overcome your anxiety and depression just as they have helped other people overcome theirs.

Again, take your time and go down the path your comfortable with but don't forget to challenge yourself and face your fears. If you need help, there are many places that can help you. For example, you can turn to friends and family. Remember, you always want to find a mentor or role model as a Stoic. You could also join an online group which focuses on Stoicism. The members of the groups are there to help people who are struggling with implementing or have questions about Stoicism. Stoicfellowship.com is a great website that can help you find a community close to your area.

Don't give up because then you could easily fall into the old habits you want to change. You could continue to feel your life is full of chaos and continue to deal with anxiety. While it will take time, Stoicism can help you overcome your obstacles, but you do need to make sure you're putting in the effort so you can achieve your ultimate potential and happiness.

Conclusion

Everyone wants to reach their full potential, live a balanced life, and become the best person they can be. One of the ways to do this is by learning and implementing the practices of Stoicism. Not only can Stoicism help calm your anxiety, but it can also help you achieve goals in your life that you never imagined you could accomplish.

Through its many exercises, values, and principles, Stoicism teaches you that you can overcome any obstacle in your life, have a peace of mind, and reach your highest potential. Even if you think you can't do this right now, start to work on some of the exercises in this book. You can start by choosing whatever five exercises you feel most comfortable doing. For instance, start off by thinking about what your ideal self is. How do you want people to remember you? Do you want to be remembered as a kind, generous, and determined? Write down the things you want to be remembered as and then go through the exercises and pick a few that you feel you can start with that will help you become the person you want to be.

Maybe you want to focus on overcoming your anxiety by creating peace of mind. You want to be able to overcome your anxiety at any moment, including out in public. Once you establish the obstacle of your life you want to overcome so you can start to become more balanced and reach your full potential, focus on a number of exercises to help you accomplish this. Remember, it's important to work on building your confidence, which you can go through a number of Stoic exercises.

There is a lot of information in this book to help you learn Stoicism, its teachings, exercises, and what you can do to help you reach your full potential. Whether you have learned and studied Stoicism previously or you are just learning about the Stoic philosophy, you can gain insight from this book to help yourself grow. On top of this, you can also gain insight on how to help other people achieve their ultimate potential.

Stoicism has been a way of life for thousands of years. Whether it was a popular philosophy at the time or not, Stoicism is a great way to help you overcome your fears, help you understand ways to control your negative emotions, help you overcome obstacles, and help you reach your highest potential. No matter where you are in life or who you feel you are, you're capable of learning Stoicism and accomplishing its exercises. Every human being is capable of reaching their highest potential and becoming the best person they can be. Stoicism can help you achieve these goals in many ways.

I want to thank you for taking the time to read this book! I am honored you chose this book to help you better understand and implement Stoicism in your life. If you enjoyed this book, I would really appreciate it if you could leave a review as it helps my work and it helps to get the message of Stoicism out to more people. Thank you!

Bibliography

10 Insanely Useful Stoic Exercises. Retrieved from https://dailystoic.com/10-insanely-useful-stoic-exercises/.

10 Practical Stoic Exercises for a Modern Stoic Lifestyle. Retrieved from https://www.njlifehacks.com/10-practical-stoic-exercises-for-modern-stoic-lifestyle/.

20 Stoic Exercises for Impressive Self-Improvement. Retrieved from https://s3.amazonaws.com/njlifehacks/20+Stoic+Exercises+-+NJlifehacks.pdf.

3 Common Misconceptions About Stoicism (And A Counter To Each). Retrieved from https://dailystoic.com/misconceptions-about-stoicism/.

A brief history of stoicism. (2016). Retrieved from https://stoicjourney.org/2016/07/28/a-brief-history-of-stoicism/.

A Stoic Response to Grief. Retrieved from https://dailystoic.com/stoic-response-grief/.

A Struggle With One Of The Stoic Psychological Techniques. (2018). Retrieved from http://whatisstoicism.com/stoicism-resources/a-struggle-with-the-stoic-psychological-techniques/.

About Stoicism Today. Retrieved from https://modernstoicism.com/about-stoicism-today/.

Anderson, K. (2012). Five Reasons Why Stoicism Matters Today. Retrieved from https://www.forbes.com/sites/kareanderson/2012/09/28/five-reasons-why-stoicism-matthttps://www.forbes.com/sites/kareanderson/2012/09/28/five-reasons-why-stoicism-matters-today/#17b0d8047a64ers-today/#17b0d8047a64.

Ben Martin, P. (2018). In-Depth: Cognitive Behavioral Therapy. Retrieved from https://psychcentral.com/lib/in-depth-cognitive-behavioral-therapy/.

Christ, S. 8 Important Lessons Stoic Philosophy Will Teach You About Being Happy. Retrieved from https://www.lifehack.org/articles/lifestyle/8-important-lessons-stoic-philosophy-will-teach-you-about-being-happy.html.

Daily Stoic Exercises for Beginners. (2017). Retrieved from https://astoicremedy.com/2017/04/17/daily-stoic-exercises-for-beginners/.

Donnelly, K. (2019). 12 Time Management Apps to Organize Your Life and Keep You on Track. Retrieved from https://www.shopify.com/blog/time-management-apps.

Donovan, J. How Stoicism Works. Retrieved from https://people.howstuffworks.com/stoicism1.htm.

Earp, B. (2019). Do Not weep for Dour Dead: How to Mourn as the Stoics Did. Retrieved from https://aeon.co/essays/do-not-weep-for-your-dead-how-to-mourn-as-the-stoics-did.

Faja, E. (2016). 10 Insanely Useful Stoic Exercises. Retrieved from https://observer.com/2016/02/ten-insanely-useful-stoic-exercises/.

Gill, N. (2019). Does the Serenity Prayer Echo the Greco-Roman Notion of Stoicism?. Retrieved from https://www.thoughtco.com/stoics-and-moral-philosophy-4068536.

Gottberg, K. 10 Lessons Stoics Can Teach Us About Living A Good Life. Retrieved from https://www.smartliving365.com/10-lessons-stoics-can-teach-us-living-good-life/.

Hamm, T. (2016). How the Principles of Stoicism Can Help Your Personal and Financial Life. Retrieved from https://lifehacker.com/how-the-principles-of-stoicism-can-help-your-personal-a-1783277251.

Holiday, R. (2017). 7 insights from the ancient philosophy of Marcus Aurelius that will change the way you think about life, death, and time. Retrieved from https://www.businessinsider.com/stoicism-lessons-life-death-2017-6#you-could-leave-life-right-now-5.

Holiday, R. (2016). 37 Wise & Life-Changing Lessons From The Ancient Stoics. Retrieved from https://thoughtcatalog.com/ryan-holiday/2016/10/37-wise-life-changing-lessons-from-the-ancient-stoics/.

Holiday, R., & Hanselman, S. (2016). The Daily Stoic. New York: Penguin Random House LLC.

Irvine, W. (2014). What Stoicism Isn't. Retrieved from https://www.huffpost.com/entry/what-stoicism-isnt_n_5346269.

Kreiss, T. Stoicism 101: An introduction to Stoicism, Stoic Philosophy and the Stoics. Retrieved from https://www.holstee.com/blogs/mindful-matter/stoicism-101-everything-you-wanted-to-know-about-stoicism-stoic-philosophy-and-the-stoics.

Modern Stoicism. Retrieved from https://modernstoicism.com/.

Monk, H. (2017). 5 Stoic Principles for Modern Living. Retrieved from https://medium.com/pocketstoic/5-stoic-principles-for-modern-living-applying-an-ancient-philosophy-to-the-21st-century-2a8e10f31887.

Morin, A. 4 Ways Emotions Can Screw Up Your Decisions. Retrieved from https://www.psychologytoday.com/us/blog/what-mentally-strong-people-dont-do/201602/4-ways-emotions-can-screw-your-decisions.

Robertson, D. (2018). What do the Stoic Virtues Mean?. Retrieved from https://donaldrobertson.name/2018/01/18/what-do-the-stoic-virtues-mean/.

Rosenberg, E. (2019). The 8 Best Expense Tracker Apps of 2019. Retrieved from https://www.thebalance.com/best-expense-tracker-apps-4158958.

Salzgeber, J. (2019). The Little Book of Stoicism: Timeless Wisdom to Gain Resilience, Confidence, and Calmness. Amazon Digital Services LLC.

Smith, M. (2018). Stoicism: Stoic Philosophy Made Easy. Kindle Edition.

Stoic Communities. Retrieved from https://stoicfellowship.com/stoic-groups.html#communities.

Stoicism. Retrieved from https://www.iep.utm.edu/stoicism/.

Stoicism - By Branch / Doctrine - The Basics of Philosophy. Retrieved from https://www.philosophybasics.com/branch_stoicism.html.

Stoicism | Definition, History, & Influence. Retrieved from https://www.britannica.com/topic/Stoicism.

The Definitive List of Stoicism in History & Pop Culture. Retrieved from https://dailystoic.com/stoicism-pop-culture/.

The Stoics. Retrieved from https://www.theschooloflife.com/thebookoflife/the-great-philosophers-the-stoics/.

Toren, A. (2015). 5 Epic Leaders Who Studied Stoicism -- and Why You Should Too. Retrieved from https://www.entrepreneur.com/article/252625.

What Is Stoicism? A Definition & 9 Stoic Exercises To Get You Started. Retrieved from https://dailystoic.com/what-is-stoicism-a-definition-3-stoic-exercises-to-get-you-started/.

What Is Stoicism? A Simple Definition & 10 Stoic Core Principles. Retrieved from https://www.njlifehacks.com/what-is-stoicism-overview-definition-10-stoic-principles

Stoicism Reveals 4 Rituals That Will Make You Confident - Barking Up The Wrong Tree. Retrieved from https://www.bakadesuyo.com/2017/12/make-you-confident/.

Printed in Great Britain
by Amazon